Studies in Military and Strategic History

General Editor: **Michael Dockrill**, Professor of Diplomatic History, King's College London

Published titles include:

Martin Alexander and William Philpott (*editors*)
ANGLO-FRENCH DEFENCE RELATIONS BETWEEN THE WARS

Nigel John Ashton
EISENHOWER, MACMILLAN AND THE PROBLEM OF NASSER
Anglo-American Relations and Arab Nationalism, 1955–59

Christopher M. Bell
THE ROYAL NAVY, SEAPOWER AND STRATEGY BETWEEN THE WARS

Peter Bell
CHAMBERLAIN, GERMANY AND JAPAN, 1933–34

Antony Best
BRITISH INTELLIGENCE AND THE JAPANESE CHALLENGE IN ASIA, 1914–41

Philippe Chassaigne and Michael Dockrill (*editors*)
ANGLO-FRENCH RELATIONS, 1898–1998
From Fashoda to Jospin

Paul Cornish
BRITISH MILITARY PLANNING FOR THE DEFENCE OF GERMANY, 1945–50

Michael Dockrill
BRITISH ESTABLISHMENT PERSPECTIVES ON FRANCE, 1936–40

Michael Dockrill and John Fisher
THE PARIS PEACE CONFERENCE, 1919
Peace without Victory?

John P. S. Gearson
HAROLD MACMILLAN AND THE BERLIN WALL CRISIS, 1958–62

G. A. H. Gordon
BRITISH SEA POWER AND PROCUREMENT BETWEEN THE WARS
A Reappraisal of Rearmament

Raffi Gregorian
THE BRITISH ARMY, THE GURKHAS AND COLD WAR STRATEGY IN THE FAR EAST, 1947–1954

Stephen Hartley
THE IRISH QUESTION AS A PROBLEM IN BRITISH FOREIGN POLICY, 1914–18

Brian Holden Reid
J. F. C. FULLER: Military Thinker

Ashley Jackson
WAR AND EMPIRE IN MAURITIUS AND THE INDIAN OCEAN

Stewart Lone
JAPAN'S FIRST MODERN WAR
Army and Society in the Conflict with China, 1894–95

Joseph A. Maiolo
THE ROYAL NAVY AND NAZI GERMANY, 1933–39
A Study in Appeasement and the Origins of the Second World War

Thomas R. Mockaitis
BRITISH COUNTERINSURGENCY, 1919–60

Bob Moore and Kent Fedorowich
THE BRITISH EMPIRE AND ITS ITALIAN PRISONERS OF WAR, 1940–47

T. R. Moreman
THE ARMY IN INDIA AND THE DEVELOPMENT OF FRONTIER WARFARE,
1849–1947

Kendrick Oliver
KENNEDY, MACMILLAN AND THE NUCLEAR TEST-BAN DEBATE, 1961–63

Elspeth Y. O'Riordan
BRITAIN AND THE RUHR CRISIS

W. J. Philpott
ANGLO-FRENCH RELATIONS AND STRATEGY ON THE WESTERN FRONT,
1914–18

G. D. Sheffield
LEADERSHIP IN THE TRENCHES
Officer-Man Relations, Morale and Discipline in the British Army in the Era of
the First World War

Adrian Smith
MICK MANNOCK, FIGHTER PILOT
Myth, Life and Politics

Martin Thomas
THE FRENCH NORTH AFRICAN CRISIS
Colonial Breakdown and Anglo-French Relations, 1945–62

Simon Trew
BRITAIN, MIHAILOVIC AND THE CHETNIKS, 1941–42

Steven Weiss
ALLIES IN CONFLICT
Anglo-American Strategic Negotiations, 1938–44

Studies in Military and Strategic History
Series Standing Order ISBN 0–333–71046–0
(*outside North America only*)

You can receive future titles in this series as they are published by placing a standing order.
Please contact your bookseller or, in case of difficulty, write to us at the address below
withyour name and address, the title of the series and the ISBN quoted above.

Customer Services Department, Macmillan Distribution Ltd, Houndmills, Basingstoke,
Hampshire RG21 6XS, England

Anglo-French Defence Relations between the Wars

Edited by

Martin S. Alexander
Professor of International Relations
University of Wales, Aberystwyth

William J. Philpott
Lecturer in Military History
Dept of War Studies, King's College London

palgrave
macmillan

First published 2002 by
PALGRAVE MACMILLAN
Houndmills, Basingstoke, Hampshire RG21 6XS and
175 Fifth Avenue, New York, N.Y. 10010
Companies and representatives throughout the world

PALGRAVE MACMILLAN is the global academic imprint of the Palgrave Macmillan division of St. Martin's Press, LLC and of Palgrave Macmillan Ltd. Macmillan® is a registered trademark in the United States, United Kingdom and other countries, Palgrave is a registered trademark in the European Union and other countries.

ISBN 0–333–75453–0

This book is printed on paper suitable for recycling and made from fully managed and sustained forest sources.

A catalogue record for this book is available from the British Library.

Library of Congress Cataloging-in-Publication Data
Anglo-French defence relations between the wars / edited by Martin S. Alexander, William J. Philpott.
     p. cm. – (Studies in military and strategic history)
    Includes bibliographical references and index.
    ISBN 0–333–75453–0
    1. Great Britain – Military relations – France. 2. Great Britain – Defenses. 3. France – Defenses. 4. France – Military relations – Great Britain. 5. Great Britain – Foreign relations – 1901–1936. 6. Great Britain – Foreign relations – 1936–1945. 7. France – Foreign relations – 1901–1940. I. Alexander, Martin S. II. Philpott, William James. III. Series.
UA647 .A7244 2002
355'.031'09410944 – dc21   2002025213

10 9 8 7 6 5 4 3 2 1
11 10 09 08 07 06 05 04 03 02

Printed and bound in Great Britain by
Antony Rowe Ltd, Chippenham and Eastbourne

Contents

Preface

Philip Bell

Relations between Britain and France are a subject of never-failing fascination for historians. Between the two world wars they were also a matter of central importance in European affairs, with a vital bearing on the origins of the second world war in Europe. It is therefore a pleasure to welcome this collection of essays on a crucial aspect of Franco-British relations between 1920 and 1940, defence and strategic policy. In those two decades the two countries were obsessed by memories of the last war (the Great War as it was almost universally known at that time), and later lived under the ominous shadow of a renewed conflict. It was a time when governments and public opinion in both countries were profoundly peace-minded, and yet could not escape from the danger of war.

The essays in this volume edited by Martin Alexander and William Philpott (themselves expert authorities on the issues under discussion) owe much of their interest to their authors' command of detail. All the chapters are firmly based on meticulous and wide-ranging research in archives on both sides of the Channel. Their side-lights, as well as their central arguments, are illuminating and thought-provoking – see, for example, Talbot Imlay's remarkable exposition of how General Pownall brought French influence to bear on internal British disputes. The footnotes in themselves provide a treasure trove for the curious. Anthony Clayton tucks away in note 54 of his chapter the remark that the first radar fitted in major French warships was German equipment provided in 1941–42. What story lies behind that nugget, one wonders?

But there is much more to this volume than detail, however striking. The main theme, presented with variations in nearly all the chapters, is put in a single sentence by Clayton: 'The capacity of two great nations with essentially common interests . . . to misunderstand one another seemed endless.' The common interests were clear enough. Britain and France were both opposed to German (and *a fortiori* Nazi German) predominance in Europe. They were both imperial powers, facing similar problems and opportunities in their empires. They were both liberal parliamentary democracies in a continent increasingly controlled by dictatorial totalitarian regimes. Why then did they fail to understand one another and co-operate in pursuit of their common interests? Vital answers to that question may be found in this book. The French and

British did not trust one another, even in the face of common danger, as embodied in Arab nationalism, as Martin Thomas's chapter on the Near East shows. They sometimes actively disliked one another – Andrew Webster quotes Ramsay Macdonald in 1930: 'France becomes the peace problem of Europe. Mentality is purely militarist.' (Could any estimate have been more wrong-headed?). Even when the two countries were at war side by side, in the winter of 1939–40, they contrived to set up a Supreme War Council which was more designed for show than action, as William Philpott explains.

These answers raise yet more questions, as we wonder why the two countries should be at cross purposes. This book, as its editors and contributors intend, will give rise to further research and historical debate. I am delighted to welcome this collection of essays, and warmly recommend it to the widest possible readership.

Acknowledgements

The editors and authors would like to thank the following for permission to cite and quote documents in their possession, or for which they hold the copyright; Her Majesty the Queen and the Controller of Her Majesty's Stationery Office; the University of Birmingham; Churchill Archives Centre, Churchill College Cambridge; the National Maritime Museum, Greenwich; the Service Historique de l'Armée de Terre, the Service Historique de l'Armée de l'Air and the Service Historique de la Marine, Vincennes; the Archives Nationales, Archives des Affaires Etrangères, Archives de l'Assemblée Nationale, and Archives du Senat, Paris; the Fondation Nationale des Sciences Politiques, Paris; the Centre des Archives Diplomatiques, Nantes; the Archivo Storico Diplomatico, Rome.

The editors would also like to thank the series editors Professor Michael Dockrill, and at Palgrave Luciana O'Flaherty, for their help and patience while this volume was being prepared. Finally they would like to thank Philip Bell for agreeing to write the preface to this volume, and for giving us both over many years the benefit of his expertise in the study of Anglo-French relations in this period. Any errors that remain are the responsibility of the authors and editors alone.

Notes on Contributors

Martin S. Alexander is Professor of International Relations at the University of Wales, Aberystwyth, and previously taught at the Universities of Southampton and Salford. He is the author of the *Republic in Danger: General Maurice Gamelin and the Politics of French Defence, 1933–1940* (1993). He is the editor of *French History since Napoleon* (1999), and co-editor (with Martin Evans and J. F. V. Keiger) of *The Algerian War and the French Army (1954–62): Experiences, Images, Testimonies* (2001).

Philip Bell is honorary Senior Research Fellow at the University of Liverpool. He is the author of *France and Britain, 1900–40: Entente and Estrangement* and *France and Britain, 1940–94: the Long Separation* (1996 and 1997).

Anthony Clayton is a Research Associate of the Conflict Studies Institute at the Royal Military Academy, Sandhurst and Senior Research Fellow at De Montfort University. His many books include *France, Soldiers and Africa* (1988), *The French Wars of Decolonization* (1994), *Three Marshals of France: Leadership after Trauma* (1992), *The Wars of French Decolonization* (1994) and *Frontiersmen: Warfare in Africa, 1950–2000* (2000).

Talbot Imlay holds a PhD from Yale University and teaches in the Department of History at the Université Laval in Quebec. He has published chapters on Anglo-French strategic policy in 1938–40 in Robert Boyce (ed.), *French Foreign and Defence Policy, 1918–1940: the Decline and Fall of a Great Power* (1998) and in Kenneth Mouré and Martin S. Alexander (eds), *Crisis and Renewal in France, 1918–1962* (2001).

Peter Jackson specializes in intelligence studies, with particular reference to France, and is a lecturer in the Department of International Politics at the University of Wales, Aberystwyth. He has a PhD from the University of Cambridge, held a John M. Olin Postdoctoral Fellowship in International Security Studies at Yale University, and has taught at Carleton University, Ottawa. Among his many publications is *France and the Nazi Menace: Intelligence and Policy-Making, 1933–1939* (2000).

Joseph A. Maiolo is Lecturer in International History in the Department of War Studies, King's College London. He previously lectured in International History at the Universities of Leicester and Leeds. He is the author of *The Royal Navy and Nazi Germany, 1933–39: a Study in Appeasement and the Origins of the Second World War* (1998) and co-author with Robert Boyce of *The Origins of the Second World War: the Debate Continues* (2002).

William J. Philpott is Lecturer in Military History in the Department of War Studies, King's College London, and was formerly Principal Lecturer in the Department of Politics and Modern History at London Guildhall University. He is the author of *Anglo-French Relations and Strategy on the Western Front, 1914–18* (1996) and many chapters and articles on Anglo-French relations in the era of the two world wars, including 'Coalition War: Britain and France' in J. Bourne, P. Liddle and I. Whitehead (eds), *The Great World War, 1914–45: Lightning Strikes Twice* (2000).

Reynolds M. Salerno holds a PhD in History from Yale University. He is the author of *March to the Oceans: Mediterranean Origins of the Second World War, 1935–40* (2002) and articles on Mediterranean security in the 1930s in the *English Historical Review* and the *Journal of Strategic Studies*. He is currently Senior Member of the Technical Staff at the International Security Center of Sandia National Laboratories in Albuquerque, NM, USA.

Martin Thomas is Reader in International History at the University of the West of England, Bristol. Besides numerous articles, he has published *Britain, France and Appeasement: Anglo-French Relations in the Popular Front Era, 1936–38* (1996), *The French Empire at War, 1940–1945* (1998) and *The French North African Crisis. Colonial Breakdown and Anglo-French Relations, 1945–62* (2000).

Andrew Webster is a Junior Research Fellow of Wolfson College, Cambridge. He completed his postgraduate studies at Pembroke College, Cambridge and gained his PhD in 2000 for a thesis on 'Anglo-French Relations and the problems of Disarmament and Security, 1929–33'.

List of Abbreviations

This list applies to both text and footnotes.

AAN – Archives de l'Assemblée Nationale, Paris
ADM – Admiralty
AN – Archives Nationales, Paris
ARP – Air Raid Precautions
ARR – Archives récupérées de la Russie, Service Historique de l'Armée de Terre, Vincennes
AS – Archives du Senat, Paris
ASD – Archivo Storico Diplomatico, Rome
BEF – British Expeditionary Force
C in C – Commander in Chief
CAB – Cabinet Office
CADN – Centre des Archives Diplomatiques, Nantes
CAS – Chief of the Air Staff
CEMA – Chef de l'Etat-major Général de l'Armée
CID – Committee of Imperial Defence
CIGS – Chief of the Imperial General Staff
CNS – Chief of the Naval Staff
CO – Colonial Office
COS – Chiefs of Staff Committee
CPDN – Comité Permanente de la Défense Nationale
CSDN – Conseil Supérieur de la Défense Nationale
DBFP – Documents on British Foreign Policy
DDF – Documents Diplomatiques Françaises
DMO – Director of Military Operations
DNI – Director of Naval Intelligence
DPR – Defence Policy and Requirements Committee
EMA – Etat-major Général de l'Armée
EMAA – Etat-major Général de l'Armée de l'Air
EMM – Etat-major Général de la Marine
FO – Foreign Office
FPC – Foreign Policy Committee
GC&CS – Government Code and Ciphers School
GOC – General Officer Commanding
HCM – Haut Comité Militaire

IIC – Industrial Intelligence Centre
JDC – Joint Defence Committee
JIC – Joint Intelligence Sub-committee of the Chiefs of Staff
Committee
JO – Journal Officiel de la Republique Française
JPC – Joint Planning Committee
LNOJ – League of Nations Official Journal
LNP – League of Nations Publications
MAE – Ministère des Affaires Etrangères, Paris
NMM – National Maritime Museum, Greenwich
PC – Preparatory Commission for the World Disarmament Conference
PREM – Prime Minister's Papers, PRO
PRO – Public Record Office, Kew
RAC – Royal Armoured Corps
RAF – Royal Air Force
RHDA – Revue Historique des Armées
SCR – Section de Centralisation des Renseignements
SDN – Societé des Nations
SFSDN – Service Française de Societé des Nations
SHAA – Service Historique de l'Armée de l'Air, Vincennes
SHAT – Service Historique de l'Armée de Terre, Vincennes
SHM – Service Historique de la Marine, Vincennes
SIS – Secret Intelligence Service
SR – Service de Renseignements
SWC – Supreme War Council
USAMHI – United States Army Military History Institute,
Pennsylvania
WDC – World Disarmament Conference
WO – War Office

1
Introduction: Choppy Channel Waters – the Crests and Troughs of Anglo-French Defence Relations between the Wars

Martin S. Alexander and William J. Philpott

In the 1990s the Channel Tunnel finally provided a physical union between Britain and France. Emotionally and attitudinally, however, the British and French still regard each other warily. Perhaps encouraged by the new geographic linkage, and certainly assisted by the release of archives, historians have re-examined many aspects of relations between these once 'troubled neighbours'.[1] This volume seeks to fill a gap by presenting new research on the defence relationship, focusing on the era between the two world wars (1919–39).[2]

The inter-war climate between the British and French armed services reflected the atmosphere of wider Anglo-French relations. In the early and mid-1920s 'there were no overriding threats to Britain', as John R. Ferris has remarked. 'Any grand strategy would necessarily be speculative, an approach which Whitehall disliked.'[3] All the same a haze, if not yet any dark storm-clouds, was starting to dim the sun that many fondly supposed might perpetually shine on Britain's empire. The Washington naval limitations conference of 1921–22 precipitated the end of the 1902 Anglo-Japanese alliance. This increasingly obliged British defence planners (institutionalized in the Committee of Imperial Defence and its chiefs of staff sub-committee) to contemplate Japan as a possible future enemy.

However, British plans in the 1920s took seriously the possibility that France, too, might be an adversary rather than an ally. The programmes designed to expand the Royal Air Force in 1921–25 particularly reflected this pessimistic outlook for Anglo-French strategic relations.[4] French policies and France's far-reaching military presence in Europe after the conclusion of the Paris peace treaties were thought, in London, to be suspiciously hegemonic. Besides the privileged commercial relations

France concluded with newly-independent states in east-central Europe such as Poland and Czechoslovakia, the signs of French influence included the establishment in 1919 of a military mission under General Louis Pellé in Prague and the appointment in 1921 of another French officer, General Louis Faury, as the first commandant of the Polish Army staff college.[5] Many British statesmen and defence chiefs estimated that French policies had the potential to provoke international tensions and even give grounds for a new war.[6]

During this time, furthermore, the United States declined to underwrite French security, Congress in 1920 rejecting pleas from Paris for a post-war guarantee of military protection, and also declining to take the USA into the newborn League of Nations.[7] In Whitehall, just as in Washington, scant sympathy existed in either political or military circles for French feelings of insecurity. Britain unsurprisingly followed the American suit, declining to push through any concrete outcome to the 1920–22 negotiations for a pact with France and Belgium.[8]

Anglo-Saxon attitudes severely perplexed French statesmen. In Paris most political and military leaders regarded the British governments of the years 1919–25 as feckless, unfaithful and short-sighted. The Marquess of Curzon, British foreign secretary of the early 1920s, had an acrimonious relationship with many French politicians and especially with Raymond Poincaré, President of the Republic from 1913 to 1920. The latter's return as prime minister in 1923–24 (and again in 1926–29) made for clashes of personality and policy with British officials. From a French standpoint, Britain did too much to aid the economic and political re-integration of the defeated but latently powerful enemy, Germany, and too little to provide long-term security to the victorious but severely mauled ally, France.[9]

The Locarno Treaty of December 1925 seemed to promise two-fold relief to France: on the one hand, an unforced German pledge not to seek to alter by force the borders with France and Belgium; on the other, a British (and Italian) underwriting of the treaty. Locarno, however, was not underpinned by any Anglo-French military staff talks or operational planning.[10] The logistical, intelligence and operational dimensions to a punitive action if Germany reneged on her signature were never worked out. This left French diplomats and defence planners uneasily aware of the misalignment between British defence policy and British diplomatic undertakings. A France brought close to the limit of her endurance in 1917, even with Britain as an ally, deeply feared the ephemeral quality of postwar security arrangements.[11] These, French leaders felt, left a far more potent, populous Germany ringed not by watchful bayonets but by pious words on pieces of paper. As expressed in a metaphor used by General Louis Maurin, French minister for war, in April 1935, a month after Germany violated Versailles by re-establishing a conscripted army:

> Germany had hitherto been surrounded by a wall of paper; within that wall she had grown and had provided herself with formidable military means [...] It was impossible to foretell with any accuracy in what direction the armed force of Germany would move once the wall of paper was completely torn down.[12]

At the end of the 1920s and in the early 1930s Anglo-French relations had cooled, however. This was in part because the erstwhile allies took sharply contrasting views of the philosophy and specific proposals embodied in the World Disarmament Conference. Neither in the meetings of its preparatory commissions from 1929, nor in the main sessions of the conference, was Anglo-French convergence and co-operation much in evidence, as Andrew Webster's chapter here (Chapter 3) makes clear.[13] The conference proper convened at Geneva in February 1932. Severely damaged by Germany's walk-out in October 1933, it staggered on into 1934.

In the naval sphere, the French remained aggrieved by the terms of the Washington treaty of 1922, which had placed the French on a par with their Mediterranean rivals, the Italians.[14] In the air, the French showed a greater enthusiasm for total prohibition of bomber aircraft than did the British. The latter increasingly turned, in the early and mid-1930s, to designing and producing longer-range bombers as the most cost-effective weapon to preserve peace through deterrence (embracing the creed that 'the bomber will always get through', in the chilling words of Stanley Baldwin, then leader of the Conservative Party, in the House of Commons in November 1932).[15] Faith that bombers packed the greatest punch for the taxpayer's pound even resisted the pressure in the late 1930s for all-out emphasis on fighters and anti-aircraft guns to defend the skies over Great Britain. After Munich the Secretary of State for Air, Sir Kingsley Wood, argued in Cabinet in November 1938 that 'if our real aim was to prevent war it was necessary that we should also have a sufficient bomber force to ensure that any country wishing to attack us would realise that the game was not worth the candle.'[16] British bombers, however, were of little use in assisting the defence of France from over-land invasion.

As regards land forces, French military leaders resented pressures from left-wingers at home and the British delegation at Geneva to make deep cuts. Behind British pressure lay a hope that concessions by France might keep an increasingly truculent Germany at the conference table. General Maxime Weygand, French army inspector-general and commander-in-chief designate between 1931 and January 1935, could not understand British policy. Successive governments steered clear of staff talks or military planning designed to flesh out Britain's Locarno commitment to preserve the Franco-Belgian-German frontiers.[17] Weygand 'found it difficult to follow us', reported Colonel Gordon Heywood, the British military attaché, in March 1933, 'when we advocated a policy, namely the reduction of French armaments to such a level as to make an attack the more likely and which thereby increased the chances of England having to honour her signature'.[18] Particularly resisted by French generals was the plan put up in 1933, over the signature of Ramsay MacDonald (then the British prime minister), to permit the German Reichswehr's expansion to a peacetime force of 300,000 men. In October 1933 Germany did quit the conference. On 17 April 1934 Louis Barthou, then French foreign minister, issued a note that signalled a return by those responsible for French security to reliance on 'old fashioned' alliances and refurbished military defences.[19] French army and navy commanders smarted over the erosion of armed strength resulting from support for the League of Nations and collective security, accompanied by reduced spending on military training and modern weapons. They felt that too many revisions of Versailles had been made, all in Germany's favour. Some claimed to have lost confidence that the French standing army could guarantee the national territory from a sneak attack, *une attaque brusqée*.[20] From about 1931, numerous 'friends of the French army', including well-briefed journalists, retired officers and writers using pseudonyms, penned articles for the *Revue Militaire Générale* and the *Revue des Deux Mondes*. Their aim was to raise doubts whether the 'skeletonised' forces could preserve the sacrosanct 'inviolability of national territory', and to force ministers to undo what were seen as baleful 'pro-Geneva' cuts in budgets and first-line troop levels.[21]

In May 1934 Weygand mobilized a protest from the entire membership of the French army's board, the Conseil Supérieur de la Guerre (CSG). The generals signed a formal note registering alarm at the tilting military balance. It recommended urgent investment to revive the French army. It cited statistics on imminent German military strength and reflected Weygand's hostility to the effects of the disarmament process.[22] In January 1935, six days before retiring, Weygand repeated his warnings in a valedictory statement to the CSG.[23]

British documents from this time reveal the great distance that the Channel represented in terms of the respective perceptions of the European military balance. We have seen how French strategists fretted that Germany was contained by just a flimsy 'wall of paper'. The contrasting British official perspective was elegantly expressed in November 1933 by Orme Sargent, deputy under-secretary at the Foreign Office:

> No doubt a convincing case can be made out to show that if Great Britain were committed to an alliance with France there would be no German danger. But the British public at present do not look at the matter in this way: they prefer to live dangerously without commitments, rather than securely with them – and perhaps they are right.[24]

In March 1934, just five weeks before the 'Barthou Note', the British government's Defence Requirements Committee, formed the previous year, resumed its inquiry into the most serious lacunae in British defensive strength. Any measures smacking of the mass commitment of British troops to Europe along the lines of 1915–18 were political anathema. Maurice Hankey, secretary to the Cabinet and Committee of Imperial Defence, warned the permanent head of the Foreign Office, Sir Robert Vansittart:

> I foresee a criticism against the idea that the Expeditionary Force should be equipped to go to France. After the meeting Sam Hoare [Secretary of State for India] said that what struck him was that we were preparing for a war of exactly the same kind as the last.[25]

Even the War Office was unsympathetic to complaints from Weygand and others, seeing them as unduly alarmist and 'typically French' histrionics. Its military intelligence division, MI3, opined after Hitler re-introduced conscription in March 1935 that 'it is not thought that a peace strength of thirty-six divisions is excessive in view of the strategic position of Germany, the length of her frontiers and the armed strength of neighbouring powers'.[26]

Against this backdrop, relations between the British and French air forces make a revealing case study – and, lacking a chapter to themselves in this collection, they merit extended scrutiny now. During the 1920s the RAF (Royal Air Force) was an independent service, formed on 1 April 1918. It was viewed with some jealousy by the Royal Navy and British army. Those wearing the RAF's light blue uniform were newcomers, even upstarts, who demanded financial resources that might otherwise have remained with those in navy blue and khaki. With the RAF desperate for arguments to fight its corner in Whitehall, France performed a crucial function. For as the nearest continental power and the most militarily powerful one, France was a useful yardstick against which the RAF could measure its own claims for men, money and aircraft. As noted earlier, it was against a hypothesis of bombing raids by a French air force that Fighter Command had, in the early 1920s, claimed to need 52 metropolitan RAF squadrons for home air defence.[27]

Ironically, France at this point had many aircraft but no air force. That is, no independent third French service existed with which the RAF could have a relationship (albeit that in 1928 a minister for air, Fernand Laurent, was added to the government). In 1933 the advent of a young, dynamic, and personally ambitious air minister, Pierre Cot, changed this. Cot instigated the rapid development of a separate French air force (the Armée de l'Air). He quickly equipped the service with an air war council (Conseil Supérieur de l'Air), an air staff with an air intelligence branch, an Air War College (Ecole Supérieur de l'Air), and air attachés posted to the most important French embassies and legations abroad.[28]

Despite the usefulness of the 'French bogeyman' to boost the case for the home RAF, British air forces in the 1920s and early 1930s were largely occupied in imperial policing and colonial defence.[29] Only from the mid-1930s onwards did Anglo-French air co-operation become substantive, particularly from 1935 when German rearmament became overt. In 1935–36 Anglo-French air staff talks occurred, on account of the risk of war after Italy invaded Abyssinia.[30] At this juncture France appeared to be in the driving seat as far as bilateral developments were concerned. Cot had initiated air rearmament in 1933, and this had been continued by the air minister in the period 1934–35, General Victor Denain. His Plan II for French air rearmament set a target of a front-line force of 1,050 modern aircraft.

The RAF gained a further reason for working more intimately with the French. In the pre-radar era, as this still was, any German air raids directed at cities, ports or factories in Britain would have to pass through Belgian and/or French air space *en route* to targets in the United Kingdom. Britain grasped that her warning time of inbound raiders, and thus RAF Fighter Command's ability to 'scramble' fighter squadrons to climb to combat altitude and seek to intercept German attacks, would be massively enhanced by access to the network of Franco-Belgian air-raid alert stations (*postes de guet*). These were connected by telephone lines to the fighter and anti-aircraft artillery controllers of the Belgian and French territorial air defence commands. It became a matter of utmost value to British home defence to become linked into this early warning system.

By 1936–37, however, leadership and self-confidence in the cross-Channel air relationship had dramatically shifted its locus. British air intelligence and diplomatic sources in Paris anxiously watched as French air rearmament stalled, and then ground almost to a halt, amid political recriminations and partisanship. The warning signs appeared even in 1934, as the Armée de l'Air launched its Plan II. 'Now that the material of the French air force is to be renewed', minuted M. J. Cresswell at the Foreign Office, 'the general reserves may be expected to increase in number, but decrease (relatively) in quality very rapidly – until it is possible to re-equip the reserves as well. . . . There will be a moment when the old reserves will be practically valueless.'[31]

But most damage to French air strength was inflicted, British observers felt sure, by Pierre Cot. His reappointment to the French air ministry in June 1936 was the work of Léon Blum's left-centre Popular Front government. Cot's ideas had a long-term soundness, indeed were in many cases essential. He understood that French aircraft production was hopelessly artisanal, fragmented among too many under-capitalized and inefficient firms, and dangerously concentrated in the industrial suburbs around Paris. These were too near to Germany, as modern aircraft developed larger payloads and longer ranges – and thus were exposed to a pre-emptive Luftwaffe strike at the very start of a war. Cot sponsored legislation in the summer of 1936 to nationalize large parts of the airframe and aero-engine industries. This was accompanied by decrees ordering the manufacturing companies Gnome-et-Rhône, Hispano-Suiza, Aviation Bloch-Dassault and Dewoitine to relocate their production to the provinces, and especially to cities in southern and south-western France, such as Toulouse. This was to distance them from Germany and reduce their exposure to destruction by Luftwaffe raids.

Strategic though these moves undeniably were, their short- and medium-term impact was disastrous. The left-wing and ideological character of the nationalizations caused furious controversy in the Chamber of Deputies and the Senate. It also aroused opposition to the minister and his policies among conservative French air force generals. Meanwhile the physical relocation of aircraft factories caused a catastrophic slide in monthly aircraft output.[32] The British monitored this crisis with growing consternation.[33] Across the Channel, meanwhile, 1936–37 saw the RAF receive top priority in British rearmament and special favour from Neville Chamberlain, Chancellor of the Exchequer from 1931 to May 1937, and then prime minister. The lamentable condition of the

French air force by 1937–38, and the politicization of its administration and doctrine under Cot, struck many British officials and politicians as proof of French unreliability and weakness.[34] This was not a France with which many British ministers, civil servants or military officers wished to become allied.[35]

Yet if the RAF had a privileged place in British rearmament policy in these years, the French judged the results to be a hindrance to closer Anglo-French strategic interests and defensive co-ordination. In the spring of 1937 exchanges of intelligence and technical information occurred between the RAF and the Armée de l'Air.[36] Meanwhile disagreement ran strongly in Whitehall. Might Britain one day have to assume a role again in the defence of Belgium and France? What would be the most effective and cost-efficient form of British military assistance in such an eventuality? 'It is not possible in the absence of experience of a war between first class air powers', noted a view from Britain's service chiefs cited with approval by General Hastings Ismay, assistant secretary to the Committee of Imperial Defence, in July 1937, 'to say whether or not air forces can stop armies . . . we agree that the allies must be capable of placing in the field considerable land forces if they are to stop a German onslaught on land'.[37]

This left open the question of whether the 'considerable land forces' could be supplied exclusively by France, perhaps supplemented by Belgium, with any British contribution to continental defence strictly limited to aircraft. In London the advocates of air power were eloquent: aircraft promised the maximum deterrent value for money. Moreover, French air weakness made the wisdom of giving priority to RAF programmes in 1937–38 appear irrefutable. British air rearmament only switched emphasis after the Inskip Report of December 1937, which reduced the priority for heavy bombers able to strike at the German industrial and urban heartland, thereby raising the role of Air Defence of Great Britain (ADGB). In part the change reflected adventitious but crucial technological breakthroughs: the coming of the first functional radar warning stations in 1937, and the proving of a new generation of monoplane, single-seat, fast fighter aircraft, the Hawker Hurricane and Supermarine Spitfire (first prototypes of each having flown in 1934 and 1936 respectively). By 1937–38 Hurricanes were re-equipping the fighter defence squadrons of the UK, whilst the first squadron of operational Spitfires entered service in 1938.

The RAF and Armée de l'Air were liaising intensively at this time. Cot personally held discussions with the British Secretary of State for Air, Viscount Swinton, in December 1937. Indeed Cot's removal from the air ministry in January 1938 and replacement by the urbane and uncontroversial Guy La Chambre promised even closer co-operation between the RAF and the Armée de l'Air. The French strengthened their embassy in London, posting an air attaché with the rank of colonel. French aero-engineers visited the Royal Aircraft Establishment at Farnborough in February 1938 and, in March, air staff officers held talks.[38] That summer the French were given details of the airfields, fuel supply and storage, and ground logistical support required by the RAF if it were to deploy an Advanced Air Striking Force (AASF) to northern France. By the Munich crisis of September 1938 preparations were well advanced for an AASF of 20 squadrons, each of 16 aircraft, organized in two Bomber Groups: in total, 320 bomber aircraft.[39]

By September 1938 French military and political leaders, including General Maurice Gamelin, the prime minister Edouard Daladier and the foreign minister Georges Bonnet, were drawing satisfaction from the increasing firmness apparent about RAF commitment to the Continent. Britain agreed to deploy the first Group of ten bomber squadrons on the allocated bases in France by the end of the first month of war; and the next ten squadrons during the second month. The air staffs discussed landings at French air force bases by RAF fighters running low on fuel after pursuing German raiders across the Channel; standardization of radio frequencies and communications procedures; aircraft recognition arrangements to permit French air controllers to identify RAF planes; and French refuelling of RAF formations.[40]

But soon after the Munich *dénouement*, the fast pace towards air co-ordination slowed again. This was not of French doing. Rather, the attenuation of air staff co-ordination resulted from changes on the British side of the Channel: the appointment of Air Marshal Hugh Dowding as Air Officer Commanding Fighter Command in 1937 and priority thereafter for construction of an integrated system of 'Chain Home' radar stations. These, initially stretching from the Isle of Wight to East Anglia, were linked by telephone and wireless to the new RAF fighter bases, now organized into sectors and groups.

These developments dismayed the French, whose chief of air staff, General Joseph Vuillemin, had warned in March and September 1938 that war with Germany in the near future would see the Armée de l'Air 'annihilated in two weeks'.[41] On the one hand, the increased priority for defending British air space was bound to keep RAF fighter squadrons in the United Kingdom. The RAF's technological and organizational improvements had removed much of the value of France and Belgium to provide advance warning of Luftwaffe raids, reducing the need to base major RAF fighter assets east of the Channel to engage raiders over France and Belgium. Dowding and his commanders now presented the British authorities with a prospect of intercepting bombers over the Channel or at the English coast. On the other hand, the proponents of a heavy RAF bomber force as 'the best deterrent to avoid war' remained, and included Kingsley Wood who had succeeded Swinton as air minister in May 1938. In a statement on the air programme to the Cabinet in November 1938, Wood presented the RAF's pressing needs as firstly to build reserve strength in depth; secondly to increase the proportion of squadrons equipped with the latest aircraft types; and thirdly to concentrate on fighters. The Chancellor of the Exchequer, Sir John Simon, and Neville Chamberlain were pleased. 'Such a programme', remarked Simon approvingly, 'was manifestly defensive'. The Cabinet authorized the air staff's full programme of 3,700 additional fighters, half of which were to be ordered immediately.[42]

The French correctly discerned that these decisions in London would curb the size of the air force that Britain would forward-deploy into France.[43] Given the parlous state of their own air rearmament in 1938–39, French anxiety was understandable and justified. The story of Anglo-French air force relations is thus another narrative of efforts in parallel that never fused into an integrated, unitary air strategy. The unravelling of Anglo-French air defence into something close to 'each ally for himself' in 1940 was something incipient in the poorly stitched fabric of pre-war air relations.[44]

Between the armies, too, relations ebbed and flowed. They too reflected the wider context of the Anglo-French political and diplomatic relationship, and the perceptions in London and Paris of the degree of threat to peace in Europe at particular moments. During the 1920s, although Britain did not guarantee France militarily, there was substantial co-operation between elements of the army general staffs. This stemmed from the maintenance by both entente powers of substantial land forces on German territory, enforcing the Versailles Treaty and supporting the work of the Inter-Allied Control Commission. The British army of occupation, stationed at Cologne and Düsseldorf, adjoined the French troops garrisoning the central part of the Rhineland (headquartered at Mainz).

Political differences between the governments, notably over how to react to German non-payment of reparations and the subsequent French military occupation of the Ruhr in 1923–24, made for tensions from time to time. Nevertheless the presence of armies enforcing the 1919 peace settlement inside Germany, along with the British and

French teams on the Inter-Allied Commission, ensured a continuing familiarity. There was a considerable store of knowledge about each other's army, troop morale, weapons systems and general fighting capabilities available down to the end of the decade. With the evacuation of the last occupation contingents in June 1930, however, this major source of Anglo-French military contacts was lost.

Thereafter, relations between the two armies became more attenuated and information grew harder to come by. The French managed to keep a more detailed watch on the British army in the early 1930s than vice versa. Their military attaché in London from 1929 to 1936, General Robert Voruz, and his long-serving assistant, Major Cuny, reported assiduously on the British army, its recruitment problems, training, and changes in the high command. These were supplemented by a long annual despatch about all aspects of life in Britain, politics and economic prospects as much as matters military, for the benefit of the intelligence branch (Deuxième Bureau) of the general staff and the War Ministry in Paris. The reports of Voruz's successor as attaché, General Albert Lelong (1936–40), were just as comprehensive.

The British attachés in Paris were less industrious. In the time of Colonel George Waterfield (1929–33) and Colonel T. G. G. Heywood (1933–36) the Paris posting was considered something of a social sinecure rather than a route to promotion and senior command.[45] Such information as the British obtained in these years was thanks to Weygand and Gamelin, the most senior French commanders. The former was chief of the general staff, 1930–31, and inspector-general of the army, 1931–35; the latter was chief of the general staff, 1931–40. Both had held important posts in the 1914–18 war involving contact with the British army. Weygand had been chief of staff to Marshal Ferdinand Foch (the Allied *generalissimo* in 1918); Gamelin had been Marshal Joseph Joffre's operations officer in 1914–15 and a corps commander in 1918. Each was highly respected by British army officers. This was a respect they reciprocated towards the British Chief of the Imperial General Staff (CIGS) in 1931–33, Field Marshal Sir Archibald Montgomery-Massingberd (who had served on the Western Front in 1915–18 as chief of staff to General Sir Henry Rawlinson, first at IV Corps and then at Fourth Army). Old contacts of this sort paid dividends for the War Office when, in both 1931 and 1933, Montgomery-Massingberd visited France at Gamelin's invitation, to see the construction of the Maginot Line fortifications in Alsace and Lorraine.[46]

Despite these friendships and the resulting privileges, the British view of the condition of the French army grew more blurred as time passed.

At the War Office, MI3 compiled a detailed and accurate assessment of the French army in December 1935, at the height of the crisis provoked by Italian aggression in East Africa.[47] In 1936 Colonel Frederick G. 'Paddy' Beaumont-Nesbitt, a Grenadier Guard, was appointed to Paris as military attaché, to succeed Heywood. A highly respected soldier who had won the Military Cross in the Great War, Beaumont-Nesbitt worked hard in 1936–37 to improve the War Office's qualitative and quantitative intelligence on the French army. He spoke frequently with Colonel Jean Petibon, head of Gamelin's military office. He also obtained extensive access to officers of the French high command and attended corps-level manoeuvres in Provence in September 1936. There he met future army commanders including General Henri Giraud and General Gaston Prételat.[48]

Despite Beaumont-Nesbitt's endeavours, however, by 1937–38 the authorities in London grew aware of how seriously incomplete and speculative a lot of their information about the French army, its armaments and its operational plans had become. In September 1937 Field Marshal Sir Cyril Deverell, Montgomery-Massingberd's successor as CIGS, was invited to attend the French army's exercises in Normandy. He detected an ulterior aim of impressing upon him how much it would serve British interests to co-operate, militarily, more closely with France.[49] In April 1938 Major C. A. de Linde, Beaumont-Nesbitt's assistant military attaché in Paris, confessed to London that he and the military attaché had 'not the same means' of intelligence gathering on the French armed forces as did Germany and Italy. It was 'intolerable', minuted Ismay, assistant secretary to the CID, that Britain was no longer provided with 'the exact position' from the French about 'what they can and intend to do with their army'.[50] Not only were details lacking about the order-of-battle of the French army, and the quality of their training and weapons; so was concrete information on the French army's intended wartime deployments and operational plans.

In this aspect of cross-Channel relations, there was a vicious circle to be broken: France would divulge the detail of concentrations and dispositions, and of her battle plans, when the British sat down to comprehensive staff talks. Yet until the scare over rumoured imminent German plans for a lightning *coup de main* against Holland in January–February 1939, the governments of Baldwin (1935–37) and Chamberlain (1937–40) regarded the price in lost political and diplomatic freedom of action as too great to warrant detailed military exchanges.

The French army high command increasingly made its demands on the War Office very specific.[51] It sought a small but highly mechanized

'Field Force' (in the terminology of the mid-1930s) to fulfil specific roles as part of Allied ground dispositions. In the early stages of a war, this British corps was sought to form a powerful, strategic mobile reserve behind the lines on a reconstituted Western Front. The protection of the frontiers was incumbent on French infantry formations in the north, and the Maginot Line and French fortress divisions from Luxembourg via Lorraine to Switzerland; behind them a mobile British field force, strongly equipped with tanks, could prepare to counter-attack any German breakthrough of the fortifications and infantry positions.[52] In the subsequent stages of a war, once the Allies took the offensive, the British land contribution would become an attacking instrument to join French armour in defeating the German forces in the field, batter through to the heart of the Third Reich, and overthrow Nazism.

This grand strategy in several stages presupposed the organization and harnessing together of the British and French war economies. The resources of the two empires overseas, as well as the respective metropolitan industries and treasuries, were to be mobilised.[53] This, it was universally agreed, was a cardinal 'lesson' of the 1914–18 war. Its significance is discussed here in Martin Alexander's chapter (Chapter 8) on British and French preparations for converting their economies to a war footing and interlocking their resources of money, materiel and men into an Allied economic war effort. Grand strategy was predicated on a war of four years' duration, and of at least two distinct phases. The first would be defensive, characterized by the build-up of Allied mobilized strength, letting a blockade squeeze the enemy whilst the Allies withstood assaults by Germany and its satellites. The second would be offensive, to destroy a weakened and war-ravaged Reich. The 'Broad Strategic Policy for the Allied Conduct of the War', agreed in the first stage of Anglo-French staff talks in early April 1939, remarked that

> Germany and Italy cannot hope to increase their resources appreciably in the course of the war: they will therefore stake their chances of success on a short war. The United Kingdom and France, on the other hand, are in a position to increase their war potential from one month to another.[54]

To harness and pool economic resources, some far-sighted moves had been initiated by 1939–40. Supply of British coal to French power stations and the steel industry was an example. There were also financial offsets, and mechanisms to share the war's fiscal burdens were included in the Anglo-French Treasury agreements of 4 December 1939.

As William Philpott's chapter (Chapter 9) shows, a comprehensive system of economic committees was envisaged as part of the allies' Supreme War Council machinery. Steps were even taken towards tank and anti-aircraft-gun manufacture that hinted at the joint weapons production commonplace later in the war. However, as in other areas of the Allied strategic relationship, what was accomplished proved to be too little and too late.

Similarly promising, but incomplete, was the arrangement of the higher direction of the war. Here, as William Philpott's contribution shows, politicians and military chiefs in London and Paris sought to embed and institutionalize the 'lessons' of 1914–18 from the outset. In particular they drew on the valuable role performed by the Inter-Allied Supreme War Council (SWC) after its establishment in 1917, and were intent on forming an identical body. This was achieved as one offshoot of the three rounds of comprehensive Anglo-French staff talks in 1939.[55] The inaugural SWC meeting took place only nine days after war was declared, at Abbeville, on 12 September 1939.[56] Sundry associated or parallel bodies designed to achieve the well-oiled integration of the French and British war efforts existed from the start of hostilities in 1939: an Anglo-French Military Committee and an Anglo-French industrial Co-ordination Committee (both located in London), and an Anglo-French Joint Purchasing Commission in the United States (identified, correctly, as a key source of raw materials, machine-tools and weapons, notably fighter aircraft).[57]

Britain and France were not just European powers in the inter-war years and in the second world war – they were imperial ones too. Indeed, in Britain's case she defined herself first and foremost as an imperial power. For British leaders, and only slightly less for those in France, attention to the German question had always to be balanced by care for other security and defence issues.[58] This was so during the reparations wrangles of the 1920s as much as when the Third Reich posed a growing military threat after 1933.[59] Reynolds Salerno (Chapter 4) shows the vicissitudes of Anglo-French co-operation in the Mediterranean theatre (France and Britain's 'near abroad'). He analyses the volatile relationship between the Abyssinian crisis of autumn 1935 and the autumn of 1938, and shows that the co-operation prompted in 1935–36 by fears of what British contemporaries termed a possible 'mad dog act' by Mussolini was short-lived. The Italian involvement in the Spanish civil war that broke out in July 1936, and Britain's increasing anxiety about the vulnerabilities of its empire in the Far East in 1937–38, pulled a temporarily harmonized French and British policy towards Italy apart again.[60]

In 1938 Italy was at the centre of British appeasement policy. Chamberlain set much store by Mussolini's potential to moderate Hitler's behaviour, even hoping to use the Anglo-Italian 'Gentlemen's Agreement' of 1937, and subsequent bilateral talks with Rome, to detach Italy from the Axis altogether.[61] This need became more pressing. In November the chiefs of staff urgently recommended that, with a growing risk of a catastrophic war against Germany, Italy and Japan together, Britain's diplomats bestir themselves to reduce the number of the nation's prospective enemies.[62] Unfortunately for Anglo-French harmony, however, French strategists and politicians became more hostile towards Italy in 1937–38. Some enthused about the Mediterranean as a promising arena for an offensive if war occurred.[63] Promoted by Admiral François Darlan, chief of the French naval staff (1937–41) and General Jules Bührer (chief of staff of colonial troops, 1938–40), plans were drafted for French army, air and naval forces to attack from Tunisia, Djibouti, Corsica and Provence to knock out fascist Italy, now seriously damaged by its imbroglio in Spain. Britain and France finally embarked on staff talks and war planning for the Mediterranean in May 1939.[64] However, the divergent policies of the previous three years meant that strategy against Italy was another subject on which Anglo-French co-ordination had an impossible amount of ground to make up.[65]

The question of Italy influenced Anglo-French relations in Europe and the colonies. Martin Thomas's chapter (Chapter 7) focuses on relations in the domain of colonial defence. Despite the importance of empire for each Entente power, the military resources they devoted to imperial security were modest.[66] Britain was gravely stretched in the Mediterranean, even though the potential enemy, Italy, was itself riddled with strategic, economic and operational weaknesses.[67] French notions of offensive action to conquer Italy's overseas possessions (Libya, Somaliland and Abyssinia) were unrealistic, because French North Africa (Morocco, Algeria and Tunisia) had not been developed as a major military base or reserve arsenal for arms manufacture.[68]

Before 1914 the French colonies further from home (West Africa, Equatorial Africa, Madagascar, Indochina) were attracting the ambitions of General Charles Mangin. It became Mangin's dream to constitute the natives into a bottomless human reservoir of fierce shock troops, and this idea was the genesis of France's legendary *force noire* in 1915–18.[69] At best the French empire was still seen in this light during the 1930s; but the long-term neglect of imperial infrastructure, arsenals and bases meant it was in 1940 a downright liability. The indefensibility of the colonies rendered academic the desperate, panicky talk, as Paris fell, of continuing the war from 'Overseas France'.[70]

Because of distance and geographical isolation, naval forces were the key to an Anglo-French strategy for imperial defence.[71] However, as Anthony Clayton's chapter here (Chapter 2) suggests, relations between the British and French naval staffs were arguably the most frosty of all between the wars. The 1935 Anglo-German naval agreement was negotiated behind the backs of the French. Worse, with cavalier disregard for French feelings, the agreement was made public on 18 June, anniversary of the Battle of Waterloo.[72] The troubled Anglo-French naval relationship of the 1930s was only temporarily eased by the joint patrols undertaken to police the 1937 Nyon Convention on non-intervention in the Spanish Civil War.[73] The more commonplace frictions and misunderstandings, however, set the fleets on course for the tragic 'end of the affair' at Mers-el-Kébir in July 1940.[74] Inadequate inter-war investment in imperial defence came home to roost for both Britain and France – not just in the Mediterranean in 1939–41, but in the exposure of both allies' Far Eastern territories (Singapore, Hong Kong and Indochina) once Japan joined the war in December 1941.[75]

The transformation of these episodic and conditional inter-war Anglo-French relationships into a genuine Anglo-French alliance was, therefore, as Talbot Imlay demonstrates (Chapter 5), very much the work of rapid improvization in 1938–39.[76] What was forced into existence at the eleventh hour reflected an increasingly frantic effort to catch up lost time.

In almost every facet of the cross-Channel relationship re-examined in this volume, the new light shed from the archives, especially from the French ones, reveals a tantalizing potential for an integrated, systematic and pragmatic partnership. A relationship of this sort was essential to defeat Germany – let alone withstand, and then defeat, the Axis as a whole. British and French military chiefs, civil servants and some ministers had hatched embryonic schemes that would be cloned much more successfully by the Anglo-American alliance of 1942–45. Time and again there is evidence of thinking, and sometimes of acting, along the lines that became second nature later in the war to their Anglo-American successors.[77]

In the case of the first, incomplete, alliance against Hitler, the Anglo-French one of 1939–40, practical lessons drawn from coalition war in 1914–18 were offset by the deep psychological scars of that conflict.[78] These scars limited the commitment and clouded the judgement of those preparing to run the new Anglo-French war strategy. Defeat in

1940 allowed the replacement of the men who began at the top on the British side, Field-Marshal Lord Gort, General Sir Edmund Ironside and Air Chief Marshal Sir Cyril Newall. Their replacements were more 'alliance-minded' in their direction of Britain's war effort. Despite the common endeavours of the first world war, separate languages and cultures, and recriminations about who had frittered away the victory of 1919 undermined Anglo-French efforts to do better in 1939–40.[79] As a result, coalition co-ordination was too fragile to withstand the blows inflicted by Germany in May and June 1940. Inter-war Anglo-French defence relations were more substantial than most accounts have allowed; but they remained much less substantial than the terrible tests of a new war would require.

Notes

1. See N. Waites (ed.), *Troubled Neighbours: Franco-British Relations in the Twentieth Century* (London: Weidenfeld & Nicholson, 1971); also P. M. H. Bell, *France and Britain, 1900–1940: Entente and Estrangement* and *France and Britain, 1940–1994: the Long Separation* (Harlow: Longman, 1996 and 1997).
2. On the post-1945 relationship see M. L. Dockrill, 'British Attitudes towards France as a Military Ally', *Diplomacy and Statecraft*, 1 (1990), pp. 49–70; R. Woodhouse, *British Policy Towards France, 1945–51* (Basingstoke: Macmillan Press [now Palgrave Macmillan] 1995); G. Warner, 'The Reconstruction and Defence of Western Europe after 1945', in Waites, *Troubled Neighbours*, pp. 259–92.
3. J. R. Ferris, *Men, Money and Diplomacy: The Evolution of British Strategic Foreign Policy, 1919–1926* (Ithaca, NY: Cornell University Press, 1989), p. 12.
4. *Ibid.*, pp. 12–186, *passim*. A 'French threat' to Britain was manipulated by Marshal of the RAF Sir Hugh Trenchard, Chief of the Air Staff, to secure funds for a 52-squadron Home Defence Air Expansion Scheme for completion in 1929. Ferris writes (*ibid.*, p. 132) of 'Trenchard's cynical use of the French air menace, in which he later claimed never to have believed', to gain advantage for the fledgling RAF in its bureaucratic and budgetary fights with the other services and the Treasury. In 1926, however, the French threat's incredibility, and a new squeeze on the defence budget, saw the 52 squadron scheme postponed to 1935–36. See Annual Reports of the Chiefs of Staff, 1926–33: Brief no. 3 for Ministers on the Co-ordination of Defence, House of Commons defence debate, 9 March 1936, Appendix B, Public Record Office, Kew (hereafter: PRO): CAB 21/450.
5. See G.-H. Soutou, 'L'impérialisme du pauvre: la politique économique du gouvernement français en Europe centrale et orientale de 1918 à 1929. Essai d'interprétation', *Relations Internationales*, 7 (1976), pp. 216–39; A. Marès, 'Mission militaire et relations internationales: L'exemple franco-tchécoslovaque, 1918–25', *Revue d'histoire moderne et contemporaine*, 30 (1982), pp. 559–86.
6. See M. Bemeke, G. D. Feldman and E. Glaser (eds), *The Treaty of Versailles: a Reassessment after 75 Years* (Cambridge: Cambridge University Press, 1998);

also M. Trachtenberg review of this rich reappraisal of the form and consequences of the peace, *Security Studies*, 9 (2000), pp. 191–205; D. Stevenson, 'France at the Paris Peace Conference: Addressing the Dilemmas of Security', in R. Boyce (ed.), *French Foreign and Defence Policy, 1918–1940: the Decline and Fall of a Great Power* (London: Routledge, 1998), pp. 10–29; D. R. Watson, 'The Making of the Treaty of Versailles', in Waites, *Troubled Neighbours*, pp. 67–99.

7. W. R. Keylor, 'France's Futile Quest for American Military Protection, 1919–22', in M. Petricioli and M. Guderzo (eds), *A Missed Opportunity? 1922: the Reconstruction of Europe* (Berne: Peter Lang, 1995), pp. 61–80; and 'France and the Illusion of American Support, 1919–1940', in J. Blatt (ed.), *The French Defeat of 1940: Reassessments* (Oxford: Berghahn Books, 1998), pp. 204–44.

8. See A. Lentin, 'Lloyd George, Clemenceau and the elusive Anglo-French guarantee treaty, 1919: "A disastrous episode"?', in A. Sharp and G. Stone (eds), *Anglo-French Relations in the Twentieth Century: Rivalry and Cooperation* (London: Routledge, 2000), pp. 104–19; J. Bariéty, 'Le projet de pacte franco-britannique, 1920–1922', *Guerres mondiales et conflits contemporains*, 49 (1999), pp. 83–99; N. Fleurier, 'Entre partenariat et alliance: Rapports diplomatiques et militaires de la Belgique avec la France en 1920', *ibid.*, pp. 23–38; C. Metzger, 'L'Allemagne: Un danger pour la France en 1920?', *ibid.*, pp. 5–22; S. Marks, 'Ménage à Trois: the Negotiations for an Anglo-Franco-Belgian Alliance in 1922', *International History Review*, iv (1982), pp. 524–52; and more generally, *Innocent Abroad: Belgium at the Paris Peace Conference, 1919* (Chapel Hill, NC: North Carolina University Press, 1981).

9. See J. F. V. Keiger, ' "Perfidious Albion?" French Perceptions of Britain as an Ally after the First World War', in M. S. Alexander (ed.), *Knowing Your Friends: Intelligence Inside Alliances and Coalitions from 1914 to the Cold War* (London: Frank Cass, 1998), pp. 37–52; S. Marks, 'Poincaré-la-peur: Poincaré and the Ruhr Crisis of 1923', in K. Mouré and M. S. Alexander (eds), *Crisis and Renewal in France, 1918–1962* (New York: Berghahn, 2001), pp. 28–45.

10. A. Sharp, 'Anglo-French Relations from Versailles to Locarno, 1919–1925: the Quest for Security', in Sharp and Stone, *Anglo-French Relations*, pp. 120–38. An important new book that presents fresh research on Locarno is G. Johnson (ed.), *Locarno Revisited: European Diplomacy, 1920–1929* (London: Frank Cass, 2002).

11. See Bell, *Entente and Estrangement*, pp. 113–65; D. Johnson, 'The Locarno Treaties', in Waites, *Troubled Neighbours*, pp. 100–24.

12. Report by Col. T. G. G. Heywood (British military attaché, Paris) on a conversation with the French minister for war, 9 April 1935, PRO, FO 371/18800/C3080/227/17.

13. See Bell, *Entente and Estrangement*, pp. 168–83; C. Kitching, 'The search for Disarmament: Anglo-French Relations, 1929–1934', in Sharp and Stone, *Anglo-French Relations*, pp. 158–79; D. Richardson, 'The Geneva Disarmament Conference, 1932–34', in D. Richardson and G. Stone (eds), *Decisions and Diplomacy: Essays in Twentieth-Century International History* (London: Routledge, 1995), pp. 60–82.

14. See J. Blatt, 'The Parity that Meant Superiority: French Naval Policy Towards Italy at the Washington Conference, 1921–22, and Interwar French Foreign Policy', *French Historical Studies*, 12 (1981), pp. 223–48; W. G. Perett, *French*

Naval Policy and Foreign Affairs, 1930–39 (Stanford University PhD thesis, 1977); P. Masson, *La marine française et la guerre, 1939–1945* (Paris: Editions Tallandier, 1991), pp. 9–32; E. Goldstein and J. Maurer (eds), *The Washington Conference, 1921–22. Naval Rivalry, East Asian Stability and the Road to Pearl Harbor* (London: Frank Cass, 1994).

15. See U. Bialer, *The Shadow of the Bomber: the Fear of Air Attack and British Politics, 1932–1939* (Woodbridge: Boydell and Brewer, 1980).

16. Cabinet Conclusions, 7 November 1938, PRO, CAB 23/96/53(38).

17. Britain's chiefs of staff referred to Locarno in their annual reports for 1929 and 1930, stating: 'We think it important that the C.I.D. should be under no misapprehensions that, so far as the Defence Forces are concerned, they are not in a state of readiness to fulfil our guarantee.' Annual Reports of the Chiefs of Staff, 1926–1933: Appendix B to Brief no. 3 on Co-ordination of Defence for Ministers in the House of Commons defence debate, 9 March 1936, PRO, CAB 21/450.

18. 'Conversation with General Weygand on the disarmament situation in Germany – note by Colonel Heywood', 15 March 1933, PRO, FO 371/16706/C2627/245/18.

19. See M. Vaïsse, *Sécurité d'abord. La politique française en matière de désarmement, 9 décembre 1930 au 17 avril 1934* (Paris: Editions Redone, 1981).

20. See R. J. Young, '*L'attaque Brusquée* and its Use as Myth in Interwar France', *Historical Reflections*, 8 (1981), pp. 93–113.

21. See M. S. Alexander, 'In Defence of the Maginot Line: Security Policy, Domestic Politics and the Economic Depression in France', in Boyce (ed.), *French Foreign and Defence Policy*, pp. 164–94; P. C. F. Bankwitz, *Maxime Weygand and Civil-Military Relations in Modern France* (Cambridge, MA: Harvard University Press, 1967), pp. 54–75, 83–8 and 94–100.

22. 'Avis motivé du Conseil Supérieur de la Guerre au sujet des besoins de l'Armée française', 11 May 1934, Daladier papers, Archives Nationales, Paris (hereafter AN), 496 AP, 4DA1/2/b; also F. Guelton (ed.), *Le 'Journal' du Général Weygand, 1929–1935* (Montpellier: Editions du CNRS-ESID, 1998), pp. 318–26.

23. 'Présidence de M. le Ministre de la Guerre. Objet: Exposé par M. le Général Weygand, Vice-Président du Conseil Supérieur de la Guerre, Inspecteur-Général de l'Armée de certaines considérations relatives à l'état présent et futur de l'Armée française', in CSG minutes, 15 January 1935, Service Historique de l'Armée de Terre, Vincennes (hereafter SHAT), 1N22. Cf. Guelton (ed.), '*Journal' du Général Weygand*, pp. 338–47; Bankwitz, *Maxime Weygand*, pp. 108–14.

24. Sargent minute of 10 November 1933, on report from Col. Heywood (Paris) on conversations with Generals Weygand and Gamelin, 24 October 1933, PRO, FO 371/16709/C9556/245/18.

25. Hankey to Vansittart, 8 March 1934, PRO, CAB 21/434.

26. 'Memorandum on the German Law for the Rebuilding of Defence Forces', by War Office Military Intelligence Branch MI3, 20 March 1935, p. 3, PRO, FO 371/18831/C2295/55/18. See also W. K. Wark, *The Ultimate Enemy: British Intelligence and Nazi Germany, 1933–39* (London, NY: I. B. Tauris, 1985); on French judgements about German rearmament and military expansion see P. Jackson, *France and the Nazi Menace: Intelligence and Policy Making,*

1933–1939 (Oxford: Oxford University Press, 2000); and *idem*, 'French intelligence and Hitler's rise to power', *Historical Journal*, 41 (1998), pp. 795–824.

27. Ferris, *Men, Money and Diplomacy*, pp. 128–32; M. S. Smith, 'The Royal Air Force, Air Power and British Foreign Policy, 1932–37', *Journal of Contemporary History*, 12 (1977), pp. 153–74.

28. See P. Venesson, 'Institution and Airpower: the Making of the French Air Force', in J. Gooch (ed.), *Airpower: Theory and Practice* (London: Frank Cass, 1995), pp. 36–67; M. S. Alexander, *The Republic in Danger: General Maurice Gamelin and the Politics of French Defence, 1933–1940* (Cambridge: Cambridge University Press, 1992), pp. 142–71.

29. This is best discussed in D. E. Omissi, *Air Power and Colonial Control: the Royal Air Force, 1919–1939* (Manchester: Manchester University Press, 1990); also M. S. Smith, *British Air Strategy between the Wars* (Oxford: Clarendan Press, 1984). Britain's land forces, too, were heavily committed in far-flung overseas duties after 1919. See T. R. Moreman, ' "Small Wars" and "Imperial Policing": the British Army and the Theory and Practice of Colonial Warfare in the British Empire, 1919–39', in B. Holden Reid (ed.), *Military Power: Land Warfare in Theory and Practice* (London: Frank Cass, 1997), pp. 105–31.

30. On the Anglo-French air, army and naval staff talks over sanctions against Italy see *Documents on British Foreign Policy, 1919–1939* (London: HMSO, 1968 et seq.), 2nd ser., XV, appendix II ('Anglo-French Staff Discussions, 9–10 December 1935: Report by Colonel T. G. G. Heywood [. . .] 18 December 1935' and 'Précis of a report by Air Vice-Marshal P. B. Joubert de la Ferté on the air [. . .] conversations' 10 Jan. 1936. For the naval talks of 29 October–9 November 1935 and 15 January 1936, ibid., nos. 148, 330, 338; also A. Reussner, *Les conversations franco-britanniques d'Etat-Major, 1935–1939* (Vincennes: Service Historique de la Marine, 1969), pp. 39–100; P. Masson, 'Les conversations militaires franco-britanniques, 1935–38', in *Les Relations Franco-Britannique de 1935 à 1939* (Paris: Editions du Centre Nationale de la Recherche Scientifique, 1975), pp. 120–3. For the context and import of these limited talks, see S. Morewood, 'The Chiefs of Staff, the "Men on the Spot" and the Italo-Abyssinian Emergency, 1935–36', in Richardson and Stone (eds), *Decisions and Diplomacy*, pp. 83–107; F. Hardie, *The Abyssinian Crisis* (London: Batsford, 1974), pp. 145–63; R. A. C. Parker, 'Great Britain, France and the Ethiopian Crisis, 1935–1936', *English Historical Review*, 89 (1974), pp. 293–332; N. Rostow, *Anglo-French Relations, 1934–36* (London: Macmillan, 1984).

31. Minute by Cresswell, 28 April 1934, on 'French Air Force Reserves and Re-equipment', air ministry memorandum, 26 April 1934, PRO, FO 371/17653/C2653/85/17.

32. Cot later defended himself vigorously against charges of administrative incompetence and fellow-travelling with Communism. From 1940–43 he lived in New York, lecturing at Yale and publishing an early riposte to his critics: 'The Defeat of the French Air Force', *Foreign Affairs* (July 1941), pp. 790–805; and a book, *Triumph of Treason* (trans. Sybil and Morton Crane: New York: Ziff-Davis, 1944).

33. For British knowledge of the crisis gripping the *Armée de l'Air* see RAF Intelligence Branch Summaries (France), 1936 and 1938, PRO, AIR 8/210, AIR 8/252 and AIR 8/287.

34. See a characteristic report by Group Captain Douglas Colyer, British air attaché in Paris, on a 12 June 1936 interview with Cot, along with appended scathing minutes by officials in the Foreign Office, PRO, FO 371/19871/C4182/172/17.
35. For British wariness about excessive intimacy with inter-war France, see J. C. Cairns, 'A Nation of Shopkeepers in Search of a Suitable France, 1919–1940', *American Historical Review*, 79 (1974), pp. 710–43; D. J. Dutton, ' "A Nation of Shopkeepers in Search of a Suitable Frenchman": Britain and Briand, 1915–1930', *Modern & Contemporary France*, 6 (1998), pp. 463–78; A. Sharp, 'Standard-bearers in a Tangle: British Perceptions of France after the First World War', in D. J. Dutton (ed.), *Statecraft and Diplomacy in the Twentieth Century: Essays Presented to P. M. H. Bell* (Liverpool: Liverpool University Press, 1995), pp. 55–73; M. L. Dockrill, *British Establishment Perspectives on France, 1936–40* (Basingstoke: Macmillan Press [now Palgrave Macmillan], 1999).
36. See, 'Exchange of information between British and French air staffs', 20 March 1937; Air Intelligence Branch AI3(b), no. 213, 'Comments on the French order-of-battle for the German Air Force', 2 April 1937; 'Exchange of information between British and French Air Staffs, March–April 1937', 21 April 1937 (minute sheet signed by Group Captain L. C. H. Medhurst, Deputy Director of Air Intelligence), PRO, AIR 40/186331/556/35.
37. 'The role of the army in a major war', sections 8–9, by Gen. H. L. Ismay, 13 July 1937, PRO, CAB 21/509, quoting the chiefs of staff from CID Paper CP 41 (37), para. 14. Cf. the secretary to the Cabinet and the CID to the prime minister, 18 months earlier: 'Continental states are not satisfied that aircraft can defend them against invasion and still look on armies and fortifications as their mainstay. If we have no efficient army they will feel that we do not mean business', Hankey to Baldwin, 15 January 1936, PRO, CAB 21/434.
38. See P. Fridenson and J. Lecuir, *La France et la Grande-Bretagne faces aux problèmes aériens (1935-mai 1940)* (Vincennes: Service Historique de l'Armée de l'Air, 1976), pp. 82–3, 86–7; Cot testimony, 1 Aug. 1947, in *Commission d'enquête parlementaire sur les événements survenus en France de 1933 à 1945: Témoignages* (9 vols, Paris, 1951–2), i, p. 273.
39. 'Aménagements à assurer par la France, nécessaires à une force aérienne avancée de bataille basée sur le Continent, selon le Plan Occidental', 6 July 1938, SHAT, CSDN, dr. 136 (Conversations franco-britanniques). This was a 40-page document of immense detail. Ten principal airfields (handling 32 aircraft each) were to be handed over to the RAF in the Rheims-Nancy area, along with ten secondary airfields, four supply aerodromes and one air base for RAF Transport Command at Nantes, the designated RAF embarkation port in France.
40. 'Note de M. le général Gamelin à MM. les ministres Daladier et Bonnet: analyse', 23 Sept. 1938, SHAT, CSDN, dr. 135/2.
41. Minutes: Conseil Supérieur de l'Air, 15 March 1938, in M. Baumont, P. Renouvin, J.-B. Duroselle, J. Laloy, and Y. Lacaze (eds), *Documents Diplomatiques Français, 1932–1939* (hereafter: *DDF*) (Paris, 1963 et seq.), 2nd ser. (1936–39), VIII, no. 447, pp. 832–49; also CPDN minutes, 15 March 1938, in M.-G. Gamelin, *Servir* (3 vols, Paris, Plon, 1946–7), ii, pp. 322–8; Vuillemin letter to La Chambre, no. 127/EMGAA, 26 September 1938, printed in La Chambre's testimony (25 Nov. 1947), in *Commission . . . Témoignages*, ii, p. 313; Alexander, *Republic in Danger*, pp. 162–71; P. Jackson, 'La perception de

la puissance aérienne allemande et son influence sur la politique extérieure française pendant les crises internationales de 1938 à 1939', *Revue Historique des Armées*, 4 (1994), pp. 76–87.

42. Cabinet Conclusions, 7 November 1938, PRO, CAB 23/96/53(38).

43. 'Etude sur la participation de l'Angleterre dans l'éventualité d'une action commune franco-britannique en cas de guerre', by Gen. A. Lelong (French military attaché, London), 8 November 1938, Papiers Daladier, 4DA8/3/b; also Ministre de la Défense Nationale et de la Guerre (Cabinet): CSDN Paper no. CU/1 for Daladier, 'La puissance des forces armées franco-britanniques', 22 November 1938, SHAT, 5N579/2. Cf. R. J. Young, *In Command of France: French Foreign Policy and Military Planning, 1933–1939* (Cambridge, MA: Harvard University Press, 1978), pp. 218–19.

44. Excellent on the air war in 1940 is P. Facon, *L'Armée de l'Air dans la tourmente: La bataille de France, 1939–1940* (Paris: Economica, 1997); see also J. A. Gunsburg, 'Armée de l'Air versus Luftwaffe in 1940', *Defence Update International*, 45 (1984), pp. 44–53.

45. A point that Gen. Sir James Marshall-Cornwall affirmed when interviewed at his home at Malton, North Yorkshire, by Martin Alexander, in August 1978.

46. See Lettre du général Moyrand, sous-chef de l'Etat-major de l'armée au général Voruz, 25 April 1933, SHAT, 7N2802; also Voruz to Moyrand, 12 May 1933, with itinerary for Montgomery-Massingberd's visit to France (12–13 July 1933), in ibid; and *Servir*, ii, pp. 110 and 172.

47. 'General Note on French army strengths, service and mobilization arrangements' by Col. Bernard Paget, MI3(a), 10 December 1935, PRO, FO 371/19870/05439.

48. Beaumont-Nesbitt to Sir G. Clerk (British ambassador, Paris), enc. no. 2, under Clerk's cover note of 22 September 1936 to the foreign secretary, Anthony Eden, PRO, FO 371/19871/C6616/172/17. Cf. Gamelin, *Servir*, ii, pp. 247–9.

49. French manoeuvres, 1937 – Note by Field Marshal Sir Cyril Deverell, 15 October 1937, PRO, CAB 21/275/14/31/108; also Beaumont-Nesbitt report on the attendance by Mr Hore-Belisha at French army manoeuvres, 8 October 1937, PRO, FO 371/20694/C7129/122/17.

50. 'Notes on the Present State of the French Army', by de Linde, 23 April 1938, PRO, FO 371/21594/C3388/55/17, and Ismay minute in CAB 21/554.

51. M. S. Alexander and W. J. Philpott, 'The Entente Cordiale and the Next War: Anglo-French Views on Future Military Cooperation, 1928–1939', in Alexander (ed.), *Knowing Your Friends*, pp. 53–83.

52. For discussion of the contemporary British assessment of the German army's capabilities, see J. P. Harris, 'British Military Intelligence and the Rise of German Mechanized Forces, 1929–40', *Intelligence and National Security*, 6 (1991), pp. 395–417.

53. Bradley F. Smith shows, in *The War's Long Shadow: the Second World War and its Aftermath, China, Russia, Britain and America* (New York: Touchstone (Simon and Schuster), 1986), that Britain put her economy and society more comprehensively on a war footing than any other second world war belligerent – albeit mostly *after* 1940 and the knockout of France. Cf. R. J. Overy, *Why the Allies Won* (New York: W. W. Norton, 1995).

54. Anglo-French Staff Conversations – UK Delegation: Report on Stage One, Chiefs of Staff paper, 11 April 1939, PRO, CAB 53/47/COS 877.

55. The re-establishment of the SWC was actually arranged at a higher level, being considered too 'political' a matter for the staff talks proper.

56. Journal de marche: Cabinet Gamelin, 12–13 September 1939, Papiers Gamelin, SHAT, 1K224/9; F. Bédarida, *La stratégie secrète de la drôle de guerre: Le Conseil Suprême Interallié, septembre 1939–avril 1940* (Paris: Presses de la Foundation Nationale des Sciences Politiques, 1979); *idem*, 'La rupture franco-britannique de 1940: Le Conseil Suprême Interallié, de l'invasion à la défaite de la France', *Vingtième Siècle*, 25 (1990), pp. 37–48.

57. On the Allied Military Committee in 1939–40, see the recollections of its senior British military member, J. H. Marshall-Cornwall: *Wars and Rumours of Wars: a Memoir* (London: Leo Cooper, 1984), pp. 129–36.

58. See Ferris, *Men, Money and Diplomacy*, passim; G. C. Peden, 'Sir Warren Fisher and British Rearmament Against Germany', *English Historical Review*, 94 (1979), pp. 29–47; *idem*, 'The burden of imperial defence and the continental commitment reconsidered', *Historical Journal*, 27 (1984), pp. 405–23; *idem*, 'Keynes, the Economics of Rearmament and Appeasement', in W. J. Mommsen and L. Kettenacker (eds), *The Fascist Challenge and the Policy of Appeasement* (London: Allen and Unwin, 1983), pp. 142–57; S. W. Roskill, *Naval Policy Between the Wars. I: The Period of Anglo-American Antagonism, 1919–1929* (London: Collins, 1968).

59. See the chapters by J. Bariéty, E. Bussière, D. Artaud and R. Boyce, in Boyce (ed.), *French Foreign and Defence Policy*, pp. 30–48, 71–88, 89–106 and 107–131 respectively.

60. See G. Stone, 'Britain, France and the Spanish problem, 1936–39', in Richardson and Stone (eds), *Decisions and Diplomacy*, pp. 129–52; *idem*, 'The European Great Powers and the Spanish Civil War, 1936–1939', in R. Boyce and E. Robertson (eds), *Paths to War: New Essays on the Origins of the Second World War* (Basingstoke: Macmillan, 1989), pp. 199–232.

61. C. Seton-Watson, 'The Anglo-Italian Gentleman's Agreement of January 1937 and its Aftermath', in Mommsen and Kettenacker (eds), *The Fascist Challenge*, pp. 267–82.

62. See M. J. Budden 'Defending the Indefensible? The Air Defence of Malta, 1936–1940', *War in History*, 6 (1999), pp. 447–67; S. Morewood, 'Anglo-Italian Rivalry in the Mediterranean and the Middle East, 1935–1940', in Boyce and Robertson (eds), *Paths to War*, pp. 167–98.

63. See the conversation between Gen. Lelong (French military attaché, London) and Henry Pownall (Director of Military Operations at the War Office), 25 February 1938, in B. J. Bond (ed.), *Chief of Staff: the Diaries of Lieutenant-General Sir Henry Pownall. Vol. I: 1933–1940* (London: Leo Cooper, 1972), pp. 135–6; also Lelong to Daladier, 18 February 1938 and Corbin to Delbos, 8 March 1938, *DDF*, 2nd ser., VIII, nos 206 and 345.

64. 'Rapport du général Noguès, 7 mai 1939, à M. Edouard Daladier, ministre de la Défense Nationale et de la Guerre, et au général Gamelin, chef d'Etat-major de la Défense Nationale, sur les conversations d'états-majors franco-britanniques tenues à Rabat (Maroc) du 4 au 6 mai 1939', Cabinet du Ministre de la Défense Nationale et de la Guerre, SHAT, CSDN, dr. 135/2; for the minutes of the 16 pre-war meetings in the Anglo-French staff

talks, with supporting memoranda and papers, PRO, AIR 9/104, 105, 116 and 117.

65. See D. Omissi, 'The Mediterranean and the Middle East in British Global Strategy, 1935–39', in M. J. Cohen and M. Kolinsky (eds), *Britain and the Middle East in the 1930s: Security Problems, 1935–39* (Basingstoke: Macmillan Press [now Palgrave Macmillan], 1995); D. C. Watt, 'Britain, France and the Italian Problem, 1937–1939', in *Les Relations Franco-Britanniques, 1935–1939* pp. 277–94.

66. M. Thomas, *The French Empire at War, 1940–45* (Manchester: Manchester University Press, 1998), pp. 10–35; *idem*, 'At the Heart of Things? French Imperial Defense Planning in the late 1930s', *French Historical Studies*, 21 (1998), pp. 325–61.

67. See R. Mallett, *The Italian Navy and Fascist Expansionism, 1935–40* (London: Frank Cass, 1998); M. Knox, *Mussolini Unleashed, 1939–1941: Politics and Strategy in Fascist Italy's Last War* (Cambridge: Cambridge University Press, 1982).

68. See M. Thomas, 'Plans and Problems of the *Armée de l'Air* in the Defence of French North Africa before the Fall of France', *French History*, 7 (1993), pp. 472–95.

69. See C. Carlier and G. Pédroncini (eds), *Les Troupes coloniales dans la Grande Guerre* (Paris: Economica, 1997); M. Michel, 'Le mythe de la "Force Noire" avant la guerre de 1914–18', *Relations Internationales*, 2 (1974), pp. 83–90; *idem, L'appel à l'Afrique. Contributions et réactions à l'effort de guerre en Afrique Occidentale Française, 1914–1919* (Paris: Publications de la Sorbonne, 1982).

70. The conclusion reached by the subject's most thorough historian is that, 'Taken as a whole, by 1939 the French empire was indefensible' (Thomas, *The French Empire at War*, p. 31). On the North African option in 1940, see E. M. Gates, *End of the Affair: the Collapse of the Anglo-French Alliance, 1939–40* (London: Allen and Unwin, 1981), pp. 235–9, 262–6, 272–3 and 300–25; A. Truchet, *L'Armistice de 1940 et l'Afrique du Nord* (Paris: Presses Universitaires de France, 1955).

71. See P. Jackson, 'Naval Policy and National Strategy in France, 1933–1937', *Journal of Strategic Studies*, 23 (2000), pp. 130–59; Masson, *La marine française*, pp. 33–53.

72. R. M. Salerno, 'Multilateral Strategy and Diplomacy: the Anglo-German Naval Agreement and the Mediterranean Crisis, 1935–1936', *Journal of Strategic Studies*, 17 (1994), pp. 39–78; C. Bloch, 'Great Britain, German Rearmament and the Naval Agreement of 1935', in H. W. Gatzke (ed.), *European Diplomacy Between Two Wars, 1919–1939* (Chicago: Quadrangle Books, 1972), pp. 125–51; Bell, *Entente and Estrangement*, pp. 184–90; J. Maiolo, *The Royal Navy and Nazi Germany, 1933–39: a Study in Appeasement and the Origins of the Second World War* (Basingstoke: Macmillan Press [now Palgrave Macmillan], 1998).

73. See M. Thomas, *Britain, France and Appeasement: Anglo-French Relations in the Popular Front Era* (Oxford: Berg, 1996), pp. 91–2 and 101–3.

74. Gates, *End of the Affair*, pp. 259–61, 268–72 287–93 and 327–73. P. M. H. Bell has written more extensively than anyone on the divorce in summer 1940: see his 'Entente Broken and Renewed: Britain and France, 1940–1945', in Sharp and Stone (eds), *Anglo-French Relations*, pp. 223–43; *France and Britain,*

1940–1994, pp. 9–26; *A Certain Eventuality: Britain and the Fall of France* (Farnborough: Saxon House, 1974), pp. 137–64; 'The Breakdown of the Alliance in 1940', in Waites (ed.), *Troubled Neighbours*, pp. 200–27; 'Prologue de Mers-el-Kébir', *Revue d'Histoire de la Deuxième Guerre Mondiale*, 33 (1959), pp. 15–36. Cf. H. Coutau-Bégarie and C. Huan, *Mers-el-Kébir (1940): La rupture franco-britannique* (Paris, Economica, 1994); and A. J. Marder, *From the Dardanelles to Oran: Studies of the Royal Navy in War and Peace, 1915–1940* (Oxford: Oxford University Press, 1974), pp. 179–288.

75. See I. Cowman, 'Defence of the Malay Barrier? The Place of the Philippines in Admiralty Naval War Planning, 1925–1941', *War in History*, 3 (1996), pp. 398–417; C. M. Bell, '"Our Most Exposed Outpost": Hong Kong and British Far Eastern Strategy, 1921–1941', *Journal of Military History*, 60 (1996), pp. 61–88; idem, *The Royal Navy, Seapower and Strategy Between the Wars* (Basingstoke: Palgrave, 2000); P. Haggie, *Britannia at Bay: The Defence of the British Empire against Japan, 1931–1941* (Oxford: Oxford University Press, 1981); J. Neidpath, *The Singapore Naval Base and the Defence of Britain's Eastern Empire, 1919–1941* (Oxford: Clarendon Press, 1981); A. J. Marder, *Old Friends, New Enemies: The Royal Navy and the Imperial Japanese Navy: Strategic Illusions, 1936–1941* (Oxford: Clarendon Press, 1981).

76. See also T. Imlay, 'France and the phoney war, 1939–1940', in Boyce (ed.), *French Foreign and Defence Policy, 1918–1940*, pp. 261–82.

77. See Alexander, *Republic in Danger* pp. 396–7 and 399; F. Vandiver, 'Foch and Eisenhower: Supreme Commanders', in J. M. Bourne, P. Liddle and I. Whitehead (eds), *The Great World War, 1914–45, vol. I: Lightning Strikes Twice* (London: Harper Collins, 2000) pp. 416–27; D. Showalter, 'Coalition War: the Anglo-American Experience', in *ibid.*, pp. 460–78.

78. In contrast, the wartime relations and linkages between Germany, Italy and Japan were always so unco-ordinated and so flimsy that theirs was arguably never an 'alliance' at all. For a recent excoriation of the 'lack of understanding of foreign countries or the practical aspects of coalition warfare' by Hitler and his principal military advisors, see R. L. DiNardo and D. J. Hughes, 'Germany and Coalition Warfare in the World Wars: a Comparative Study', *War in History*, 8 (2001), pp. 166–90.

79. See W. J. Philpott, 'Coalition War: Britain and France', in Bourne, Liddle and Whitehead (eds), *Lightning Strikes Twice*, pp. 479–91.

2
Growing Respect: the Royal Navy and the Marine Nationale, 1918–39

Anthony Clayton

On a grey day and in heavy weather in late November 1939 a powerful naval task force assembled in the English Channel; its task was to engage German 'pocket battleships'. The force included the battle-cruiser *Hood*, the pride of the Royal Navy. The force was commanded by the French Admiral Gensoul from his flagship, the fine modern small battleship *Dunkerque*. That *Hood* was under command of a French admiral was testimony to the respect for the French navy that had developed in the 1930s, and to how much the two navies had moved closer together on three levels – policy, material and ships at sea – levels that in the 1920s had not always been harmonious.

A battle task force under French command would have been inconceivable in 1918, at the end of the first world war.[1] Both navies, British and French, were in sensitive, touchy states of mind at the time. For the British, Jutland had not been the Trafalgar-scale victory that the Royal Navy's reputation warranted and public opinion had anticipated; further, it was evident that the Royal Navy's pre-1914 lordship of the seas was now to be challenged by the United States Navy, which was, in terms of modern super-Dreadnought capital ships, becoming the equal of the Royal Navy. At ship-officer level there was also a 'Grand Fleet snobbery'. The minority of officers who had, as it happened, formed a wholesome respect for the French navy in the Dardanelles operations or in the Adriatic were nevertheless seen as having indulged in naval 'sideshows' – only American battleships had served with the Royal Navy in the North Sea, while the French capital ships had not. The economic climate of post-1918 Britain was one that called for drastic cuts in government spending. The High Seas Fleet having been scuttled, the Royal Navy was an obvious target for a huge scrapping programme. In the fleet's squadrons and flotillas that remained OUNE

(Owing to the Urgent Need for Economy) was the cry. Construction to surpass the big-gun battleship programme set in motion by the United States during the war was politically out of the question.

The Marine Nationale, for its part, could never pretend to have suffered the experience of thousands of *poilus* on the Western Front. Its senior officers – some, but not all, still products of traditional anti-English 'Trafalgar must be avenged' folk-lore – had not developed the same emotional ties of mutual military respect that had formed between the French and British generals on the Western Front. Much of the French navy's most useful work, escorting convoys and patrolling sea-lanes, had been unglamorous. Almost all naval construction had been stopped during the war, industrial resources being given to the army. The general public had, as a result, little or no interest in or understanding of the navy. For many it seemed an unnecessary burden on the taxpayer; as in Britain, the navy seemed an obvious target. With admirals uncertain of their role and sailors badly paid and badly cared for, morale at all levels was low.

It is easiest to follow the complex story of Anglo-French naval relations in the 1920s at each level of the relationship – policy and international relations, *matériel*, and events at sea; in the 1930s the policy and events at sea interface and are set out in sequence.

1920–29: Choppy seas

International relations in the decade immediately following the first world war were characterized by an increasing divergence of interest between the two great allies of 1914–18. The French, profoundly distrustful of Germany, sought to create a new security architecture by making treaties with successor states of the Romanov and Habsburg empires. Such a set of treaties was to complement the other vital piece of French defence thinking in the years 1919 to 1939, the need to balance the superior population, and therefore larger army, of Germany with African troops, *Spahis* and *Tirailleurs* from the three North African territories and, if necessary, Black African *Tirailleurs Sénégalais*. It was correctly foreseen that this need would increase with the fall in the French birth rate in the 1930s when the correlation of forces would be highly adverse. Only a small number of these troops could be garrisoned permanently in France, and the majority would have to be ferried over from Algeria, Tunisia and Moroccan ports.

The London Foreign Office believed that the French treaty plans were divisive and security would be best attained through support of the

League of Nations and the re-creation of a balance of power in Europe. In this balance France should equate with Italy; Germany was to be limited by the Versailles Treaty and consequently no power would be strong enough to dominate the continent.

The French resented the equation with Italy and saw British naval policy as a sign of weakness; only by a scaling down of fleets the world over, the French argued, could Britain secure the reduction of the United States Navy to the level equal to that of the Royal Navy and so divert the loss of prestige consequent upon no longer being the world's most powerful navy. Moreover the French perceived, correctly, that Italy was in a resentful mood, believing that the rewards of victory due to her had been denied, and in consequence might be tempted into an alliance with a revanchist Germany.

These factors quickly led to friction in international negotiations, and also later in crisis management in several areas of the world. At the outset the British and French naval delegates at the Versailles conference in 1919 differed sharply over two issues: the future of the submarine and the distribution of the surrendered German warships. The British, having been driven almost to the point of defeat in early 1917 by German submarines, an experience Admiral Lord Wester Wemyss could hardly forget, hoped that such vessels could be totally outlawed.[2] But the French delegation, headed by Admiral de Bon, argued that while abolition was no doubt suitable for nations prepared to spend money on large warships, it was against the interests of weaker powers for whom, if used in accordance with the rules of war, submarines were an important defensive weapon.[3] The second bone of contention, German warships, was settled by the Germans themselves scuttling the majority of the ships at Scapa Flow, but not before French resentment had been aroused by British and American agreement that most of the ships be scrapped or sunk, and their total opposition to any division that would have provided France or Italy with any major units. In the end France and Italy both received a very limited number of the surviving German cruisers, destroyers and submarines.

Further, and sharper, acrimony was to follow at the 1921–22 Washington Naval Conference. In Britain by this time, each armed service was appraising its most likely opponent. The army was equipping itself as a colonial army to oppose a Soviet incursion into India. The Royal Navy resented American strength but its more serious strategists were looking ahead to Japan. The newly formed Royal Air Force was, however, vociferously pointing with much exaggeration at France and her growing air force. The British accordingly entered the negotiations with a renewed desire to abolish submarines, and an almost paranoid desire to secure a reduction in French air and naval power.[4] If this proved impossible, then French power should be checked by ensuring that Italy would form an effective counter-balance. France's real needs, her links with North Africa, were simply not understood, while, more realistically, the practical limitations on her battleship-building capabilities, whatever she might demand, were not appreciated.

These British misunderstandings, together with French suspicions that Britain and America had arranged a pre-conference deal, led to French objections to the painfully negotiated 5.5.3 agreement between Great Britain, the United States, and Japan on the ratio of capital ships, an agreement that had also envisaged 175,000 tons of capital shipping each for France and Italy – five or six ships depending on tonnage, compared with the 15 for Britain and America. At the outset the French prime minister, Briand, had realistically accepted the 175,000 figure, but strong public and naval objection, the latter led by Admiral de Bon, led to a demand for a tonnage of 350,000, or ten ships, as a matter of national prestige. The fact that a capital-ship construction programme, with four keels already laid, had just been cancelled was conveniently forgotten. Briand was persuaded to overrule de Bon by the American Secretary of State, Hughes, but the French flatly refused any discussion on reduction of the numbers of other categories of surface warship or submarines below their own projections, with the one exception of a 60,000 total tonnage limit for aircraft-carriers.[5]

The low watermark of the conference was however reached later when the French contemptuously rejected an offer by Britain to scrap its entire submarine fleet, including many modern boats, if other countries would do the same. An especially sour note entered the controversy – a curious mixture of ethics of war and practicalities – following an article in *La Revue Maritime* by Captain (later Admiral) Castex, a leading French naval theorist. The article had been written earlier and might have been forgotten had it not been for the appointment of Castex as a lecturer on senior officers' courses. The British First Lord of the Admiralty, Lord Lee, in an attack on the French position, argued that in the article Castex had justified the German U-boat campaign as a successful naval strategy.[6] The French government disavowed the article, but they also rejected the British interpretation of it, and the general furore aroused marked the lowest point in Anglo-French relations since the Armistice.

Further diplomacy took place in the years 1926 to 1929 at sessions of the League of Nations' Preparatory Commission for the Disarmament Conference and, later, in 1929, during preparations for a Naval

Conference in London planned for early 1930. The main controversies, between Great Britain, the United States and Japan, lie outside the scope of this work. Anglo-French naval relations remained distrustful, proposals by each side being rejected by the other with one exception, an unofficial French proposal accepted by Britain, but subsequently disavowed by Paris. The proposal's significance however was the antagonism it aroused in the United States.[7] The French also continued, throughout, to oppose any project of reducing the French Navy to parity with Italy, or for the abolition of submarines.

Throughout the early to mid-1920s the French navy battled with its inheritance of obsolete or obsolescent ships (219 units condemned in 1920) and unhappy morale. Its saviour was a lawyer politician born in a town far from the sea: Georges Leygues, the greatest French naval administrator since Colbert.[8] In his three periods of office as navy minister from 1917 to 1920, 1925 to 1930 and 1932 to 1933, Georges Leygues provided the navy with a rationale, modernized its institutions, and began the construction of a modern fleet. His vision throughout was clear; that France must possess a navy equal to that of Germany and Italy combined. The prime role of the French navy must be to secure the lines of communication between France and French North Africa, especially with Algeria. Unlike his increasingly powerful naval officer son-in-law, François Darlan, George Leygues was never at any time anti-British.[9] He saw security in the Mediterranean as the key role for the navy, and the various construction programmes he authorised were all designed to meet the changing needs of this role.

Initially, Georges Leygues thought this role might be fulfilled by defensive light forces, light cruisers and powerful destroyers. After his departure from his first period in office his successor initiated a large-scale submarine construction programme which, on his return to office, Georges Leygues took every opportunity to reassure London was not to be seen as a threat to Britain.[10] There was good reason for this, for by the time he returned to the rue Royale for his second spell as minister in November 1925 Mussolini had taken power in Rome and laid down the keels of two big 8-inch-gun cruisers, a clear warning that the Italian navy now had ambitions beyond its (earlier) Adriatic interests – inevitably posing a threat to France's North African communications. France began to move from resentment of the size of Britain's Mediterranean fleet to a desire that the fleet remained there. Even with the ending of the Anglo-Japanese alliance and increasing evidence of Japanese ambitions Britain continued to keep a powerful force in the Mediterranean – from the mid-1920s onwards a battleship squadron of three or four oil-burning ships, an aircraft-carrier, two cruiser squadrons, three destroyer flotillas and one submarine flotilla, between a third and a half of the Royal Navy's combat-ready units. The Mediterranean fleet's location had also the additional advantages of securing vital fuel-oil supplies, and after the harsh conditions of Scapa Flow, providing officers and men with a highly agreeable lifestyle.

It is not surprising, in the uneasy diplomatic climate of the 1920s, that there seems to have been only limited formal co-operation at *matériel* level between the British and French navies. The most important example was that of British help in the conversion of the *Béarn* from a battleship hull into an aircraft-carrier from 1923 to 1927.[11] Informally, the yearly pattern of courtesy visits by ships of both navies to each other's ports, with the crews visiting each other's ships and displaying equipments with pride, represented a, perhaps unconscious, exchange. Particularly admired by the British were the first French postwar light cruisers of the Duguay-Trouin class.[12]

At the third level, at sea on specific operational tasks, co-operation varied from the happy to the disastrous. The most successful example was that of operations in the Baltic, notably the liberation of Latvia. Latvia had declared itself independent, with a provisional government, following the collapse of Russia, but the country was occupied by German troops who refused to withdraw after the Armistice, and who supported a faction of German landowners and others hoping instead to create German Baltic client states. These in turn were challenged by the Bolsheviks. Unrest and violence followed all through 1919, and the Allies, Britain and France, whose policy was to support a truly independent Latvia, were obliged to accept the Germans as a protection against the Bolsheviks. In October and November a German-sponsored force twice attempted to take Riga. On both occasions Allied naval forces – British light cruisers and destroyers together with a small French naval force of destroyers, torpedo boats and sloops – repulsed the attacks by naval gunfire; the British admiral, Sir Walter Cowan, and the French commander, Capitaine Brisson, being linked by mutual personal regard and enjoying each other's full co-operation. The Germans were forced to withdraw and Latvia secured her freedom.[13]

While the small French naval contingents in the Allied intervention forces in the north Russian and Siberian lands of the former Russian Empire generally worked smoothly with the British, in the major areas of French responsibility, Bessarabia, the Crimea and the Ukraine, there was friction and resentment.[14] In December 1918 a French-led force (which included Greeks, Poles and Romanians) occupied Odessa and a small French contingent also replaced British marines at Sevastopol. The force at first achieved some success, advancing northwards. But the French personnel, troops and sailors, were war-weary and disaffected, and easily succumbed to Communist propaganda. In March Ukrainian partisans rallying to the Bolshevik cause reversed the French successes, driving the force south. The French authorities, alarmed by the worsening disaffection, decided on an immediate and complete withdrawal from both the Ukraine and the Crimea. The withdrawal, accomplished by 6 April, and subsequent open mutinies in the French ships, were viewed by the British force commander in the Black Sea, Admiral Sir Somerset Gough-Calthorpe, with disgust.[15] A force including one or two large cruisers and destroyers did, however, return in 1920 to work alongside the British in the final evacuations from Novorossisk, Batum and Theodosia in the Crimea following the collapse of General Denikin's army.[16] Over 100,000 Russian soldiers were evacuated, more than a quarter with arms and ammunition. The majority were placed in a camp on the Gallipoli peninsula where they very quickly became a new Russian threat to Constantinople [Istanbul], albeit in a strange form. To contain this threat necessitated further Anglo-French military and naval co-operation.

Divergences over policy were to have their worst consequences in the operations that followed the surrender and subsequent collapse of the Ottoman Empire. Early policy differences arose following initial British opposition to a French mandate for Syria, although these have relevance to naval relations only in so far as the context, the soured atmosphere created by the Syrian differences, heightened the resentments and bitterness over policies towards the Turkish heartland.

Behind both the Syrian and Turkish mainland issues was the British wish, both for strategic reasons and to safeguard oil supplies, to secure a hegemony in the Middle East, and a French desire, for reasons both of national prestige and national interest, not to allow Britain to have matters all her own way. Syria was soon seen by Britain as expendable, but from the moment of Ottoman surrender Great Britain set out to assert political ascendancy in Turkey and Turkish waters with a massive naval presence: squadrons of battleships and cruisers and flotillas of destroyers, all with unrestricted fuel consumption. The French navy could not muster more than one capital ship, one cruiser and a handful of destroyers, all with fuel-consumption limits.[17] At the actual signing of the armistice on board a British battleship the French were not present, and in March 1920 it was an exclusively British force, of 3,600 sailors, that landed to occupy Constantinople as a preliminary to the imposition of a peace treaty. The local French naval commander, Admiral de Bon, attempted to use his limited resources to create links with Turkish educational and commercial institutions. He also warned of the dangers to all foreigners, including members of the numerous French community, posed by the arrival of Greek troops in Smyrna [Izmir], which had been authorized by the Allied governments at Versailles. Tension worsened when on 6 July 1920 Royal Navy warships opened fire on French installations at Mudania. This action was said to have been a reprisal for a shot fired by the French, but details of the incident remain murky.

The treaty arrangements eventually proposed reflected prime minister Lloyd George's support for the Greek cause and the longer-term project of a Greek 'client state' serving British interests. By the Treaty of Sèvres of August 1920 the Greeks were to gain territory in Thrace and a five-year hold on the Smyrna area with sufficient time to arrange a suitable plebiscite result; France was to gain a sphere of influence in Cilicia and Italy in Adalia. The renaissance of Turkish military power under Kemal Ataturk, however, rendered the Sèvres treaty void and created new Franco-British rivalries.

Paris appreciated that the hidden agenda of the Sèvres treaty was British regional hegemony and that long-term French interests might be better served by an understanding with Kemal and the nationalists. Ships were first ordered not to open fire on the nationalists; then to try to show them the advantages of a French alliance; and finally not to recognize Greek sovereignty in Anatolia. The nationalists, however, remained xenophobic towards all foreigners; the French were defeated in Cilicia while the Greeks in Smyrna began harassing French residents and institutions.[18]

While the British continued to try to maintain some vestige of the now outdated pro-Hellenic policy (repudiated in Greece following a change of government), and the Sèvres settlement, the French faced the new reality of a major Turkish defeat of the Greek army in September 1921, the Greeks being forced back to the coast. The Greeks then demanded to occupy Constantinople, which produced a last glimmer of Allied unity – a threat of joint naval action, either bombardment of Piraeus or confiscation of Greek shipping – if the Greeks attempted to enter the city.[19] In October, however, without the agreement of the other Allies, the French signed an agreement with Kemal by which they abandoned claims on Cilicia and recognized Kemal's administration. They also began to supply weaponry to the nationalists. This recognition produced a furious diplomatic reaction in London, the

French being denounced as unscrupulous and treacherous. In the field it produced, in early September 1922, a crisis at Smyrna. British, American and French battleships and other vessels had to evacuate foreigners – Greeks and Armenians in the case of the British and Americans, and French and French-protected personnel in the case of the French – while the victorious nationalist forces entered, looted and burnt the city, massacring in an orgy of ethnic cleansing those who could not escape. A second and final crisis occurred further north later in the same month. After Smyrna Kemal moved his army to Chanak on the east shore of the Dardanelles, opposite Constantinople, where a British garrison with a small contingent of French troops was still stationed under the arrangements for enforcing the Sèvres agreement. At this juncture Poincaré, the French prime minister, ordered the withdrawal of the French troops from the Asiatic coast, leaving the British troops (supported by warships) to face the nationalists alone. Incandescent charges of disloyalty, double-dealing and betrayal, made by the foreign secretary Curzon, were met with cold indifference by Poincaré. The British had to choose between a war or a diplomatic climb-down, and the negotiations of a more generous treaty accepting the territorial integrity of Turkey.[20] Lloyd George was forced to accept the latter and his own political extinction. Franco-British relations were strained to breaking point.

However, even while the final stages of the Turkish intervention were taking place a new Mediterranean menace, which would draw the British and French navies together, was taking shape. In September 1923 Italian battleships bombarded Corfu, and subsequently Italian marines and troops landed on the island. This action was a reprisal for the assassination of an Italian general and his staff working on the Greek-Albanian frontier commission. The Greek government had already apologised and agreed compensation, but Mussolini chose this event for his first display of bombast.

The action placed Great Britain in a dilemma. Italy had been an ally in the first world war but recently and unsuccessfully had been helping Greece. In 1864 Britain had guaranteed the neutrality of Corfu, and was bound to support the League of Nations. While Italian naval assertion only 300 miles from the entrance to the Suez Canal was clearly a challenge, almost all of the Mediterranean fleet was in Turkish waters. While the crisis was eventually settled by negotiation, the events of 19 September 1923 were illuminating for both Great Britain and France. To humiliate the Greeks two Italian battleships and six destroyers, with aircraft overhead, entered Phaleron Bay, near Athens; the Greek warships in the bay had to fly Italian colours and fire a salute in respect. A British and a French cruiser were reduced to the role of impotent witnesses.[21]

As the decade wore on the common interests of Great Britain and France continued to draw the ships at sea together. A small gesture, appreciated by many Frenchmen, was the escort provided by two Royal Navy destroyers in 1925 for a liner carrying Marshal Lyautey, made a scapegoat by the Paris government and Marshal Pétain for the Rif uprising, back to France from the Moroccan protectorate he had created.[22]

The Far East provided another example of local co-operation when in 1927 the safety of the large international communities living in Shanghai appeared threatened by increasing civil unrest and xenophobia. Western European nations, the United States and Japan reacted effectively and quickly. At the height of the crisis (February 1927) 35 warships from seven navies were in the port. Great Britain and France contributed the most ships, the former also contributing by far the largest military force.[23]

The last months of the decade saw a development ominous for both navies. The keel was laid of the *Deutschland*, the first of the so-called 'pocket battleships' – a clear sign that Germany intended a return to sea power. For France, with a one-ocean navy, a challenge was now appearing upon a second sea, and for Britain, with a two-ocean navy and even more dependent on sea communications than France, a three-ocean challenge loomed.

1930–39: Growing mutual respect

Anglo-French relations, both general and naval, present a paradox in the 1930s. Beneath the recurrent and sometimes bitter diplomatic wrangles there survived the sentiment, and the recognition, that the two nations shared a common interest in opposing aggressor nations, and in France, an acceptance that Britain must necessarily be the leading partner.[24] But on the one hand the British rejected the French view that security would best be secured by attempting to rejuvenate alliances with Poland and the Little Entente; and on the other, the French viewed the British philosophy that the League of Nations should provide security, and that Britain, placing its empire before any European commitment, could arbitrate in continental European quarrels, as humbug. These differences precluded any really effective naval staff discussions until the spring of 1939. The instability and occasional scandals of Third Republic governments on the one hand, and the Royal Navy's increasing concern over Japan – a threat not seen as a priority in Paris – also served to skew attempts to co-ordinate policies, while economic weaknesses and pacifist groups in both countries slowed rearmament until the end of the decade.

Policy and international relations differences were sub-implicants of these widely different political and economic conditions. After George Leygues' death in office in 1933, power over French naval policy passed from the politicians to the admirals; initially to Durand-Viel, then and above all to François Darlan, first as *chef de cabinet* in the navy ministry from October 1929 to October 1934 and then from January 1937 as Chief of the Naval Staff. His power was however limited by two major constraints: in any clash over strategy or policy, the voice of the army usually prevailed, and France's economic difficulties and industrial weakness severely constrained naval shipbuilding.

It is extraordinarily difficult to sum up Darlan's complex personality.[25] His best qualities as a naval administrator and strategist were all displayed before 1940. He had no illusions about the naval threats posed to France by Italy and Germany, and accepted that Britain would have to be France's major ally. But signs of the less attractive side of his personality, his overweening ambition and latent anglophobia, aggravated by frustration over British policies and attitudes, were evident before 1939. After the collapse of France these emerged more openly.

Darlan claimed to be the descendant of a sailor at Trafalgar, although it is more likely that he was descended from a sailor in the navy at the time but, as it happened, not at Trafalgar. Although his career was advanced by his relationship to Georges Leygues, his own ability would have secured him flag rank. As a sailor he was a 'guns' admiral with, certainly until 1942, little faith in naval aviation. His dislike of Britain was to be seen in his creation of a small circle of officers (a favouritism), Auphan, Leluc and others of known anti-British views, to whom he signalled secretly on policy matters.[26] The circle did not, however, include Admiral de Laborde, despite his overtly expressed anglophobe views which were to lead him to scuttle the French navy rather than attempt to join the Allies in 1942. Laborde, a count, viewed Darlan with aristocratic disdain, and as a partisan of naval aviation rather than guns, also with professional distrust. Darlan resented the fact that the British honoured General Gamelin with an award which he saw as more prestigious than that given to him. In the late 1930s Darlan's proposal to give the latest class of destroyers the names *Xaintrailles, du Guesclin* and those of other French commanders in the Hundred Years War had to be vetoed by Paris. One anglophile French admiral even warned the British on several occasions of Darlan's latent antipathy. In fairness, however, it should be noted that until Mers el Kébir in 1940 Darlan never envisaged hostilities with Britain.

As had been the case with the previous conferences, the London Naval Conference which opened in January 1930 was chiefly concerned with the relationships between the British, United States and Japanese navies, on which some limited agreement was reached.[27] The British again sought the abolition of submarines. The French delegation, which included Darlan, riposted with a demand for a large increase in their submarine tonnage. The French reiterated requests for a Mediterranean Security Pact, which the British judged obstructive, and an attempt to manoeuvre Britain into guaranteeing support in a conflict with Italy. The French continued to object to any concept of parity with Italy, claiming an overall tonnage of 800,000 tons, which was regarded by Britain as excessive. At one point, in exasperation, the British even talked of an Anglo-German-Italian agreement to contain France.[28] Soon after, specifically to meet the challenge of the German pocket battleships, the French in 1932 laid the keel of the *Dunquerque*, the first of two small battleships, faster and more powerful than the Deutschlands.

In February 1932, in the shadow of the Depression and the September 1931 Japanese aggression in Manchuria, the League of Nations General Disarmament Conference opened in Geneva. The Germans demanded to be permitted a naval strength equivalent to that of France, injecting a new and disturbing factor,[29] while the British put forward a proposal that all nations abandon conscription, an idea unacceptable to France. A renewed British proposal to abolish submarines was again rejected by France.[30] A French proposal for security to be guaranteed by an international League force was unacceptable to Britain; a British proposal to abolish naval and military aircraft was talked out by the French. Regarding the German demand for naval equality with France, the British, fearing a pre-1914-type arms race and consequential conflict, tried in vain to persuade the French to concede. Proposals and counter-proposals all foundered on the same rocks, the British wish for a reduction of armaments and French insistence on armaments perceived as essential for security. Even before Japan's January 1933 notice of withdrawal from the League, and the abrupt October 1933 announcement by the new German Chancellor, Adolf Hitler, of Germany's withdrawal from the conference, it was clear nothing could be achieved, though the conference meandered on until June 1934.

With the international situation deteriorating fast, Britain sought, ever more frantically, to secure stability and a balance of forces in

Europe. To the Admiralty it seemed a priority to try to limit German rearmament, to ensure that the Royal Navy could, if necessary, concentrate sufficient force to fight Japan. A remark of Hitler's, that he would be content with a navy 35 per cent the size of the Royal Navy, appeared to be a concession from the earlier German demand for parity with France. In the midst of preparations for a further naval arms limitation conference, the negotiations opened which led to the 1935 Anglo-German Naval Agreement permitting this level of rearmament.[31] The agreement broke an undertaking given to France that there would be no unilateral deals with Germany, as neither France, nor the League of Nations nor Italy, were consulted. The French government concealed its anger, but Darlan saw the agreement as yet one more example of British perfidy, and another indication that for Britain the naval power whose ambitions were to be contained was not Germany, who would gain from the agreement, but France.[32]

Earlier in the preparatory talks the French, to the irritation of Whitehall, had taken an uncompromising stance, insisting on the right to build a navy equal in size to that of Germany and Italy combined.[33] The conference itself, which dragged on until March 1936, chiefly revolved around the eternal triangle of American, British and Japanese strengths, and reached only very limited conclusions.[34]

Italian ambitions in Ethiopia precipitated further Anglo-French disagreements. The detail of policies and events are set out elsewhere in this volume (Chapter 4) and need only be summarized here.[35] Initially, for France, Ethiopia mattered little, though later public opinion became critical; what did matter was maintaining friendly relations with Mussolini, who had reacted sharply to Nazi designs on and activities in Austria. The army saw an Italian alliance as offering the possibility of a 'southern front', with the Italians able to deploy a far larger force than Britain ever could against Germany in the event of a war that might be precipitated by a reoccupation of the Rhineland or a take-over of Austria. France's senior admirals, notably Durand-Viel, Chief of the Naval Staff, and Decoux, the navy's leading strategist, accepted this view on the basis that a war with Italy would weaken France at a time of growing German strength. Darlan, at the time in a sea command, had no such illusions, assessing correctly Mussolini's Tunisian and other ambitions, fearing a renewed Italian demand for naval parity, and himself acutely aware of France's inability to match Italian shipbuilding. He saw clearly that by 1939–40 the Italian navy would be at least the equal of the French navy.[36] British naval support would therefore be even more important, if it could be relied upon.

British policy was confused. Overtly opposed to Italian aggression, many, including the foreign secretary, Samuel Hoare, were nevertheless prepared to seek accommodation in the interests of peace. Although the Mediterranean fleet commander, the exceptionally able Sir William Fisher, was confident that he could destroy the Italian fleet, others, notably the First Sea Lord, Sir Ernle Chatfield, were more cautious, fearing that in a conflict there would inevitably be some loss and damage, a dehydration of strength which could not be risked in view of the growing Japanese threat.[37] Chatfield insisted that if the navy was to be asked to fight, it must be allowed to use Toulon and Bizerta, as Malta would become insecure and Alexandria and Haifa alone were inadequate; also that the navy must have the support of the French navy and air force.[38] Faced with the choice of Italy or Britain as an ally (a choice which it was French policy to try to avoid) Laval, the French foreign minister, initially refused the British requests.[39] Under pressure he later agreed to allow docking and repair facilities to British ships, with operational support if necessary. Some naval staff talks, apparently concealed from the Quai d'Orsay, and notable chiefly for revealing the French lack of preparations, followed. A rough demarcation line was agreed – the eastern Mediterranean was to be a British responsibility and the western area French – albeit reluctantly accepted by the French who noted that the major concentration of British ships was in the eastern Mediterranean, in their view leaving them dangerously exposed not only to Italy but also to Germany.[40] A little later, in January 1936, French naval staff officers agreed to a wider, but even more vague series of co-operation measures in the event of war, but as these were never officially approved by the French government doubts remained on the British side.[41]

The whole business worsened relations; the French resented the British naval demands, while the British resented France's reluctance to confront an aggressor. Furthermore, the French saw Britain's abandonment of the Hoare-Laval proposals for a negotiated settlement (involving a partition of Ethiopia) in favour of rhetoric and ineffective League of Nations sanctions as hypocrisy. The policies of both countries turned Italy towards Germany, the conclusion of the Rome-Berlin Axis following later in the year, while in French naval circles anxiety was increased by the rapid construction of the two powerful German battle-cruisers *Scharnhorst* and *Gneisenau*, and rumours of the arrival of German U-boats, in sections, at Trieste.

The immediate consequences of the Italian realignment were to be seen in the German militarization of the Rhineland in March 1936. The

Rhineland reoccupation, coupled with exaggerated claims of German rearmament and the decline in French manpower caused by the 'lean years', accentuated France's dependence on African troops and the communications to secure their arrival. The French prime minister, Flandin, arrived in London and claimed somewhat tentatively that France had made preparations for a naval blockade of Germany, but the British government was in no mood for action other than staff conversations limited to discussing possible naval deployments in the Western Approaches.[42]

The opening of the Spanish civil war in July 1936 led to increasing German and Italian aid for the nationalists and the presence of powerful German and Italian warships in the western Mediterranean, all at a time of French naval weakness. The possibility of a pro-Axis government in Madrid, and in particular an Axis naval presence in the Balearic islands if the nationalists were to win, added greatly to French anxieties. It led to a request, at first resisted by Britain for fear of irritating the Italians, for formal joint naval staff talks.[43] Almost from the outset, ships of both navies were involved in evacuating nationals, and later, sometimes under attack from one or other side in the civil war, escorting refugee ships from both the Atlantic and Mediterranean coasts of Spain.[44]

By the summer of 1937 two developments led to a more proactive approach. Firstly, the French Popular Front government had appointed Darlan as Chief of the Naval Staff in January. Secondly, Italian warships, mostly submarines, were covertly intercepting and, on occasions, sinking Soviet and other ships furnishing supplies to the republican forces.[45] In August, inadvertently, one Italian submarine attacked a British destroyer, HMS *Havock*, which counter-attacked with depth charges. For the first time in the decade the British and French navies entered into a large-scale working agreement, following an international conference at Nyon in September 1937. An anti-piracy force was set up to patrol fixed routes, the British around Gibraltar, Malta, Cyprus and in part of the Aegean, the French in Tunisian waters. Powers to retaliate were permitted if a submarine was found near a scene of piracy, and powers to arrest if a submarine were only a moderate distance away.[46] British naval forces, depot-ships and flying-boats were permitted to operate from French and French North African ports. The British force at times included one or more capital ships and 36 destroyers, the French 28 destroyers. There was some British suspicion that the French turned a blind eye on republican vessels flying the red ensign. The Soviet Union initially objected to Italian vessels patrolling the Tyrrhenean Sea

(Italy having made a self-righteous turn from sinner to saint), but overall the system succeeded, though it much later became clear that the Italian decision to end piracy operations was primarily the consequence of *Havock's* retaliation, which nearly sank her Italian attacker. Both navies gained valuable intelligence and submarine-tracking experience in the eight months of full patrolling which followed the Nyon agreement. The British, however, refused to be drawn into Darlan's most proactive project, the countering of an Italian air force base on Mallorca by establishing a Franco-British naval base on Minorca. Overall the significance of the working agreement was limited to partnership for a particular purpose rather than laying any broader foundations for an alliance.[47]

The whole sequence of events worried Darlan; not only Italy's construction but also Germany laying down two major battleships, the *Bismark* and *Tirpitz*; and the ever-increasing evidence that in certain circumstances Britain might either not join in a war against Italy (or Germany), or might despatch almost all the Royal Navy to the Far East. Darlan's response was to urge French naval rearmament to the French government. Darlan's answer to the strategic dilemma was a 'Mediterranean first' strategy, aimed at neutralizing Italy by massive air and naval strikes against Eritrea, Libya, the Dodecanese and Italy herself, a strategy which incurred uncompromising opposition from Gamelin. Darlan was also sharply opposed to the idea, favoured in some circles in Britain, of returning any of Germany's pre-war colonies, which he believed would become naval bases.

Darlan's strategy, in many ways clear-sighted, suffered from two drawbacks. The first was opposition from the British, who still persisted in opposing any proactive measure that might provoke Mussolini; the furthest the Chamberlain government would go at this stage (early 1938) was permission for limited army and air staff talks only. After the Anschluss with Austria some similarly limited naval exchanges, confined to technical exchanges between attachés, were authorized. The second drawback was the presupposition that the two European Axis powers would enter any war at about the same time, a misapprehension the British did not hesitate to exploit.

In the August/September 1938 Sudetenland crisis both navies recalled reservists and mobilized for war. The French permitted large numbers of Royal Navy reservists to travel across France to Marseilles where a Cunard liner transported them to the Mediterranean fleet. The crisis does not appear, however, to have produced any developments in joint naval planning other than a reiteration of the broad areas of responsibility agreed at the time of the Ethiopian crisis.[48]

After the Sudetenland crisis a compromise between the views of Gamelin and Darlan was reached, which envisaged diversionary offensive naval action in the Mediterranean and Red Sea. The First Sea Lord, Sir Roger Backhouse, personally favoured a pre-emptive attack on the Italians (so freeing the Fleet to move to the Far East if necessary), but the staff talks, still low level, continued to lack realism. The British delegation, empire-minded and led by opponents of the Mediterranean offensive strategy, even hoped that perhaps, with some British reinforcement, France might assume full responsibility for the entire Mediterranean, or would at least station the two new small battleships *Dunkerque* and *Strasbourg* permanently at Brest for work in the Atlantic. The French were aghast at the concept of the Royal Navy's main effort being focused on the Far East, and pointed out that the loss of the eastern Mediterranean was likely to be more damaging in the long term than the loss of Singapore.[49]

The Italian invasion of Albania served usefully to highlight the European dangers. At the time the home fleet was in British waters, the Mediterranean fleet scattered around in courtesy visits and at Haifa; and a powerful German squadron was on its way for an official visit to Lisbon. The only protection for Gibraltar available, had there been a crisis, was that of three French battleships fortunately in the area.[50]

With minds concentrated by the German threat to Poland, the staff talks, now at a higher level, eventually resulted in agreements to last until May 1940; the assumption that war would involve both Germany and Italy from the outset remained, however, and these arrangements had to be amended in several respects when, in September 1939, it appeared that Germany was to be the sole adversary. The Royal Navy would assume responsibility for the North Sea and Atlantic approaches and would co-operate closely with the French navy in the Channel. In the Mediterranean, the east would remain a British and the west a French responsibility. As a result five task forces, four British and one French, were created to deal with German raiders, the French force requiring the stiffening of a British 15-inch gun unit.[51] For the first time, however, the British were prepared to permit major capital ships to serve under a French admiral.

There was a measure of co-operation between the French and the British in the Far East, although it was limited by the weaknesses of both navies in the region. Two small French warships, together with American and British river gunboats, confronted the Japanese attackers at Hankow in October 1938; they were unable to secure the city but neutral property and lives were protected. In May 1935 a force of two

British, two French and two American cruisers with other smaller ships assembled at Amoy to safeguard the residents of the foreign concession.[52] An Anglo-French Defence Conference was held at Singapore in June 1939, but could achieve little.

In terms of *matériel* collaboration in the 1930s the design of the small battleships *Dunkerque* and *Strasbourg* was assisted by access being given to British files relating to the building of the *Nelson* and *Rodney*. Specific technical advice was also made available for the modernization of the battleship *Lorraine* in the early 1930s. Otherwise little advice was on offer until the 1939 staff talks. Thereafter expertise on ASDIC antisubmarine equipment was made available, together with some wireless technology, particularly in the field of equipment for direction-finding from signals emissions.[53] British assistance did not, however, extend to the provision of radar equipment – in any case only a very few Royal Navy ships were fitted with radar up to the time of the French collapse – but the technology itself was revealed to an amazed visiting party of French officers some months before the outbreak of war.[54] The French navy surprised the Royal Navy with a gunnery display by a visiting cruiser squadron in the summer of 1939. The shell splashes of each ship were a different colour, facilitating spotting and aim correction.[55]

Right up to the actual outbreak of war the British government and the cautious new First Sea Lord, Sir Dudley Pound, persisted in the hope that Italy could be detached from the German embrace, Pound additionally warning of the attrition that a war with Italy would cause the Royal Navy in view of the strength of Italian submarine and air forces. The Japanese June 1939 blockade of Tientsin strengthened the voices of caution. Darlan's final pre-war strategy, envisaging naval bombardments of Italy and Sicily, which was offered to the British at a conference in Malta in July 1939 as a way of compelling Italy to enter a war, had no real chance of success and was dealt a final blow by the Nazi-Soviet Pact of August. Gamelin was able to argue that if there was no prospect of Soviet help in containing Hitler, there would be no war on two fronts for Germany and the one front, his, must count on a neutral Italy.

The absence of any effective firm policy agreement between the French army and navy and between France and Britain served only to weaken the alliance, and can be argued to have played a part in the tragic circumstances in which HMS *Hood*, which had in November 1939 sailed so proudly under Admiral Gensoul, was to open fire on the *Dunkerque* and her admiral seven months later.

If any summary of all these events is possible, perhaps one point emerges: Anglo-French naval relations were a microcosm of wider

Anglo-French relations at the time and since. The capacity of two great nations with essentially common interests nevertheless to misunderstand each other seemed endless. In these misunderstandings the insularity of the British, clinging to an illusion that in some way Britain had a moral authority to rise above, and arbitrate between, continental European nations, was more often to blame.

Notes

I would like to record my appreciation of the help that I received from M. Philippe Vial of the Service Historique de la Marine, and Colonel André Martin-Siegfried in the preparation of this chapter.

1. The prevailing, if deliberately exaggerated 1919–20 view was that of Captain Pound (later, as Admiral Sir Dudley Pound, to be First Sea Lord at the outbreak of the second world war) that the French navy was not worth a 'hatful of crabs'. A. J. Marder, *From the Dardanelles to Oran* (Oxford: Oxford University Press, 1974), p. 181.
2. Admiral Wemyss had been appointed First Sea Lord in the winter of 1917–18, following the dismissal of Admiral Jellicoe who was held responsible for the failure of the anti-submarine campaign.
3. S. Roskill, *Naval Policy Between the Wars* (2 vols, London: Collins, 1968 and 1976), i, p. 92.
4. 'I hope we will *insist* on abolition of submarines, and that *France* is *made* to reduce her Navy, Army and Air Force which will otherwise become a danger to the peace of the world.' King George V to Sir Edward Grigg, November 1921, quoted in Roskill, *Naval Policy*, i, p. 306, n.4.
5. Italy was allowed the same tonnage, in practice three ships. Britain and America were allowed 135,000 tons, Japan 51,000.
6. Castex wrote 'on doit reconnaître que les Allemands étaient absolument fondés à l'employer . . .'. Translation at the time rendered this as 'absolutely justified' with its moral connotation, but it is also possible to translate 'fonder' as 'to place hopes upon' with a purely functional meaning. However, elsewhere in other writing, Castex argued that the use of submarines was no more immoral than the use of other types of warship.
7. The original French proposal was to limit the aggregate of individual ship tonnages of all classes of ships employed for home defence and overseas defence, together with limits on the tonnages and main armament calibres of individual classes. The British proposal favoured limits on tonnages of individual ships and tonnages and gun calibres for nine classes of warship. A first French compromise, suggesting four categories of ship with tonnages transferable from one category to another, was rejected by Britain. The unofficial proposal that aroused United States ire suggested limitations on all classes of warship mounting guns of more than 6-inch calibre. Roskill, *Naval Policy*, i, xii, xiv.
8. J. Raphael-Leygues, *Georges Leygues* (Paris: France-Empire, 1983) provides a fine biography. A useful career summary appears in E. Taillemite, 'Georges

Leygues 1917–1933. Une politique maritime pour la France', in *Revue Historique des Armées* (RHDA), 4/1995, pp. 31–42. In all French writing Georges Leygues is never shortened to a simple Leygues; this practice is followed here.

9. Raphael-Leygues, *Georges Leygues*, p. 261, on the basis of 57 letters written by Georges Leygues to Darlan, notes that none contained any hatred or even aversion to the Royal Navy.

10. The subject is technical, and in its detail relevant. It relates to oil fuel supply. Until Georges Leygues's second ministry, French naval fuel was spot-bought. From 1926 the supply was arranged from Romania and from Iraq via a pipeline to Syria, but with the provision that a switch to Venezuelan oil might be necessary in the event of a war with Italy. Of the submarines built in the years 1924–38, 41 were large (one the largest in the world) and were designed with trade protection in mind. Georges Leygues's assertion was therefore an honest one even if it represented an incorrect deduction of the lessons of 1914–18. Interestingly, the Soviet navy was thinking along the same lines.

11. R. A. Burt, *French Battleships 1876–1946* (London: Arms and Armour Press, c.1990).

12. These vessels built between 1922 and 1925 were the first 6-inch-gun cruisers to mount all their main armament in turrets rather than in gun shields open to the elements. The first British cruisers with 6-inch gun turrets, the Leander class, did not appear until 1933.

13. Matelot L. Cherutschi, 'L'intervention navale alliée en Lettonie, octobre-novembre 1919, exemple d'une collaboration Franco-Brittanique', *RHDA*, 1/1995, pp. 105–16, sets out the detail of this event.

14. An Anglo-French Convention, agreed in December 1917 and reaffirmed in November 1918, had assigned specific areas for the support of anti-Bolshevik movements and forces. Britain was to be responsible for the Caucasus, Armenia and the Caspian, France for western and central Black Sea lands. The French naval contribution to the Murmansk force included one large but very old cruiser.

15. J. Swettenham, *Allied Intervention in Russia 1918–1919* (London: Allen and Unwin, 1967), pp. 248–50 and Roskill, *Naval Policy*, i, pp. 156–7 offer useful accounts of the fiasco. Raphael-Leygues, *George Leygues*, pp. 197–201, describes the mutinies. K. Edwards, *The Grey Diplomatists* (London: Rich and Cowan, 1938), p. 34, claims that Gough-Calthorpe tactfully arranged for the ships in mutiny to be escorted out of the area by Greek rather than British ships.

16. 'The French and British men o'war also embarked entire battalions' wrote Captain E. P. Cameron in *Goodbye Russia* (London, 1934), p. 87. At Novorossisk the warships of both navies bombarded the advancing Bolsheviks on a common fire plan.

17. The strengths appear in M. Nouschi, 'Les Forces Navales Françaises et le problème Turc', *RHDA*, 1, 1985, pp. 63–70. The British could also actually control the amount of coal available to the French ships through domination of an inter-Allied coal committee. Additionally, the British naval commander, Admiral Gough-Calthorpe, was also British High Commissioner, with political authority, at Constantinople.

18. The Italians had withdrawn from their zone by June 1921.

19. Roskill, *Naval Policy*, i, pp. 196–9.

20. A French military and naval presence remained at Constantinople until September 1923 after the signing of the Treaty of Lausanne in July. Together with the forces of Britain and other allies they served to contain excessive demands of the nationalists during the negotiations.

21. For a full account, see Edwards, *Grey Diplomatists*, pp. 81–9.

22. This gesture was almost certainly the work of Admiral Beatty. There was no French escort, or official welcome, for Lyautey on his arrival.

23. A. Temple Patterson, *Tyrwhitt of the Harwich Force* (London: Macdonald, 1973), ix. Admiral Tyrwhitt was the British naval commander.

24. The full significance of Vichy in 1940 is only to be understood when seen as the *fracture* of this general common interest. De Gaulle represented, in his own style, the continuity.

25. H. Coutau-Begarie and C. Huan, *Darlan* (Paris: Fayard, 1989) provides an excellent biography of this figure reminiscent of French classical tragedy, a man of immense ability but with a flawed character.

26. A source confidential to the author states that the British broke the code of these signals. The statement cannot be confirmed or disproved but merits mention.

27. The conference principally revolved around the highly technical issues of definitions of categories of warship and possible tonnages for each. It opened in the Royal Gallery of the House of Lords with its huge murals of Waterloo and Trafalgar. Darlan commented sourly in a letter to his wife, 'Charmant'. Begarie and Huan, *Darlan*, p. 52.

28. Darlan had earlier commented that the whole conference would be a repeat of Washington, and acceptance of parity with Italy would be 'l'abdication définitive de la France sur les mers et nous laisserions les Anglo-Saxons libres d'exercer à leur seul profit le controle des communications maritimes'. Darlan to Georges Leygues, 10 November 1929, quoted in Begarie and Huan, *Darlan*, p. 91.

29. Roskill, *Naval Policy*, ii, v, describes the negotiations in detail.

30. The French offered to accept 1,200 as the maximum tonnage for a submarine – an ocean-going tonnage and of no interest to Britain.

31. Specifically the agreement provided for 35 per cent of all categories except submarines, for which Germany was to be allowed 45 per cent, with the right to move to 100 per cent if Berlin assessed this as necessary.

32. Begarie and Huan, *Darlan*, p. 161.

33. Roskill, *Naval Policy*, ii, pp. 292–3.

34. All that was agreed was a 'non-construction zone' of ships between 8,000 and 17,000 tons. The Japanese withdrew, the Italians refused to sign and the limitation was generally ignored in the years that followed. The agreement did however leave Britain free to re-arm in the major categories of warships.

35. Indispensable for the study of Franco-British naval relations throughout the 1930s is the Service Historique de la Marine's collection of documents and commentary presented in *Les Conversations Franco-Britanniques d'Etat-Major (1935–1939)* (Vincennes: Service Historique de la Marine, 1969). See also R. M. Salerno, 'The French Navy and the Appeasement of Italy', *English Historical Review*, CXII (1997), pp. 68–104.

36. The first two Littorio class 15-inch-gun battleships laid down in 1934 were due for completion in mid-1940, before France's new 15-inch-gun ships. The

Littorios, with four very thoroughly modernized older capital ships, would give Italy the advantage over France's two modern but small battleships and four or five older, obsolescent units. The concentration of these ships would in any case leave the Atlantic denuded, a risk no French admiral could accept without grave disquiet.

37. Marder, *Dardanelles to Oran*, pp. 84–5.

38. In November 1935 Fisher sent a destroyer to Bizerta to test French reactions after the Italian invasion of Ethiopia had commenced. Laborde, the French commander, in awe of the Italian residents, proved unreceptive. Roskill, *Naval Policy*, ii, pp. 262–3. The destroyer's commander, Mountbatten, wrote later that he was told to wear 'some clothes that did not look obviously English and speak only in French'. P. Ziegler, *Mountbatten* (London: Collins, 1985), p. 91.

39. Although reminded that Italy was an aggressor, Laval took refuge in a proviso that France would not consider the obligation for mutual support to be applicable if the Italians alleged that the British naval build-up was excessive.

40. Marder, *Dardanelles to Oran*, p. 94. The agreement provided for British assistance in escorting troops from Morocco to Bordeaux; exchange of liaison officers; the possibility of French destroyers assisting in anti-submarine work or more offensive action in the western Mediterranean; the possibility of French submarines attacking Italy's communications with Libya in the eastern Mediterranean; and a re-drawing of inter-fleet boundaries leaving the extreme western Mediterranean to the British Home Fleet. *Conversations Franco-Brittaniques*, pp. 61–2, 82, notes French anxiety over the British naval dispositions.

41. Marder, *Dardanelles to Oran*, pp. 90–1. British officers wondered whether, in the event, the French government would actually honour the agreements, an anxiety confirmed by the brief and virtually useless army and air force staff talks.

42. At the time, in the waters around the United Kingdom, only one cruiser and 17 destroyers were in full commission.

43. The British also rejected a covert request made by Darlan to Chatfield for help for the republican forces. Roskill, *Naval Policy*, ii, p. 374. The British had earlier been irritated by French foot-dragging over non-intervention, with supplies reaching the republicans across the Pyrenees.

44. For accounts of the naval operations see A. Clayton, *The British Empire as a Superpower 1919–39* (London: Macmillan, 1986), pp. 348–62, and Vice-Admiral Sir P. Gretton, 'The Royal Navy in the Spanish Civil War', *Naval Review*, LXII, 1974, pp. 8–17, 96–103 and 203–13.

45. The Italian ships flew the Spanish flag and were said to be manned by 'volunteers'.

46. The fact that it was known through signals intelligence that the Italians had stopped their attacks does not alter the significance of the agreement in terms of Anglo-French naval relations. The submarines of all states which had attended the Nyon conference (which did not include Germany and Italy) were ordered to remain in port or operate only in certain particular sea areas. A full text of the agreement is included in *Conversations Franco-Britanniques*, pp. 190–1.

47. Curiously, in the end the Balearic problem solved itself. An agreement, brokered by a Royal Naval cruiser captain, provided for the republican evacuation of Minorca, and an Italian withdrawal from Majorca.

48. The compiler of *Conversations Franco-Britanniques*, M. A. Reussner, commented, p. 210: 'Mais l'historien de la coopération navale franco-brittanique, s'il prend une vue d'ensemble des mesures communes arrêtées par les deux marines dans cette crise conclura qu'elles portent la marque d'une improvisation hâtive et insuffisante'.

49. The French had good reason for their horror. By an informal understanding Britain had undertaken to keep four modernized or partly modernized battleships in the Mediterranean. These, together with two or three of France's obsolescent units, would at least have deterred the Italians from a sortie to cut the Atlantic, and perhaps the western Mediterranean, shipping routes. Without the four British ships, and with the advent of the two Littorios in the summer of 1940, Italy would have her *Mare Nostrum*.

50. A. Wassilieff, *Un Pavillon sans tache* (Paris: B. Grasset, 1986), p. 19.

51. The terms of the agreement, concluded at Portsmouth in August 1939, are outlined in P. Bergongnoux, 'Le Réarmament de la Marine Nationale', *RHDA*, 4, 1985, 34. *Conversations Franco-Britanniques*, pp. 230–1 notes the French anxieties over the exposure of *Dunkerque* or *Strasbourg* to a numerically superior German force. The weakness in the design of these two ships lay in the concentration of their main armament in two forward four-gun turrets. Two well-aimed shots, or even one, could have knocked out both turrets. The British battle-cruisers all mounted turrets aft as well as forward. A particular difficulty was the proposed British contribution to surveillance of the Canaries, a flotilla of submarines based at Freetown, which the French regarded as inadequate.

52. M. Brice, *The Royal Navy and the Sino-Japanese Incident, 1937–41* (London: Allan, 1973), pp. 96 and 119–20.

53. ASDIC was a method of detecting submarines by means of reflections caused by pulse waves emitted from a hunting vessel transmitting the waves from a quartz crystal fitted beneath the ship. It was very far from one hundred per cent reliable.

54. Professor J. F. Coales to the author, 1 June 1998. The earliest radar actually fitted to major French warships was German equipment provided in 1941–42.

55. The point is technical, but there had been instances in the first world war of German ships left unscathed with British ships' fire ill-distributed and inaccurately corrected.

3
An Argument without End: Britain, France and the Disarmament Process, 1925–34

Andrew Webster

One of the key elements shaping the Anglo-French defence relationship during the inter-war period was the issue of disarmament: how to balance the tide of popular enthusiasm for an end to 'militarism' which followed the first world war with the needs of national security and international stability.[1] Regarded by many as the litmus test (or indeed the very purpose) of the League of Nations, the success of disarmament became a shorthand expression for a postwar return to peace. Yet years of intricate negotiations came to nothing, for the disarmament talks revealed underlying differences of intent between Britain and France over how to create security in the postwar era. There was a constant tension between the two powers' status as former wartime allies both ostensibly dedicated to the peaceful management of international affairs through the League of Nations, and their conflicting interests as the only two unrestricted great powers in Europe. Fundamentally, the innumerable technical disagreements that divided the two countries' governments over how to limit armaments reflected political differences between the perspectives of a maritime and a land power. The British argued that with peace now restored to Europe, significant cuts to continental armies were possible. These cuts would in and of themselves create an even stronger ethos of peace and security. They dismissed all demands for an extension of their obligations to Europe, insisting that the League Covenant and the 1925 Treaty of Locarno represented the maximum possible British commitment. Safe from invasion as a result of geography and seapower, Britain did not share the same security concerns as a continental power such as France, which was obsessed by the potential threat from Germany, and to a lesser extent Italy. French policy-makers rejected the idea that a disarmament agreement was the most direct route to European stability. On the contrary, they insisted that the organization of security had to precede disarmament: the only way to ensure peace was to create a system that could, if necessary, enforce it. Until such additional and substantive security guarantees materialized, France would rely for its safety upon the artificial military superiority over the defeated enemy provided by the Treaty of Versailles. This dilemma of disarmament versus security paralysed and finally doomed the general disarmament process between the wars.

By 1925 the search for a general disarmament convention already had a complex history.[2] The years since the war had produced an unmanageable raft of unco-ordinated and often competing initiatives; what disarmament had taken place was either the result of independent agreement (such as the Washington Naval Treaty of 1922) or of unilateral national decisions driven primarily by financial constraints. In neither case was disarmament carried out under League auspices as part of an overall settlement or in a form subject to general international supervision. However, the League Assembly's 1925 call for renewed preparations for a general conference resulted in the creation of a Preparatory Commission (PC) by the League Council in December 1925, to be composed of political and diplomatic (but not military) representatives from 19 interested powers.[3] Expectations were that the conference would be held in the near future – by early 1927 at the latest – but a snail's pace of progress by the PC defeated all such hopes. From its very first session, the commission became bogged down in unproductive technical discussions about the nature of armaments. It would take six sessions scattered over five years before the PC, always in the public eye, at last produced a draft disarmament treaty.[4]

At the heart of the long deadlock were the differences between Britain and France. Where the British felt themselves already secure, and presented their consequent postwar demobilization as unilateral disarmament, the French sought specific new provisions for supervision and sanctions in any agreement before they would materially reduce their military superiority over Germany. Competing draft conventions submitted at the third session in early 1927 by the British and French representatives, Lord Robert Cecil and Joseph Paul-Boncour, served to emphasize this Anglo-French division. Both drafts provided for the limitation and not the reduction of armaments, but their respective technical proposals advanced the interests of sea and land powers respectively. The two drafts were ineffectually amalgamated to produce a 'first reading' draft convention. This was little more than a catalogue of Anglo-French differences over such technical issues as methods of naval limitation, the status of 'trained reserves' and international inspection of national armouries.[5] The PC's sixth session in April 1929, which produced a more complete 'second reading' draft convention, demonstrated that real progress could only follow from Anglo-French compromise. The meeting came on the heels of several failed attempts to advance disarmament instead through private negotiations among the major powers – the Geneva Naval Conference of 1927 and the 1928 Anglo-French 'compromise' on armaments.[6] When the PC reconvened, these failures and the long pause in practical discussions meant that it found itself under heavy pressure from an aroused world public to make substantive progress.[7]

The setbacks of the previous two years had left the major powers in a chastened mood and willing to find conciliatory positions. Following a period of fierce Anglo-American altercation and with an election only weeks away, a more positive British approach sprang from the Conservative Cabinet's feeling that the electorate demanded progress. In the cynical belief that Britain would not have to deal with any unwelcome results because no overall agreement would be reached, it was decided to accept any land and air arrangements that were adopted unanimously.[8] French concerns not to fall out with Britain, or give the Anglo-American group cause to accuse them of militarist ambitions, similarly led to a moderation of approach in Paris and the adoption of a less dogmatic attitude.[9] The principal effect at the commission was the abandonment by Britain and France of the contested proposals for limiting trained reserves and war material and of the principle of international supervision. This resulted in a set of anodyne technical provisions that limited arms only in the weakest of fashions and did not reduce them at all. The fundamental Anglo-French divergence over the political problem of security remained unaddressed and unresolved.

Nonetheless, the majority of the delegates still considered the unexpected amount of agreement satisfactory and the session was adjourned to allow for further private discussions by the main naval powers. The unfortunate result of this adjournment was the paralysis of work on general disarmament for another 18 months. When the PC finally resumed its task in November 1930, the European political situation had become noticeably darker. German dissatisfaction was manifest, and their assertions of the 'legal obligation' of the powers to disarm down to Germany's level now became increasingly strident. These claims were in reality simply a political strategy aimed at winning concessions in order to cover illegal German rearmament. This, however, made no difference to their propaganda value inside or outside Germany.[10] In the meantime,

Anglo-French disputes over disarmament became distinctly sharper and more divisive. The initial basis for this was a change of government in Britain. The Labour Party returned to power in June 1929 and quickly demonstrated a desire to press France to make concessions in its military and naval preponderance over Germany and Italy respectively, just at a time when the worsening European political and economic situation seemed to the French to make any such alterations impossible.

With James Ramsay MacDonald as prime minister, Arthur Henderson as foreign secretary and Cecil as a special adviser on League questions, the new government made its presence felt on disarmament questions almost at once. A resolution was presented to the League Assembly in September 1929 that sought to reopen several of the disputed topics apparently settled at the PC's last session in April, particularly its dropping of limitations on trained reserves and the feeble 'indirect' means adopted to limit war material. Unsurprisingly, this focus on greater restrictions for land armaments raised considerable anger among the French, who were already suspicious about possible Anglo-American collusion in their private talks on naval disarmament. General Edouard Réquin of the war ministry insisted that it had to be made clear to the British 'that we will create difficulties for them in naval discussions unless they finally abandon their perpetual attacks against our land forces'.[11] It was Labour's declared belief, however, that sufficient specific security guarantees to permit French disarmament to take place either already existed or would soon be in place through their initiative to extend the system of League-centred arbitration and conflict resolution. To this end, the British signed the 'Optional Clause' and advocated the re-examination and eventual approval of several schemes drawn up over the previous two years by an ancillary body to the PC, the Committee on Arbitration and Security – measures intended to create a general climate of security in Europe which would in turn promote meaningful disarmament. These included the General Act, the Model Treaty, the Treaty for Financial Assistance and the so-called 'harmonization' of the League Covenant and the 1928 Kellogg-Briand Pact outlawing war.[12] To Henderson in particular, this appeared a way out of the disarmament-security dilemma which did not involve new British commitments. 'The French would come to trust in arbitration, have a feeling of security, and feel that they could do without calling up all their available manpower every year', he told a British journalist.[13] Security did not come from 'military systems', MacDonald insisted. It was primarily a question of psychology, which disarmament would significantly promote.[14]

French policy-makers did not see matters in this light. Their unvarying attitude, maintained consistently despite sometimes rapid changes in ministries, was to insist ever more strongly that 'disarmament can only be the consequence of security organised through a compulsory peaceful settlement of all disagreements, and an automatic mutual assistance, effective and immediate, against a future aggressor'. This view rejected as misguided and dangerous the British attitude that 'security is above all a question of sentiment, of spiritual *détente*, sufficiently assured by agreements of a general type such as the Briand-Kellogg pact'.[15] To the French, security *was* a matter of concrete commitments to action. In this light, the Kellogg-Briand pact was all very well 'but it cannot be said that in its present state it is sufficient to guarantee the security of nations'.[16] The British attempts to promote arbitration were treated politely in Paris, so as not to appear obstructionist, but were regarded as essentially insignificant. The main French interest was the hope that these measures could bring a return to the philosophy of the Geneva Protocol of 2 October 1924 (a scheme that proposed the pacific settlement of international disputes by compulsory arbitration), through their extension to include provisions for the automatic definition of the aggressor and for sanctions.[17] But such commitments to action were exactly what the British wished to avoid. Consequently, despite the effort expended by Henderson, this attempt to resolve the dilemma came to nothing. French security concerns were further heightened with the ending of the Allied occupation of the Rhineland (to be completed by 30 June 1930) which had been conceded by Aristide Briand under great pressure from Henderson at the Hague Conference in August 1929. Without the safeguard of those troops, in perfect position to enter Germany at short notice, fears of exposure to a sudden German attack only grew. So did the perceived dangers of France standing alone against its old enemy. The French response was to place greater reliance on the long-running project of the Maginot Line, which secured final approval of funding in December 1929, and to be even firmer both in demanding new commitments to their security and in refusing all concessions to Germany over armaments. Finally, there was yet another cause for concern: Italy was stridently demanding the concession of naval parity with France in all classes of warships, an issue of great importance as the independent pursuit of naval disarmament again took centre-stage.

It was MacDonald, obsessively pursuing an Anglo-American agreement, who provided the main driving force for another attempt to advance naval disarmament outside the PC. For diplomatic, political and financial reasons a treaty with the US extending the limitation of naval armaments was highly desirable; certainly it was more central to the prime minister's concerns than relations with France. His efforts were rewarded by the summoning of another conference of the five major naval powers to meet in London in January 1930. In Paris, however, there were doubts about the wisdom of participating in the conference. Armaments were indivisible, French policy-makers argued. The management of land, sea and air arms were interdependent: isolating and settling the naval sphere in a private conference would both undermine the authority of the PC and jeopardize France's case on land and air armaments.

> The Anglo-Saxons, being satisfied, will become the arbiters between Germany (or Italy) and us, when the debate on land and air forces opens. We will have lost all means of leverage on them, as their naval claims, which give us strong arguments, will have been already satisfied.[18]

But unlike the 1927 naval conference in Geneva which France had avoided for this very reason, in the end the pressures of public opinion in late 1929 meant that the French had no choice but to attend the London Naval Conference.

While British interests in pursuing naval disarmament centred on protecting their global position by securing as stable and advantageous a naval regime as possible, the French did not wish to see their own naval power, particularly *vis-à-vis* Italy, casually overturned simply to protect 'Anglo-Saxon' superiority. France's naval figures could only be reduced, they insisted, if the Italians dropped their claim to parity (which they never did) or if a new security agreement that included British participation was created to cover the Mediterranean. The British Cabinet rejected the idea of a Mediterranean pact as dangerous and unnecessary. Instead it continued to exert powerful pressure on the French to reduce their claims. A French statement to the conference of their naval needs in mid-February attracted bitter criticism, MacDonald complaining in a well-known diary entry that 'France becomes the peace problem of Europe. Mentality is purely militarist.'[19] As any extension of Britain's obligations beyond Locarno was totally unacceptable in London, mounting anger at the repeated French insistence upon security before disarmament convinced the British that France did not want any agreement at all. The diplomat Sir Robert Craigie, the chief British naval negotiator, protested to his French counterpart, René Massigli, that 'it was little use offering France fresh guarantees since she simply pocketed them without apparently experiencing any increase in her sense of security.'[20]

The conference ultimately produced an Anglo-American-Japanese agreement, but the Franco-Italian impasse proved unbreakable. It was finally decided in April to adjourn the naval conference with a three-power treaty and continue separately the negotiations for French and Italian adherence. Because the hard-won treaty remained at risk so long as France and Italy were free to build without restraint, the British took an active part in the continuing naval talks, trying to set French naval figures at as low a level as possible. French pretensions to seapower were considered unjustifiable and in no way comparable to Britain's unique position. The French, in contrast, continued to insist upon their entitlement, as an imperial power with world-wide interests, to a large and modern fleet. As the negotiations dragged on into 1931 – continually defeated by the inability of the negotiators 'to find some formula which would enable Italy to show that she had obtained parity, and France to show that she had not accorded it'[21] – further recriminations followed on all sides. When a settlement apparently reached on 1 March 1931 (the 'Bases of Agreement'), almost immediately came undone amid mutual misunderstandings, MacDonald protested that 'the French are solely to blame. I do not believe that they ever meant to agree.'[22] Among British policy-makers, the failure of the 'Bases of Agreement' became just another sign of French unwillingness to disarm. In contrast, the chief of the French naval staff complained that 'little does our colonial empire matter, little do our justifications matter – only one thing counts, the language of the Lion'.[23]

The work of the PC had been suspended to allow the naval talks to continue, and so the adjourned sixth session only reopened in Geneva in November 1930. In the meantime the European economic and political situation had steadily deteriorated, large gains being made by the National Socialists in the German Reichstag elections of September. But British sentiments about disarmament did not alter in turn: Henderson told the 1930 League Assembly that 'of all security measures, disarmament is, in itself, the most important'.[24] The British continued to press for cuts to the French navy. With regard to land forces it still seemed in London both that 'the most formidable military power in the world [France] is not yet satisfied that her armaments are sufficient to ensure her military security' and that 'we have gone as far as it is possible to go in the way of meeting France in the matter of security'.[25] Neither had the basic thrust of French policy changed. The prime minister,

André Tardieu, leader of the centre-right coalition, repeated that 'France believes today as yesterday that the basis of the organisation of peace lies in the formula: security, arbitration, disarmament . . . [and] refuses to allow the order of these three words to be changed'.[26] As for French armaments, General Maxime Weygand, the chief of the general staff, insisted that 'the minimum corresponding to the present conditions [of European security] has already been reached'.[27] Given French concerns, particularly with no Allied troops remaining in the Rhineland, it seemed both more urgent and less likely that the quest for general disarmament should succeed.

Once again expectations were confounded when, at long last, the commission managed to produce a full draft disarmament convention.[28] But despite five years of work, it mentioned everything and finalized nothing; it consisted only of explanations of methods of limitation and blank tables that included no specific figures. As such, it circumvented the whole disarmament-security problem by putting it off to the future. The draft convention was the product of compromise as, during a time of political scandal in Paris, Cecil bent to some of the French *desiderata* while securing key British demands. Forced to recognize that France would not surrender its superiority over Germany, Britain faced a difficult choice: pursue partial measures and accept higher French armaments as the price of agreement, or see the PC fail and give up the whole idea of disarmament. They chose the first option: it was the only way to ensure that a general disarmament conference finally met. Cecil compromised with French demands on some issues (trained reserves, conscription) in order to get a settlement; he was willing to accept weak provisions on other issues (supervision, 'direct limitation' of armaments) in order to protect Britain's own interests; and, partly as a result of his personal annoyance at the 'obstructionist' tactics of their delegate Count Bernstorff, he refused to listen to German protests about the ineffectiveness of the resulting treaty. The result was Anglo-French agreement that was as illusory as it was unexpected. The most contentious point in the draft treaty was Article 53. This stated that the convention 'shall not in any way diminish the obligations of previous treaties'. Included at British behest in order to protect the Washington and London naval treaties, the French exploited its wording and enraged the German representatives by insisting that the article also covered Germany's disarmament obligations under Versailles. While criticisms of the draft convention were many, it could be defended in one crucial regard, as highlighted in the French press: '*Ce document a une grande vertu qui est d'exister.*'[29]

Barely a month later, the much-awaited opening of the World Disarmament Conference (WDC) was set by the League Council for 2 February 1932. Ironically, the long additional delay was considered necessary so that states could complete their preparations! But the *annus terribilis* of 1931 would not be an auspicious year. Against a background of political and financial crisis, the German government's demand for 'equality of status' in armaments grew steadily louder, although what exactly this entailed remained undefined. Britain and France also faced increasing pressure from public opinion which was insisting upon concrete advances in disarmament.[30] This made it impossible, for example, for them to resist an Italian proposal advanced at the League Assembly in September for a year-long 'arms truce', even though both countries feared it might inflict disproportionate cuts to their own forces. Viewed from abroad, France appeared as the overwhelming military power. But the appearance was deceptive – French ground forces were massive, but this was an army in crisis with low morale, poor organization, a divided command and outdated equipment.[31] Furthermore, the government insisted that France had already taken significant steps in reducing all three spheres of its armed forces 'which have thus been brought down to a level that appears to her strictly to represent the lowest point consistent with her national security in the present state of Europe and the world'. The 'real task' facing the conference was 'the organisation of a solid and durable peace'.[32] The basic issue for France remained unchanged: further security had to precede further disarmament, and German claims to 'equality' were rejected absolutely.[33] As the WDC approached, French policy-makers considered that France had to be ready with specific proposals when the conference opened, 'in order to prevent and to fight likely extreme proposals in the matter of disarmament, as well as to demonstrate that her thesis on security guarantees is not a mere pretext for refusing disarmament'.[34] A determined attempt would be made from the outset to set the agenda of the WDC's political discussions, yet in truth French policy was nevertheless still no more than a defence of the *status quo*.

British political opinion, essentially unaltered by the advent of a National Government in August 1931, maintained its established belief in French militarism and inflexible attitudes. Policy-makers saw only the size of France's forces, not the quality; they considered the French army 'undoubtedly the most formidable military machine in the world today'.[35] And since it was felt that the French 'had little or no intention of disarming at all . . . [and] were heavily over-insured', British policy-makers also stuck rigidly to the idea that Britain alone had disarmed to the limit of national security.[36] The Foreign Office in November and the Cabinet policy committee on disarmament in December both posed the question of whether Britain was prepared to pay the price of gaining reductions in French armaments and stabilizing Europe by offering some kind of guarantee to France.[37] The response was an emphatic 'no'. The Cabinet decided that they were 'not prepared to enter into some form of guarantee over and above Locarno under which, in conceivable circumstances, British forces might be engaged in a war on the continent of Europe'.[38] The idea of German 'equality' was considered far more favourably, in contrast, although German rearmament was not contemplated. The rather vague intention was that Britain could serve as a mediator between the French and German points of view, finding a solution which both limited French arms and incorporated a symbolic change in Germany's status in order to grant 'equality'. The fundamental gap in British and French views over disarmament and its relationship to security was as wide as ever. Britain was not going to the WDC with any real solutions to bridge the gulf; France still refused any additional arms reductions, even at the cost of further estranging the British; and, unless some agreement was reached on 'equality', it seemed clear that Germany would never agree to remain bound by the restrictions of the Treaty of Versailles.

The World Disarmament Conference, which opened in Geneva on 2 February 1932 and would meet discontinuously until mid-1934, was the sorry climax to the inter-war pursuit of disarmament.[39] It had been seven years in the making. In theory its only task was now to insert into the draft convention the figures each nation would be allowed for different types of armaments. Incredibly, the convention, drawn up at the cost of such intense labour, was simply discarded in the first weeks of the conference and attention turned to brand-new schemes and the reconsideration of previously rejected proposals. This distraction was possible, even inevitable, because the central political problem among the key European powers remained unsolved. It was the disarmament-security relationship that would determine the fate of the WDC, not technical measures. But in the absence of some settlement among Britain, France and Germany, the way was left open for talks to descend further and further into the realm of theoretical minutiae. The genuine idealism with which the conference opened steadily dissipated as days, then weeks, months and finally years slipped by with no appreciable results. Its many complexities and repetitive submissions are beyond the scope of any brief description. Suffice it to say that the conference proceeded in four broad phases: from February to July, technical discussions were in the forefront as the real political questions were simply avoided; Germany's withdrawal in protest at the lack of progress towards 'equality' provoked a series of private negotiations among the major powers between August and December 1932 that ultimately secured Germany's return; a second substantive session of discussions followed, marked particularly by the presentation of a British draft convention in March, extending effectively until October 1933 when Germany again withdrew from the conference; a series of British, French and German proposals and counter-proposals were then bandied about until the WDC finally ended with a whimper in July 1934.

At the heart of all the WDC's political negotiations was the fate of Germany. The Germans would never voluntarily accept a new disarmament agreement that did not substantially lessen the disparity between French and German forces. Yet the French would never concede such a change in their relative strengths without new commitments from the British that were not forthcoming. Foreign secretary Sir John Simon told Tardieu (once again French prime minister from February to April 1932), that Britain desired to meet 'Germany's strong and natural objection' to being treated unequally while still reaching an agreement that did not accord German rearmament. Tardieu replied that 'no French government would be able to contemplate . . . any treatment of the problem which would release Germany from existing obligations in regard to her level of armaments'.[40] But British and French concerns about Germany's on-going secret and illegal rearmament were completely opposed. While the British considered the Reichswehr to be no military threat, the French were positively alarmist.[41] The latter's approach was thus immediately to take the initiative at the conference, proposing even as it opened a new plan to augment international security through the creation of an international force under the control of the League.[42]

The main object of the French 'Tardieu plan' was to promote the discussion of security measures and to postpone any discussion of concessions to Germany until after the French elections scheduled for May. As such, it was more a negotiating gambit than a serious proposal to solve the security-disarmament dilemma. For Britain, Simon was similarly less interested in advocating a sincere plan to break the deadlock than in seeking to avoid an early 'violent clash of ideals' between France and Germany.[43] He therefore proposed that the conference should pursue 'qualitative disarmament' – the prohibition of weapons which were primarily 'offensive' in character – and effectively sidetracked its discussions for two months.[44] The fundamental problem had not changed. Britain wished to increase security, MacDonald insisted, but only through 'strengthening the expression and influence of international opinion'.[45] In contrast, Joseph Paul-Boncour, now French minister of war, reminded the British that the reduction of French armaments was still dependent on 'the degree of organisation of security'.[46] Little help arrived from other quarters. The Germans constantly demanded that they be furnished with 'equality', while carefully refraining from defining what exactly would satisfy them. The Japanese pursued their own interests, as did the Italians; and the Americans for the most part tried to avoid any direct involvement.

The German and French elections in May brought significant changes. In Berlin, President Hindenburg dismissed Chancellor Heinrich Brüning and replaced him with Franz von Papen, a political light-weight who ushered in an eight-month period during which the forces of conservatism in Germany became increasingly entrenched. In Paris there were signs of hope, however, with the leader of the leftist Radical party, Edouard Herriot, becoming prime minister. He was particularly interested in restoring a sense of Anglo-French *entente*, to foster an active co-operation between the two powers in dealing with Germany. But Herriot was out-manoeuvred at the Lausanne Conference (16 June–9 July 1932) when he happily accepted MacDonald's promise of an Anglo-French consultative political agreement as part of the settlement that ended German reparations payments. To the French leader's disillusionment, MacDonald promptly detached his country from any concrete implementation of the consultative agreement, which he now insisted was nothing more than a friendly assurance of the two powers' desire to co-operate.[47] This disappointment was compounded in late July by the German withdrawal from 'active participation' in the conference, on the grounds that no substantive progress had been made towards 'equality'. The move was a gamble. Yet it proved successful because the withdrawal was met in London, and less willingly in Paris, by a recognition that no agreement was possible without German participation. Definite opposition to German rearmament did exist among British policy-makers, but the overriding objective was to support the conference by ensuring that Germany returned and accepted an agreed limitation. 'Minor' increases could be tolerated as the price of agreement, for the real fear was that, if left outside the WDC, the Germans might declare themselves free to re-arm without restriction. Britain would then be left to take the blame for not acting positively enough to meet Germany's claims.[48] The French in contrast were prepared to reach a settlement without Germany and hoped for a joint

Anglo-French response. The government in Berlin would then either have to accept the agreement or face being isolated as the militarist state that destroyed the chance for disarmament.[49] But British and also American pressure forced the French to negotiate, for they too feared diplomatic isolation. The focus was slowly beginning to change from arranging disarmament, still primarily that of France in most eyes, to accommodating some measure of German rearmament.

After several months of sparring, agreement was reached in mid-December on a Five Power formula. The WDC's work was to proceed on the basis of 'equality of rights in a system which would provide security for all nations'.[50] But these were empty words. What security system was contemplated, and was equality a starting point or the final goal? The imperfect melding of the Franco-German theses merely glossed over the fundamental problem: without a British commitment to security, the French would never concede equality; and unless the French conceded equality, Germany would never accept a disarmament agreement. This had been perfectly illustrated by the 'Herriot plan' of November 1932, a French scheme offering progressively increasing amounts of security commitments for different states, depending upon their location and membership of the League. It was an arrangement specifically tailored to accommodate Britain's reticence while achieving France's goal. Paul-Boncour insisted to MacDonald that 'in drafting this plan the French government had been at the utmost pains to have a proper regard to the British point of view', but that 'any far-reaching reduction of armaments . . . [was] dependent upon the improvement of security'.[51] Despite Foreign Office urgings that such French attempts to meet Britain's needs should be encouraged, the National Government continued to reject any additional obligations. The Under-Secretary of State for Foreign Affairs, Anthony Eden, told the conference at its resumption in February 1933 that Britain, in the League Covenant and Locarno, had 'gone as far as it could and should in assuming definite commitments in Europe'. Instead, he insisted that existing guarantees of security were already sufficient for 'a real measure of disarmament'.[52]

In many ways, by the start of 1933 the effective life of the WDC was over. While discussions continued on the same themes that had dominated since the creation of the PC in 1925, there was no longer the luxury of time. The Far East situation was steadily worsening, leading to Japan's withdrawal from the League in February, and on 30 January Adolf Hitler became German Chancellor. Within days he was privately informing leading generals and ministers of his intention to re-arm Germany, physically and morally, as rapidly as possible. Hitler's public speeches, in contrast, emphasized his regime's pacific intention to pursue a moderate policy of peaceful treaty revision. He called for other states to disarm down to Germany's level and asserted his constant readiness to conclude non-aggression pacts.[53] His tactics would produce differing responses in Britain and France over the following two years, though the importance of the governmental change in Germany was not immediately appreciated abroad. In London, policy planning continued on the basis that negotiation with Hitler was possible and that he could be trusted to carry out any agreement reached. In Paris, a new government led by Edouard Daladier came to power in January 1933. It was hopeful that an understanding could be reached with Germany, despite warnings from the intelligence services about the threat presented by the Nazis. Daladier was more concerned with the financial crisis brought on by the Depression; the cuts he imposed on French armed forces incurred the ire of Weygand, his commanding general, who stormed that France was being left 'undefended' against the German danger. Paul-Boncour, now foreign minister, was as convinced as Daladier that 'France must continue to seek security through international agreements rather than through rearmament'.[54] Yet from this time onward, the entire conference was acting in an air of unreality.

Despite the deadlocks and frequent complaints of hopelessness, the quest for disarmament went on. Popular expectations meant that it simply could not be dropped, and no government wished to be put in a position where it could be blamed for failure. It was this negative motivation which spurred the initiatives of the WDC's second year. The fear that the stagnation of the conference's work might be attributed to Britain finally induced MacDonald to agree to a new British effort on 16 March, the presentation of a complete draft convention which included, for the first time, suggested figures for each nation's armament levels.[55] Acting in great trepidation, the British prime minister was surprised to discover that the 'MacDonald plan' was greeted as a huge success and taken as the basis for further discussions. It included provisions for a consultative agreement that laid down procedures to be followed in the event of a breach of the Kellogg-Briand Pact. However, the formula outlined was for little more than the summoning of a conference to discuss what steps might be taken against an aggressor. It included no provisions for sanctions. As such it was much weaker than the 'Herriot plan', to which it did not refer, and offered no inducement for the French to accept the increases in German armaments which the British plan proposed. The Cabinet nonetheless decided in June that this represented 'the maximum distance which His Majesty's Government are prepared to go under present circumstances'.[56]

French policy-makers considered the MacDonald plan unacceptable, but were unwilling to cause friction by opposing it directly. Instead they framed their counter-proposals as 'amendments' to the plan. Their crucial change was the division of the proposed convention into two 'stages' of four years each with real disarmament only to begin during the second stage. These amendments formed the basis of private discussions that ran through September; meanwhile, the French promoted the possibility of security compensations through supervision and sanctions.

> If Germany continues to rearm [Daladier told British and American representatives during June], France will increase its armaments so as to maintain its superiority. . . . France would greatly prefer an effectively supervised disarmament regime. The question remains to find out if this effective control can be instituted. . . .What will be the consequences of recognised violations?[57]

Despite the obviously worsening situation in Germany, the British remained unwilling to accept the French desire for sanctions. The Cabinet felt, as Simon stated, that 'we could accept no new responsibilities'.[58] At most, ministers would accept that a breach of the convention should result in all other parties being absolved of their obligations. In other words, once one state re-armed, all could. British policy-makers were now more convinced than ever that either the WDC had to bind Germany while it was still possible, which meant reaching an agreement that conceded some limited rearmament, or that Germany should be forced to take the responsibility for breaking up the conference by publicly rejecting the proposals. As there was no deep-rooted attachment to the MacDonald plan, acceptance of France's amendments was enticing because it would protect Britain from isolation and free it from the responsibility for failure.

A 'compromise' plan was therefore presented by Simon in Geneva, on 14 October. It was based on the French amendments while still maintaining reservations on sanctions and supervision. A key Foreign Office adviser perceived, more-or-less correctly, that 'the idea of our Cabinet is to break the conference and put [the] blame on Germany'.[59] But the British were now out-manoeuvred, for their proposal became the pretext for a premeditated German withdrawal not only from the WDC but from the League itself. This walkout was given cover by Hitler's loud denunciations of Britain as the power responsible due to the repeated denial of Germany's claim to 'equality' and by his quick offer of new 'disarmament' proposals of his own, making it seem that Germany had in fact been driven from the conference. Hitler's *démarche* revealed once again the full extent of the Anglo-French divide. His proposals called for the legalization of extensive German rearmament, leading Anglo-French discussions back to their constant theme. France flatly refused to disarm whilst Germany was illegally rearming or to sanction any German rearmament within an agreement. In British eyes, however, Hitler's proposals provided a stark choice: either acceptance of some controlled German expansion within an agreement or unchecked rearmament. They made what seemed to them the obvious decision and in late January 1934 proposed a compromise that conceded substantial German armaments increases. A consultative scheme was all that they offered by way of security guarantees. Unsurprisingly, the French rejected the British proposal outright in an official note of 17 March. In London there was some support in the Cabinet for concessions to French security fears. However, despite these signs of dawning recognition, it was decided on 22 March that 'given the conditions in France today, to ally ourselves to France was a terrible responsibility'. The final French word came less than a month later, on 17 April, when an official memorandum declared that France could not continue Anglo-French negotiations if the British were advocating the effective legalization of German rearmament.[60] To the British, it seemed clear that the French were simply no longer interested in disarmament. Several commentators would later assert that this was the moment when France missed its last real opportunity to bind Hitler.[61]

At the end of May, a final attempt in Geneva by Simon to have the WDC proceed by taking the British compromise of January 1934 as a basis for negotiations was rejected by French foreign minister Louis Barthou, who made it clear that France could not accept 'a draft convention in which . . . in the very first year, France was to disarm while Germany's rearmament was legalised'.[62] On 11 June, the WDC was adjourned *sine die*; everyone knew it would not meet again. By the end of the year, Simon could tell the Cabinet that 'hopes of a worldwide agreement limiting the number and type of armaments . . . did not exist any longer, although there were still political arguments against making a public statement to this effect'.[63] It was a dismal end to the inter-war quest for general disarmament.

Despite the international appeal of disarmament, it was always going to be the national interests of a very small number of major powers that determined its fate. Chief among these powers were Britain and France. Neither was willing to make the political choices necessary for the disarmament process to succeed, choices that required a recognition that disarmament and security were actually two sides of the same coin. To obtain security, France would have to make the essentially political decision to engage in structured reductions to its military preponderance over Germany. To induce France to disarm, Britain would have to agree to commit itself to involvement in a European security system, a political decision which involved a recognition that British and French security was integrally linked. But neither was willing to take the necessary steps. The gulf in Anglo-French perspectives was never more clearly demonstrated than in a conversation between Craigie and Massigli during the London Naval Conference. The Frenchman insisted that 'since 1922, France had been constantly striving for some international agreement which would give her the only guarantee worth having, namely, some form of international protection in the event of her being subjected again to a flagrant attack'. To this, Craigie replied:

> France should surely realise that, if her policy were a genuinely pacific one, the League of Nations would never leave her to stand alone against any unprovoked act of aggression on the part of another power. This fact was so certain and so obvious that it was difficult to see how French security could really be increased by the multiplication of treaties of guarantee.[64]

For the British, no security problem existed, and they therefore ruled out from the start any new commitments by themselves. For the French, however, the security gap was obvious and the British refusal to recognize it was a source of perpetual frustration.

In the final analysis, the crux of the problem was the British willingness to accept revisions of the Versailles regime in Germany's favour, and the French refusal to do so. British policy-makers saw no threat to their country from Germany, and by the end of 1932 felt that as some degree of German rearmament was inevitable, the best solution was to secure a settlement that could manage and limit it. They over-estimated France's strength and refused to take on an interventionist role in Europe, and subsequently under-estimated the new danger posed by Hitler. French policy-makers believed that if Britain would stand firm alongside France against German demands, they would not have to accept any German rearmament at all. But they never explicitly formulated a coherent vision of what exactly would constitute sufficient 'security' for them, and refused to make real cuts in their own armaments even though Germany presented no realistic threat until 1932. For all their many demands, French policy had no overarching strategic concept other than the sterile defence of the Treaty of Versailles.

It was an endless argument and the short-sightedness implicit in the attitudes of both powers was fatal to the entire disarmament process. It stretched out the different stages of negotiations over nine years, to the point where positions became unalterably entrenched, all enthusiasm evaporated and the process was eventually overwhelmed by the advent of Hitler. The endless technical disputes throughout these years were insoluble until the underlying political issues had been addressed. Yet perhaps the disarmament problem was simply beyond solution during the inter-war period. Powers had to be reassured that they had nothing to fear from disarming. This, however, was an almost impossible task at a time when notions of 'collective security' were only incompletely understood even by their most vehement exponents and when it also seemed to many policy-makers that it was armaments themselves that provided stability. Public expectations meant both Britain and France felt obliged to grasp for the poisoned chalice of disarmament, but sadly this merely exposed the differing perceptions of where their interests lay. The possibility of joint action – through a compromise security-disarmament regime which could have been driven through at Geneva regardless of German objections – was lost in the fierce arguments that ensued. Despite all the hopes it engendered, the disarmament process did far more harm than good to Anglo-French relations between the wars.

Notes

1. Part V of the Treaty of Versailles imposed limitations upon the armaments of Germany alone. The Allied powers 'committed' themselves to disarmament in the wording of the preamble to Part V, in their official reply to German protests (the 'Clemenceau letter' of 16 June 1919) and in Article 8 of the League Covenant. They later restated their intentions in the final protocol of the Locarno conference, 16 October 1925.
2. Useful are P. Towle, 'British Security and Disarmament Policy in Europe in the 1920s'; Z. Steiner, 'The League of Nations and the Quest for Security'; and M. Vaïsse, 'Security and Disarmament: Problems in the Development of the Disarmament Debates, 1919–1934', all in R. Ahmann, A. M. Birke and M. Howard (eds), *The Quest for Stability: Problems of West European Security, 1918–1957* (London: German Historical Institute, and Oxford University Press, 1993).

3. The commission initially consisted of the ten members of the Council, the three major non-League powers (US, Germany and USSR) and six other interested states (all European). A total of 13 other states also later took part in some fashion.
4. The PC met at Geneva in six sessions over seven meetings: first session, 18–26 May 1926; second session, 22 and 27 September 1926; third session, 21 March–26 April 1927; fourth session, 30 November–3 December 1927; fifth session, 15–24 March 1928; sixth session (first part), 15 April–6 May 1929; sixth session (second part), 6 November–9 December 1930. The second session was merely a formality. The fourth and fifth sessions were hijacked by the Soviet delegate's totally unrealistic proposals for immediate and universal disarmament, delaying practical discussions for two years.
5. France refused any limits on numbers of 'trained reserves' (men who received military training and then passed into the reserves); Britain refused strict supervision of national armouries; Britain wanted naval limitation by category of ship, in order to ensure superiority within each category, while France wanted limitation by global fleet tonnage, so that it could concentrate its strength in certain categories.
6. The 1927 naval conference produced only stalemate and Anglo-American antagonism, with France and Italy refusing even to attend. The abortive 1928 'arms compromise' was a secret deal in which Britain dropped its insistence on limiting trained reserves and France agreed to back Britain's position on limiting cruisers; this apparently cynical manoeuvring also produced American anger. D. Carlton, 'Great Britain and the Coolidge Naval Conference of 1927', *Political Science Quarterly*, 83 (1968); R. Fanning, 'The Coolidge Conference of 1927: Disarmament in Disarray', in B. J. C. McKercher (ed.), *Arms Limitation and Disarmament: Restraints on War, 1899–1939* (Westport, CT: Praeger, 1992); D. Carlton, 'The Anglo-French Compromise on Arms Limitation, 1928', *Journal of British Studies*, 8 (1969); B.J.C. McKercher, *The Second Baldwin Government and the United States, 1924–1929: Attitudes and Diplomacy* (Cambridge: Cambridge University Press, 1984), pp. 55–76 and 140–70.
7. The details of the PC's meetings are tortuous in their repetition and infuriating in their special pleading, which perhaps explains why there is no standard history of the commission. Given the almost contemptuous treatment of its work by modern historians, contemporary sources remain very useful. See: League of Nations, *Documents of the Preparatory Commission for the Disarmament Conference*, series II–X, League of Nations Publications (LNP) series 'IX.Disarmament' (1926–1930); J. Wheeler-Bennett, *Disarmament and Security since Locarno, 1925–1931* (London: Royal Institute of International Affairs, 1932), pp. 43–141 and 281–306; and the 1926–30 volumes of A. Toynbee's annual *Survey of International Affairs* (London: Royal Institute of International Affairs, 1928–31).
8. 'Policy in regard to the next meeting of the Preparatory Commission', 22 March 1929, PRO, CAB 24/202/CP 91(29).
9. Report by Massigli, for Briand, 14 May 1929, MAE, SDN, I.I., vol. 856, fos. 208–16.
10. W. Deist, 'The Rearmament of the Wehrmacht', in Militärgeschichtliches Forschungsamt (ed.), *Germany and the Second World War. Volume I: the Build-up of German Aggression* (Oxford: Clarendon Press, 1990), pp. 375–86;

'Note sur les possibilités actuelles de mobilisation de l'Allemagne', memo by War Ministry, 15 January 1930, SHAT, 7N/2620; 'The military situation in Germany, January 1930', memo by War Office, 11 February 1930, PRO, CAB 4/19/979-B. German violations of the disarmament clauses of the Treaty of Versailles, ongoing since the mid-1920s, were well-known in Britain and France. While the British considered them relatively insignificant and chose to ignore them, the French became increasingly agitated by this evidence of German duplicity.

11. 'Mémento remis par le Général Requin à M. Berthelot', 8 October 1929, in file 'Position de la Guerre', SHM, 1BB/2/191.

12. These measures all aimed to lessen the chances of war either by creating machinery to settle disputes peacefully or by increasing the League's powers to prevent conflicts. States signing the 'Optional Clause' of the Statute of the Permanent Court of International Justice, for example, agreed in advance to submit certain classes of international disputes to the court and to regard its decisions as binding. The work of the Committee on Arbitration and Security, which met four times between December 1927 and May 1930, is summarized in F. P. Walters, *A History of the League of Nations* (London: Oxford University Press, 1952), vol. I, pp. 377–87.

13. A. L. Kennedy diary, 18 September 1929, Kennedy papers, Churchill College Archives Centre, Cambridge, LKEN 1/8.

14. Speech by MacDonald, Geneva, 3 September 1929, *League of Nations Official Journal (LNOJ)*, Special supplement no. 75 (Geneva, 1929), pp. 33–6.

15. 'Projet de rapport au CSDN', memo by Col. Lucien (war ministry), 30 November 1929, MAE, SDN, I.H., vol. 723, fos. 140–5.

16. Memo by French government, on French policy at the naval conference, 20 December 1929, *Documents on British Foreign Policy (DBFP)*, series II, vol. 1, no. 123.

17. 'Arbitrage, sécurité, désarmement', memo by SFSDN (Geneva), for Massigli, 30 August 1929, MAE, SDN, I.I., vol. 859, fos. 19–24; CSDN report, 17 January 1930, *ibid.*, I.H., vol. 720, fos. 191–4.

18. Memo by Réquin, 18 October 1929, in file 'Position de la Guerre', SHM, 1BB/2/191. Also 'Conférence navale et interdépendance des armements', memo by SFSDN, for Briand, 9 October 1929, MAE, SDN, I.I., vol. 1115, fos. 112–16.

19. MacDonald diary, 12 February 1930, PRO, PRO 30/69/1753/1. See also entries for 14 and 16 February and 23 April 1930.

20. Note by Craigie on a conversation with Massigli, 25 February 1930, PRO, CAB 29/129.

21. Campbell (Paris) to Henderson, 16 September 1930, PRO, FO 371/14271/A6198/1/45.

22. MacDonald diary, 30 March 1931, PRO, PRO 30/69/1753/1.

23. Memo by Violette, 31 March 1931, in file 'Négociations navales: 1 mars-1 avril 1931', SHM, 1BB/2/193, p. 118*bis*.

24. Speech by Henderson, 11 September 1930, *LNOJ*, Special supplement no. 84 (Geneva, 1930), p. 42.

25. 'The French military budget for 1930', memo by War Office, 5 June 1930, PRO, CAB 4/19/994-B; Henderson to Tyrrell (Paris), 10 November 1930, PRO, FO 800/282, fos. 188–9.

26. Speech by Tardieu, at Alençon, 28 September 1930, quoted in Tyrrell (Paris) to Henderson, 10 October 1930, PRO, FO 371/14905/W10707/198/17.

27. Weygand to Commission d'Etudes (CSDN), 17 October 1930, SHAT, 2N/11/4, pp. 133–71.

28. The text of the draft convention of 9 December 1930 is in J. Wheeler-Bennett (ed.), *Documents on International Affairs, 1931* (London: Royal Institute of International Affairs, 1932), pp. 17–39. On British and French policy preparations for this meeting, see: memo by Henderson, 2 October 1930, PRO, CAB 16/98/RA27-A; memo by General Serrigny (CSDN), 29 October 1930, SHAT, 2N/11/5.

29. Wheeler-Bennett, *Disarmament and Security*, p. 102.

30. See N. Ingram, *The Politics of Dissent: Pacifism in France, 1919–1939* (Oxford: Clarendon Press, 1991) and M. Ceadel, *Pacifism in Britain, 1914–1945: the Defining of a Faith* (Oxford: Clarendon Press, 1980).

31. See the classic work on French disarmament policy in this period: M. Vaïsse, *Sécurité d'abord: La politique française en matière de désarmement, 9 décembre 1930–17 avril 1934* (Paris: Publications de la Sorbonne, 1981), pp. 54–77.

32. Memo by French government, on French disarmament policy, 15 July 1931, *DBFP*, II, 3, no. 213. On the drafting of this memo, May–July 1931, see: MAE, SDN, I.H., vols. 724–5, *passim*.

33. Vaïsse, *Sécurité d'abord*, pp. 82–7 and 104–24. See: 'La thèse française en matière de sécurité et de désarmement', memo by SFSDN, March 1931, MAE, SDN, I.I., vol. 862, fos. 178–85; 'Conférence du Désarmement', memo by SFSDN, 27 August 1931, *ibid.*, vol. 863, fos. 179–86.

34. 'Projets d'avis de la Commission Spéciale', 19 December 1931, MAE, SDN, I.H., vol. 726, fos. 185–209. Meetings of Commission Spéciale (CSDN), November–December 1931, are in *ibid.*, *passim*.

35. 'Military appreciation of the situation in Europe, March 1931', memo by War Office, 31 March 1931, PRO, CAB 16/102/DC(P)3.

36. General Sir George Milne (Chief of Imperial General Staff) to CID subcommittee on the Disarmament Conference (Three Party Committee), 7 May 1931, PRO, CAB 16/102/DC(P) 3rd meeting.

37. 'Changing conditions in British foreign policy', memo by Foreign Office, 26 November 1931, and 'Appreciation of elements in political problem involved', interim report of the Cabinet committee, 12 December 1931, PRO, CAB 24/225/CP 301(31) and 322(31).

38. Cabinet minutes, 15 December 1931, PRO, CAB 23/69/91(31). See also Cabinet minutes, 14 January 1932, PRO, CAB 23/70/3(32).

39. The proceedings of the WDC, officially titled 'The Conference for the Reduction and Limitation of Armaments', are in: League of Nations, *Records of the Conference for the Reduction and Limitation of Armaments* [hereafter 'Conference documents'], LNP series 'IX.Disarmament' (1932–36). There is no single definitive study of the conference, but see: B. J. C. McKercher, 'Of Horns and Teeth: the Preparatory Commission and the World Disarmament Conference, 1926–1934', in McKercher (ed.), *Arms Limitation and Disarmament*; D. Richardson, 'The Geneva Disarmament Conference, 1932–1934', in D. Richardson and G. Stone (eds), *Decisions and Diplomacy: Essays in Twentieth-Century International History* (London: Routledge, 1995); E. Bennett, *German Rearmament and the West, 1932–1933* (Princeton:

Princeton University Press, 1979), pp. 131–505; Vaïsse, *Sécurité d'abord*, pp. 193–594.

40. Conversation between Simon and Tardieu, 12 March 1932, *DBFP*, II, 3, no. 236.

41. 'The extent and effects of the military breaches of the Treaty of Versailles', memo by War Office, for Foreign Office, 1 March 1932, *ibid.*, appendix iv; General Gamelin (war ministry) to Tardieu, 7 March 1932, MAE, SDN, I.I., vol. 1001, fos. 5–33. See also P. Jackson, 'French Intelligence and Hitler's Rise to Power', *Historical Journal*, 41, (September 1998), pp. 799–802.

42. Speech by Tardieu, 8 February 1932, Conference documents, *Series A: Verbatim Records of Plenary Meetings, vol. I: 2 February–23 July 1932* (Geneva, 1932), LNP 1932.IX.60, pp. 60–4.

43. Simon to Ministerial Committee on Disarmament, 21 March 1932, PRO, CAB 27/505/DC(M)(32), first meeting.

44. Speech by Simon, 20 April 1932, Conference documents, *Series B: Minutes of the General Commission, vol. I: 9 February–23 July 1932* (Geneva, 1932), LNP 1932.IX.64, pp. 94–6. The results of such an approach should perhaps have been obvious: each state defined those weapons which threatened it as 'offensive' and those weapons on which it primarily relied as 'defensive'.

45. Meeting of British and American delegations, Geneva, 23 April 1932, *DBFP*, II, 3, no. 240.

46. Meeting of British, French and American delegations, 19 June 1932, *ibid.*, no. 245.

47. On the Anglo-French agreement, see: *ibid.*, nos. 172, 184, 189, 190; *Documents Diplomatiques Français (DDF)*, series I, vol. 1, nos. 16, 17.

48. Cabinet minutes, 11 October 1932, PRO, CAB 23/72/50(32); British statements of view, 15 September and 17 November 1932, *DBFP*, II, 4, nos. 92 and 183.

49. On French policy, see: *DDF*, I, 1, nos. 132, 169, 235, 244; Vaïsse, *Sécurité d'abord*, pp. 276–91.

50. Five Power declaration, 11 December 1932, *DBFP*, II, 4, no. 220.

51. Conversation between MacDonald, Simon and Paul-Boncour, Geneva, 2 December 1932, *ibid.*, no. 204. The 'Herriot plan' of 14 November 1932, also known as the 'Paul-Boncour plan' or the 'constructive plan', is in *DDF*, I, 1, no. 331.

52. Speech by Eden, 3 February 1933, Conference documents, *Series B: Minutes of the General Commission, vol. II: 14 December 1932–29 June 1933* (Geneva, 1933), LNP 1933.IX.10, pp. 222–4.

53. Comments by Hitler to meeting of leading generals, 3 February 1933, in J. Noakes and G. Pridham (eds), *Nazism, 1919–1945: a Documentary Reader. Vol. 3: Foreign Policy, War and Racial Extermination* (Exeter: University of Exeter Press, 1998), no. 472; Conference of Ministers, in the Reich Chancellery, 8 February 1933, *Documents on German Foreign Policy*, series C, vol. 1, no. 16; W. Wette, 'Ideology, Propaganda and Internal Politics as Preconditions of the War Policy of the Third Reich', in *The Build-up of German Aggression*, pp. 96–102, 125.

54. General Weygand to Daladier, 9 February 1933, SHAT, 1N/42, dr. 3; memo by Paul-Boncour, 10 March 1933, Archives Nationales, Paul-Boncour papers,

424 AP, vol. 21. See Jackson, 'French Intelligence', pp. 811–13 and 821–2; Vaïsse, *Sécurité d'abord*, pp. 364–70.

55. The text of the MacDonald plan is in *DBFP*, II, 4, appendix iv.

56. Cabinet minutes, 27 June 1933, PRO, CAB 23/76/42(33).

57. Meeting of French, British and American representatives, Paris, 8 June 1933, *DDF*, I, 3, no. 376. Also: *ibid.*, nos. 135, 229; *ibid.*, 4, nos. 173, 260, 261.

58. Simon to Cabinet, 20 September 1933, PRO, CAB 23/77/51(33).

59. Alexander Cadogan diary, 11 October 1933, Cadogan papers, Churchill College Archives Centre, Cambridge, ACAD 1/1.

60. British memo on disarmament, 25 January 1934, *DBFP*, II, 6, no. 206; Barthou to Corbin (London), 17 March 1934, *DDF*, I, 4, no. 16; Cabinet minutes, 14, 19 and 22 March 1934, PRO, CAB 23/78/9(34), 10(34) and 12(34); memo by French government, 17 April 1934, *DDF*, I, 6, no. 104.

61. For example, A. C. Temperley, *The Whispering Gallery of Europe* (London: Collins, revised edition, 1939), pp. 260–7.

62. Speeches by Simon and Barthou, 30 May 1934, Conference documents, *Series B: Minutes of the General Commission, vol. III: 16 October 1933–11 June 1934* (Geneva, 1936), LNP 1936.IX.1, pp. 661–70.

63. Cabinet minutes, 29 October 1934, PRO, CAB 23/80/56(34).

64. Note by Craigie on a conversation with Massigli, 25 February 1930, PRO, CAB 29/129.

4
Britain, France and the Emerging Italian Threat, 1935–38

Reynolds M. Salerno

In early 1935 Britain, France and Italy signed a series of agreements that seemed to indicate genuine international co-operation in the tradition of collective security. By the beginning of 1938, the Anglo-French-Italian harmony of 1935 had entirely unravelled, exposing differences that precluded any sort of enduring reconciliation. Although they had not turned against each other, Britain and France now addressed the Mediterranean situation – and especially Italy – in contrasting ways. The growing divergence of British and French interpretations of Italian policy during this period reflected a fundamental shift in their under-standing of Italy's role in European affairs. In early 1935, the British and French saw Italy as a nation committed to collective European security but, by 1938, they recognized that the Fascist regime attached signifi-cant importance to its relationship with Nazi Germany.

While this evident change in Italian policy placed the Mediterranean at the centre of both British and French defence and security calculations, the two nations arrived at starkly different conclusions about how to address the altered Italian factor. The British believed that the Fascist leaders could be conciliated, detached from Hitler and persuaded to mollify Germany's ambitions, whereas the French perceived a permanently antagonistic foreign policy on the part of the Italians and an unassail-able link between Fascist Italy and Nazi Germany. The British embarked upon a policy aimed at ensuring peace in the Mediterranean, arguing that any preparation for war in that area would damage the impending appeasement of Italy. Insisting that Fascist Italy would resort to force if the democracies did not relinquish all their possessions in the Mediter-ranean, the French by contrast began anticipating a Mediterranean war.

Tracing for the first time the gradual divergence of British and French Mediterranean policies, by examining British and French interpretations of Italy from the Anglo-German Naval Agreement of June 1935 to the German Anschluss of Austria in March 1938, this chapter will offer an important contribution to the literature that compares British and French foreign and defence policies before the Second World War, which has hitherto almost exclusively focused on the two powers' assessments of the threat posed by Nazi Germany.

The year 1935 started positively for Anglo-French-Italian relations. On 7 January, Benito Mussolini, the Italian *duce*, and French foreign minister Pierre Laval signed an agreement that proclaimed the 'necessity of maintaining the independence and integrity of Austria'.[1] In an Anglo-French *communiqué* the following month, Britain expressed approval of the Franco-Italian accords and the two states promised to consult with other interested powers if any state menaced Austrian independence or integrity.[2] Following Nazi Germany's first open repudiation of the Treaty of Versailles – proclaiming the existence of an air force, reintroducing conscription and initiating construction of 12 submarines – representatives of Britain, France and Italy met in Stresa in early April and adopted a resolution that accepted 'no unilateral repudiation of international obligations', reaffirmed the intention to consult one another if any power threatened the independence of Austria and stated that they would actively pursue an air pact.[3]

Although these three agreements could have contributed to the creation of a formidable anti-German coalition, their value was damaged by the Anglo-German Naval Agreement of June 1935 and the subsequent crisis in the Mediterranean. France interpreted the naval agreement, which sanctioned the expansion of the German *Kriegsmarine* up to 35 per cent of the size of the Royal Navy, as not only a revision of Versailles but also an open rejection of the London *communiqué* and the Stresa front. The French inferred that Britain had forsaken its commitment to a broader European settlement in favour of national security. Moreover, the naval treaty – and the shift out of the Mediterranean by British and French naval forces that followed it – provided Mussolini with an opportunity to pursue the extension of the Italian empire into east Africa for which he had long been planning. On the day the naval treaty was signed, Mussolini made specific Italian claims on Ethiopia (Abyssinia). Four days later Laval, now the French premier, reaffirmed France's commitment to that part of the January agreement that gave Italy a 'free hand' in Ethiopia.[4]

Confident that Britain and France would not resist Italian expansion into east Africa, Mussolini intensified the conflict with Ethiopia during the summer and repeatedly rejected British and French proposals for a negotiated settlement. At the end of August, with Italy's designs on Ethiopia evident to the entire world, Britain and France reinforced their Mediterranean defences and eliminated Italy's naval superiority. Although the balance of naval tonnage in the Mediterranean had suddenly shifted in favour of Britain and France, the two powers did not attempt to forestall Mussolini's drive into east Africa. Facing no military opposition, Mussolini ordered Italian troops to invade Ethiopia on 3 October.[5]

Britain and France also decided not to take up arms to oppose Italy's flagrant transgression of the League of Nations' principles of national sovereignty and collective security. Concluding that a war with Italy 'would be a grave calamity', the British Cabinet believed that if Britain committed itself to a naval conflict against Italy in the Mediterranean and especially if Britain lost any warships in the process, the naval balance in the North Sea would tip in Germany's favour and all of China and south-east Asia would lie open to Japanese expansion.[6] Yet much of the hesitation to act militarily came from the French, who rejected Britain's request for unconditional French commitments against Italy in the Mediterranean. Laval wished to avoid any hostilities in the Mediterranean, confident that an overt Franco-Italian conflict would drive Mussolini into the German camp and further complicate French continental strategy and defence. Along with many other officials in Paris, Laval still hoped that the Stresa front could be reconstituted.[7]

Instead of using force, Britain and France arranged for the League to impose sanctions on Italy. At Laval's insistence, though, the League excluded the two punitive measures – an oil embargo and the closing of the Suez Canal – that might have forced Mussolini to reconsider his east African adventure. Moreover, the Laval government attempted to minimize the effect of sanctions by delaying their application until late November, refusing to enforce them in French Morocco or in territories under French mandate, and maintaining commercial and financial relations with countries that did not apply sanctions. Even so, the imposition of sanctions on Italy infuriated Mussolini, who had been led to believe by the 1935 Franco-Italian accord and the Stresa pact that Britain and France would quietly acquiesce in Italy's annexation of Abyssinia.[8]

Interpreting France's action during the sanctions episode as treachery, and recognizing that Italian foreign policy was fundamentally opposed to Britain and France, Mussolini in January 1936 notified the Germans that Italy was willing to reconsider its defence of Austrian independence in return for an Italian-German understanding. 'Stresa', claimed the

Duce, 'is dead and buried once and for all'. As recently as August 1935, Mussolini had concentrated Italian troops near the Brenner, inciting indignation on the part of the Germans in the South Tyrol and Austria. Mussolini started withdrawing these forces in December.[9] This subtle Italian action in favour of Germany persuaded many in London and Paris to search for a diplomatic solution to the Italian-Abyssinian crisis. But news of a proposal under consideration whereby Ethiopia would relinquish about half of its territory in order to settle the conflict with Italy (the infamous Hoare-Laval Pact) enraged British and French public opinion, scuttling all efforts to conclude the Mediterranean crisis.

Germany's reoccupation of the Rhineland in March 1936 and Italy's capture of Addis Ababa in May rekindled attempts to resolve the crisis in the Mediterranean. Britain and France did not respond forcefully to Germany's abrogation of the Locarno treaties because not only were the two powers unprepared militarily but they also faced a potentially hostile Italy in the Mediterranean. Rather than seek concessions from the Ethiopians, the British and French now began reconsidering their sanctions policy in the Mediterranean. Initially, the French government continued to support the embargo against Italy. The Popular Front, which took office at the beginning of June under the premiership of Léon Blum, reaffirmed France's commitment to sanctions.[10] But France's military leaders, who had argued since March that the enhanced German threat made pursuing an alliance with Britain and resolving the crisis in the Mediterranean essential, lobbied for lifting sanctions, recognizing Italy's Ethiopian empire and signing a 'Mediterranean Locarno' with Italy.[11]

Strong British pressure also persuaded the French to abandon the embargo against Italy. The most important voice in London on Mediterranean issues was Chancellor of the Exchequer Neville Chamberlain, who claimed that the new reality on the continent compelled Britain to end the sanctions regime in order to rebuild the Stresa front. The Admiralty complemented this perspective by persuading the Chiefs of Staff Committee (COS) that security for the British Isles and the empire required a resolution of the Mediterranean crisis and a return to normal fleet distribution. As the First Sea Lord, Sir Ernle Chatfield, explained, 'We have to divide our fleet and be able to meet the German fleet at home and the Japanese fleet in the Far East'. The COS then outlined the strategic rationale for lifting sanctions: 'Our hopes lie in a peaceful Mediterranean, and this can only be achieved by returning to a state of friendly relations with Italy.' In June, the Baldwin government proposed that the League lift sanctions against Italy.[12]

The League voted to endorse the British proposal on 4 July 1936, and within two weeks the British and French fleets had returned to their pre-1935 deployments. The crisis in the Mediterranean had reached its conclusion but the Anglo-French-Italian conflict in the Mediterranean had only begun. Even though the French had ensured that the embargo was not imposed stringently on Italy, the Fascist government heaped indignation on the French for not being responsible for ending the sanctions regime. As the new Italian foreign minister, Galeazzo Ciano, stressed to a prominent French publicist, 'Italy will always remember with regret that England and not France brought about an end to the injustice of sanctions'.[13]

The League's decision to lift sanctions on Italy coincided with the outbreak of civil war in Spain. The emotional, ideological and strategic aspects of the Spanish affair turned the fracture in Franco-Italian relations that had opened during the Italian-Abyssinian conflict into a genuine chasm. Immediately after the first army uprisings in Spain, the Republican government approached Blum for help. Blum, a Jewish socialist, had always regarded Mussolini and Hitler as dictators whose ideological affinities destined them to align with each other. He envisioned the Popular Front as a product of generic anti-Fascism and was thus ideologically obligated to support the Republicans with arms. He also claimed that a Fascist Spain would add a third European front to France's already tortuous security dilemma. However, many others in the French government urged non-intervention, fearing Comintern influence in France and claiming that French involvement in Spain could lead to a general conflagration in Europe for which France was unprepared.[14] This position was supported by those at the Quai d'Orsay who advocated integrating Italy into various diplomatic schemes, and those within the French military who believed that a friendly Italy was an essential element of French security.[15]

Added to this contentious French debate over how to respond to the Spanish civil war was the British case for non-intervention. In late July, Anthony Eden, the Foreign Secretary, informed the French that the Cabinet believed General Francisco Franco, the leader of the generals revolting in Spain, would quickly overthrow the Republic, and that Anglo-French intervention would jeopardize peace in Europe. Despite Britain's perspective, French domestic concerns proved decisive. For the stability of the government, the viability of his social-reform programme and the preservation of civil peace and order, Blum steered a middle course by closing the Pyrenees frontier to French exports bound for Spain, permitting foreign arms and volunteers to move across French borders into Spain, and proposing an international non-intervention agreement. By 15 August, the French non-intervention proposal had become Anglo-French policy and, on 9 September, France joined Britain at the first meeting of the Non-Intervention Committee to reaffirm their policy.[16]

While the French tried to straddle anti-Fascism and non-interventionism in the Spanish civil war as a way to retain Anglo-French unanimity in the Mediterranean, the British reacted to the steadily increasing level of Italian and German intervention in Spain by unilaterally adopting a new policy for the Mediterranean. Arguing that many eastern Mediterranean states now questioned Britain's predominant position in the region, the Foreign Office advocated signing a defensive treaty with Greece and Turkey and warning Italy against any alteration of the *status quo* in the Mediterranean. The service chiefs, however, insisted that it was 'most important to avoid any measures which . . . merely tend to further alienate Italy'. Britain's lack of adequate naval bases and weak military strength in the eastern Mediterranean would require the British to be on the defensive if Italy became hostile, regardless of the number of Britain's allies there. A simultaneous war at home or in the Far East would only exacerbate Britain's strategic predicament in the Mediterranean. In September, the Cabinet rescinded the diplomatic assurances that Britain had made in the eastern Mediterranean during the Italian-Abyssinian crisis, and began searching for a diplomatic accommodation with Fascist Italy.[17]

The opportunity to improve relations with Italy arose when Mussolini, during a speech in November 1936 celebrating the formation of the Rome-Berlin Axis, obliquely expressed interest in an Anglo-Italian *entente*. Britain responded favourably to Mussolini's overture and the two countries signed a declaration known as the Gentlemen's Agreement in January 1937, recognizing common but not conflicting Mediterranean interests and a mutual commitment to the Mediterranean *status quo*. The agreement paved the way for the COS to designate the security of the Mediterranean region as their least pressing military obligation, behind protecting the British Isles, the Far East and imperial communications. In February, the Cabinet approved the recommendation of the Committee of Imperial Defence (CID) that 'Italy could not be counted on as a reliable friend, nor yet in present circumstances a probable enemy', annulling the government's position of early 1936 that war with Italy should be considered as a possibility.[18]

Although France was indignant about Italy and Germany's military interventions in Spain and apprehensive about the new Rome-Berlin

Axis, French policy toward Italy did not begin to shift decisively until the Italo-Yugoslav friendship treaty of March 1937. The French perceived this development as an overt attempt to secure Italian pre-eminence in the Mediterranean and Adriatic regions at France's expense. The potential loss of Yugoslavia as a French ally meant not only the sudden evaporation of France's influence in the Balkans but also the beginning of the end for France's network of central European allies and for the eastern front – one of the most important deterrents to German aggression. By defecting from the French-sponsored Little Entente, Yugoslavia could indirectly destroy France's relationship with Czechoslovakia and Romania.[19]

The timing of the Italo-Yugoslav pact led the French to attribute yet another motivation to Italy's diplomacy in the Balkans. Two days before signing the treaty, the Italians informed the Non-Intervention Committee that Italy would not withdraw any 'volunteers' from Spain until Franco defeated the Republicans. The connection between Italy's almost simultaneous actions in Belgrade and London was inescapable. The Quai d'Orsay suggested that the Italians were attempting to eliminate their Balkan preoccupations so that Mussolini could confidently 'bring his effort to bear on the Mediterranean'. This theory became a widely shared conviction in official French circles by early July, when the Comité Permanent de la Défense Nationale (CPDN) studied the organization of French colonial defence, particularly in the Mediterranean, for the first time since the Great War.[20]

While the French had begun to consider the possibility of war in the Mediterranean, most British statesmen remained confident that a resolute policy of conciliation would ensure peace in the Mediterranean. Even Mussolini's almost immediate violation of the spirit of the Anglo-Italian Gentlemen's Agreement – by dispatching reinforcements to Franco on the day the treaty was signed, and then fortifying the island of Pantelleria and sending a large number of troops to Libya during the spring of 1937 – did not shake the British conviction that imperial defence depended on a tranquil Mediterranean. At the Imperial Conference of May–June 1937 the British revealed that 'our policy must be governed by the principle that no anxiety or risks connected with our interests in the Mediterranean can be allowed to interfere with the despatch of a fleet to the Far East'. The Admiralty planned to send a strong naval force to Singapore soon after the outbreak of hostilities with Japan even if Britain were already at war in Europe. Britain's willingness to extend these guarantees to the Dominions at a time of declining British naval strength and escalating international intervention in the Spanish civil war demonstrated the enduring importance of the British empire and the confidence that any British losses in the Mediterranean could be recovered whereas those in the Far East could not.[21]

Lingering doubts about this perspective among British military officials were suppressed by a confirmation of government policy. In June, the COS's Far Eastern Appreciation demanded that 'all measures necessary for the protection of the Suez Canal and for the security of our defended ports and our air and other routes to the Far East must be put into operation'. In particular, the Admiralty worried that recent Italian activities in the Mediterranean – especially the military build-up in Libya – could only be valuable to Italy in a war against Britain. Nevertheless, after government officials expressed their intention to initiate yet another 'frank interchange of views' with Italy, the CID at the end of July reaffirmed that Singapore and home defence had a decisive priority over ground and air defences in the Mediterranean. Reluctant and unable to prepare for a Mediterranean war, British strategists placed their faith in a Mediterranean reconciliation even if it required acquiescing in the Fascist government's demand for Abyssinia to be recognized as part of the Italian empire – something the French categorically refused to consider in light of Italy's recent actions in Spain and Yugoslavia.[22]

The course of the Spanish civil war during the spring and summer of 1937 exacerbated tensions in Italy's relations with Britain and France and brought Italy still closer to Nazi Germany. At the end of May Germany and Italy withdrew from the multilateral maritime control system and increased their military commitment to the Nationalists. The British and French demanded that Italy either withdraw her 'volunteers' or submit a detailed plan for their gradual removal. The Italians refused both overtures, insisting that Italy's troops in Spain were protecting western Europe from the communist menace. The 'crisis in Anglo-Italian relations' subsided at the end of July, when Mussolini accepted an invitation from Chamberlain, now prime minister, to start conversations that would remove 'all causes of suspicion or misunderstanding'.[23] Meanwhile, the gulf in Franco-Italian relations continued to widen.

Only four days after consenting to new Anglo-Italian talks, Mussolini agreed to Franco's request to intercept Russian shipments of weapons and supplies steaming from the Black Sea to Spanish government ports. Mussolini, who was optimistic that a naval campaign might precipitate an end to the Spanish civil war, ordered the *Regia Marina* to attack merchant ships heading for Republican Spain. Beginning on 6 August, half of the Italian fleet – unmarked and mostly operating only at night – patrolled the Mediterranean, firing 43 torpedoes at 24 vessels, sinking four merchant ships and damaging one Republican destroyer before the campaign was halted in early September.[24]

Despite an international outcry, Italy publicly denied responsibility for the 'pirate' submarine campaign in the Mediterranean. Even though the Soviets were infuriated by the apparent targeting of Russian merchant ships travelling to Republican Spain, the most openly upset were the French. Blum viewed the submarine campaign as yet another blatant example of Italy's determination to assist the Nationalists and spread fascism throughout Europe. Many French officials found Mussolini's speech in Palermo in late August, at the height of the submarine campaign, particularly revealing. Mussolini not only celebrated the imminent capture of Santander by a joint Italian-Spanish Nationalist contingent but also promised that the current historical epoch would witness the 'foundation of the second Roman empire' with Sicily as the 'geographic centre'. For the French, this speech affirmed the strategic – and not only ideological – nature of Italy's involvement in Spain.[25]

In contrast to France's indignation, the British response to the pirate submarine campaign was cautious and conciliatory. Although they informed the Italians that a British steamship had been attacked by planes based at Palma, the British emphasized that they 'did not wish to make the least protest'. In fact, they hoped the planned conversations with the Italians would go forward.[26] The Admiralty also lobbied for a peaceful resolution of this new Mediterranean crisis. Within a week of the first assaults on merchant ships, the Admiralty identified Italian submarines as the principal culprits. Yet the British decided that, unless a submerged submarine was found close to a recently attacked British ship, they would only seek to ascertain the nationalities of unknown craft. No action would be taken against hostile surface ships or airplanes and no attempt would be made to protect non-British merchant ships headed for Republican ports.[27]

The pirate submarine campaign placed France in an extremely uncomfortable position *vis-à-vis* Britain, the power with which the French most desired a lasting *entente* and alliance. Confident that Italy was responsible for the piracy, the French wanted either to raise the issue of a Mediterranean pact at the next League meeting or to discuss Italy's transgressions at the next Non-Intervention Committee meeting. Although Eden had recently supported the idea of a Mediterranean pact rather than *de jure* recognition of Italian Abyssinia, he feared that both of France's suggestions were specifically designed to alienate the

Italians. Instead, Eden proposed a conference, outside both the League and the Non-Intervention Committee, to address Mediterranean piracy. France agreed to participate as long as the Soviets, who had accused Italy of sinking their merchant ships, were also invited to attend.[28]

Undeterred by the weak British pleas to discontinue his operation in the Mediterranean, and stimulated by the French fury, Mussolini continued his campaign until an Italian submarine accidentally attacked a British destroyer on 30 August. The British, although not prepared to issue a formal protest, indicated to the Italians that the situation in the Mediterranean had now become 'intolerable'. After receiving a note from Franco that the campaign had run its course, Mussolini suspended offensive submarine operations in the Mediterranean on 4 September – one week before the British, French and Russians met at Nyon to establish an international anti-submarine patrol to stop Mediterranean piracy.[29]

At the Nyon Conference, Britain and France agreed to patrol specific zones of the Mediterranean and to destroy any unidentified submarines. The Admiralty categorically rejected the French suggestion that the Mediterranean patrol extend to hostile surface ships and aircraft threatening merchant ships, rather than Britain's plan only to take action against submerged submarines.[30] Privately, the Admiralty admitted that the objective of the proposed Mediterranean patrol was not to initiate hostilities with any other power or even to pursue aggressively the identity of the Mediterranean pirates, but to address a political predicament without increasing the tension in the Mediterranean. According to Admiral Andrew Cunningham, the deputy chief of the naval staff, 'It is obvious that, so long as the attacker is a submarine, the risk of its identity being established is comparatively small.'[31]

The most significant British accomplishment, however, followed the conference, when the British compelled the French to allow the Italians to co-operate in the patrol system established at Nyon. Italy accepted the invitation but demanded 'absolute parity' in patrol responsibilities; the British agreed and secured French consent. Italy acquired patrol zones in the central and eastern Mediterranean, between the Balearic Islands and Sardinia, and inside the Tyrrhenian Sea, permitting the Italians to continue sending supplies to the Nationalists without detection. In the end, the political grandstanding at Nyon benefited only the Fascists, inspiring Ciano to exult: 'It is a fine victory. From suspected pirates to policemen of the Mediterranean. . . .'[32]

While Italy's pirate submarine campaign angered many French statesmen and strategists, the fortification of an Italian air base in the Balearics alarmed them. The September 1937 build-up of Italian bombers in Majorca and the coincidental increase in the scale of aerial attacks on Republican ports and shipping in the Balearic Sea were perceived as an overt Italian attempt to seize the Balearics in preparation for a future war against France. Successive French proposals to counter this threat were rejected by the British. Consequently, and much to Britain's consternation, the French reopened the Pyrenees frontier to Republican Spain in October and did not close it again until January 1938. This French policy provoked Mussolini to declare publicly that Italy and France were on 'opposite sides of the barricade' in the Spanish affair, precluding any kind of amicable Franco-Italian relationship.[33]

Admiral François Darlan, chief of the French naval staff, was infuriated at Britain's reluctance to recognize that the nature of the Spanish war, especially when combined with Mussolini's visit to Germany in September, suggested that France and Britain could soon find themselves at war with Germany, Italy and Spain. In late 1937 Darlan argued for a comprehensive and geographic reorientation of French foreign policy which would focus on littoral and imperial, rather than only continental, security. French industry and France's eastern alliances, not to mention supplemental defence for the western front, relied on secure Mediterranean transportation.[34] In the event of war, French strategy should envision first subjugating the western and central Mediterranean and menacing Italy – destroying the Italian fleet and occupying Libya, Spanish Morocco and the Balearics – while remaining on the defensive on the western front in Europe and in the eastern Mediterranean. Only after Mediterranean communications were secured and provisions assured should France launch an assault against Germany.[35]

The French army and air force countered that such a Mediterranean orientation would either incite the Nazis to attack France through Belgium or Switzerland or provoke a conflict with Italy that would jeopardize France's network of eastern European alliances. Even worse, such an alignment could precipitate both of these possibilities simultaneously. French strategy, according to General Maurice Gamelin, chief of the general staff, should not stray from its current emphasis on Germany and the western front.[36] However, Édouard Daladier, the French minister of defence, reasoned that, although the British were reluctant to offer France support on land against Germany, they too were vulnerable in the Mediterranean. Yet in this region France had something significant to offer: French troops in North Africa and a formidable French navy that controlled the western basin and important Atlantic trade routes. Moreover, the Mediterranean offered France a sea route to eastern Europe that could bypass hostile continental powers. The Mediterranean provided France with not only the basis for building the coveted Anglo-French alliance but also a viable alternative to the stark, unpleasant choice between relinquishing eastern Europe or confronting Germany. By late 1937, Daladier had persuaded both the army and the air force that 'France must remain ready to pursue eventually, as a matter of first urgency, the defeat of Italy'.[37]

The escalation of the Sino-Japanese conflict in late 1937, however, encouraged the British to reach conclusions about Italy and the Mediterranean which were in direct opposition to those favoured by France. Sceptical about the United States' ability or willingness to send a fleet to the Far East in the event of trouble, Chamberlain argued that the British and the Americans should pursue conciliation in the Far East. The possibility of a crisis with Japan also motivated the prime minister to resolve the tension in the Mediterranean. Thus he again pressed for granting *de jure* recognition of Italian Abyssinia.[38]

Eden and Sir Robert Vansittart, the permanent under-secretary at the Foreign Office, argued that Fascist Italy's decisions in late 1937 to withdraw from the League, to recognize Manchukuo, to adhere to the Anti-Comintern Pact and to continue to expand its military presence in both the Balearics and Libya compelled Britain to strengthen her defences in Egypt, to accelerate British rearmament and to discard Mediterranean appeasement. But Chamberlain resolutely resisted these suggestions and, instead, relied on the arguments of Sir Maurice Hankey, secretary to the Cabinet and the CID. In November Hankey wrote:

> We have our danger in the West (Germany) and our danger in the Far East (Japan), and we simply cannot afford to be on bad terms with a nation which has a stranglehold on our shortest line of communications between the two possible theatres of war ... [*De jure* recognition of Abyssinia is] *vital to the existence of the Empire and of the United Kingdom as a first-class Power.*[39]

Many in the British government, as well as their service advisers, were reluctant to respond to Fascist Italy's unsettling behaviour in late 1937 because they had begun to recognize that, as William Strang of the Foreign Office succinctly summarized it, 'the worse our relations with Italy, the closer we must be to France'. The COS were particularly conscious of Strang's truism and acted to ensure that close co-operation with the French would not be necessary. In a January 1938 planning document that considered Britain's position in the event of a

Mediterranean war, the COS recommended no improvement of existing defences and no demonstration of British strength in the region. Britain could not contemplate war in either the Far East or western Europe if tensions existed in the Mediterranean. The Cabinet soon endorsed the COS's perspective, insisting that any provocative British military response in Egypt would disrupt the prime minister's regional agenda.[40]

The German Anschluss with Austria in March 1938 solidified the contrasting British and French views of Italy. Reports in February that Mussolini would possibly try to restrain Hitler from violence against Austria if Anglo-Italian talks began spurred Chamberlain to direct his ambassador in Rome to meet officially with Ciano. Following Eden's resignation, the new foreign secretary, Lord Halifax, emphasized to the Cabinet the 'importance of the conversations with the Italian government'.[41]

As they had been two years before during the Rhineland episode, the French were mired in domestic political turmoil at the time of the Anschluss. The resignation of premier Chautemps on the first day of the Austrian crisis precluded any resolute French response to Germany's latest affront to the continental *status quo*. For many on the political Left and Centre in France, the Anschluss foreshadowed an inevitable war in the Mediterranean and emphasized the need for an alliance with Britain. That Mussolini refused to support Austrian sovereignty with even a verbal protest indicated to many that 'the *entente* between Germany and Italy has never been more serious', and that Germany had agreed to compensate Italy in Egypt, Tunisia and Spain in return for Italian capitulation on Austrian and probably Czechoslovak sovereignty. Even the political right in France conceded that reconstituting the Stresa front was no longer a reasonable expectation. Terrified that the Anschluss would encourage the Italians to extend their intervention in Spain, the new Blum government again reopened the Pyrenees frontier, allowing French and Russian arms to flow freely into Republican Spain.[42]

For the French, the rapid German incorporation of Austria revealed both that the French military was unprepared for even a limited war and that European peace was increasingly tenuous. Aside from the general staff's heightened concerns about an Anglo-French alliance and a German move against Czechoslovakia, naval and military appreciations after the Anschluss focused increasingly on Italy and the Mediterranean. Even Gamelin, who stressed Germany's augmented military and strategic strength on the continent and the elevated threat to Czechoslovakia, now understood the menacing tendency of Italian foreign policy. 'Recent events confirm the solidarity, at least for the moment, of the Rome-Berlin Axis', opined Gamelin to the CPDN.

'[Mussolini's] price for the Anschluss was without doubt the promise of Mediterranean mastery.'[43] Italy's quiescent reaction to events in Austria suggested to the naval staff not only a durable Italian-German *entente*, but the possibility that Mussolini would try to match Germany's action. The Italian bombing of Barcelona and the resumption of raids on Republican ports in early March heightened these suspicions. It was feared that Italy could employ its air base in the Balearics to achieve a quick aero-naval success in the western Mediterranean at France's expense.[44] Following reports that Italy now had new expansionist desires and that a Franco victory was an 'absolutely essential' element of Italian foreign policy, the Quai d'Orsay endorsed the *Marine's* obsession with the Balearics and again impressed these concerns on the British.[45]

Free of alliances or treaty obligations to the states of eastern Europe, the British were less concerned than the French about the potential international repercussions of the Anschluss. On the very day that Nazi troops entered Vienna, Chamberlain expressed relief that the Austrian 'question was now out of the way'. Instead of inspiring Chamberlain to re-evaluate his European policies, the Anschluss only persuaded the prime minister to redouble his efforts; specifically, Italy was to be the primary short-term target of British appeasement, in the hope that a friendly Mussolini would mollify Hitler's long-term ambitions. As Chamberlain told his sister on the day after the Anschluss, 'We must abandon conversations with Germany, we must show our determination not to be bullied by announcing some increase or acceleration in rearmament, and we must quietly and steadily pursue our conversations with Italy'.[46]

Britain's strategists also believed that the Anschluss compelled Britain to address the Italian factor diplomatically rather than the German factor militarily. The dispatch of two 'seriously deficient' British divisions to the continent – all the policy of 'limited liability' would permit – would not deter Germany from further aggression and would only jeopardize Britain's interests in the Mediterranean. Most importantly, the COS feared the military implications of Japan and Italy joining Germany in a general war. Thus all French proposals to augment Mediterranean defences or prepare for a Mediterranean war should be rejected.[47]

The COS received support for this view from Britain's diplomats, who now accelerated their efforts to achieve a new Anglo-Italian understanding. While the British ambassador in Rome insisted that the Anschluss improved the likelihood of reaching an agreement with Italy, many at the Foreign Office now believed a new Stresa front was possible. In late March the Cabinet agreed that British rearmament and a durable Mediterranean peace should be pursued fervently.[48] The Anglo-Italian Easter Accords of April 1938, in which the British promised *de jure* recognition of Italy's conquest of Abyssinia in return for Italy's 'settlement of the Spanish question' and unspecified reduction of the Libyan garrison, represented the culmination of this British undertaking.[49]

The years 1935–37 were a critical transition period for British and French estimates and analyses of and policies toward Italy. In 1935–36, as British and French policy-makers struggled with a crisis in the Mediterranean instigated by the Italian-Abyssinian conflict, and the outbreak of the Spanish civil war, Britain and France found ways to ensure that their polices in the Mediterranean were compatible. They agreed not to use force to prevent Mussolini from invading Ethiopia; they agreed to impose sanctions on Italy rather than intervene militarily in the conflict; they agreed to lift the embargo when the crisis subsided; and they agreed on a non-intervention policy in Spain.

The escalation of Italy's participation in the Spanish civil war and the founding of the Italo-German Axis in late 1936, however, began to splinter Anglo-French unanimity on Italy. These developments led British statesmen and strategists in late 1936 and early 1937 to jettison their diplomatic commitments in the eastern Mediterranean and to place Mediterranean defences at the bottom of their list of priorities for imperial security. The Italo-Yugoslav treaty, the pirate submarine campaign and the Italian fortification of the Balearics – together with Italy's withdrawal from the League and adhesion to the Anti-Comintern pact – motivated the French in late 1937 and early 1938 to focus on the Italian threat in the Mediterranean as much as the German threat on the continent. In particular, France began preparing for war in the Mediterranean. By contrast, the British now placed concessions to Italy and a general Mediterranean appeasement at the forefront of their policy designed to ensure European peace.

By the spring of 1938, the conflicting British and French views of Fascist Italy and the Mediterranean were firmly established at the centre of each nation's foreign and defence policies. As a result of this divergence, the emerging Italian threat failed to elicit any significant Anglo-French defence co-operation with regard to the Mediterranean in 1938 and the coveted Anglo-French alliance remained elusive. Attempts at defining a joint Mediterranean strategy, though tentative and ineffectual, were not taken until the following year, when Britain and France finally agreed to hold joint staff conversations which envisaged a war against Germany and Italy. Even then the profound Anglo-French conflict over an appropriate Mediterranean strategy crippled British and French efforts throughout 1938–40 to respond to the Axis menace in a co-ordinated fashion.

Notes

1. 'Franco-Italian Agreements concluded at Rome on January 7', 22 January 1935, Public Records Office, Kew [PRO], CAB 21/413. See also D. C. Watt, 'The Secret Laval-Mussolini Agreement of 1935 on Ethiopia', *Middle East Journal*, 15 (1961), pp. 69–78.
2. *Documents on British Foreign Policy, 1919–1939* [DBFP], 2, xii, no. 400, annex, pp. 482–4. See also N. Rostow, *Anglo-French Relations, 1934–36* (London: Macmillan, 1984), pp. 83–119; A. Wolfers, *Britain and France between Two Wars* (New York: W. W. Norton, 1968), p. 118.
3. *DBFP*, 2, xii, no. 722, pp. 880–90. See also E. Serra, 'La questione italo-etiopica alla conferenza di Stresa', *Affari Esteri*, 9 (1977), pp. 313–39; L. Nöel, *Les illusions de Stresa: l'Italie abandonnée à Hitler* (Paris: France-Empire, 1975), pp. 70–86.
4. P. Laval, *Laval parle* (Paris: C. Béranger, 1948), p. 245; *Documents Diplomatiques Français 1932–1939* [DDF], 1, xi, nos. 109, 120, pp. 155–60 and 180–2. See also R. M. Salerno, 'Multilateral Strategy and Diplomacy: the Anglo-German Naval Agreement and the Mediterranean Crisis, 1935–36', *Journal of Strategic Studies*, 17 (1994), pp. 45–64.
5. A. Marder, 'The Royal Navy and the Ethiopian Crisis of 1935–36', *American Historical Review*, lxxv (1970), pp. 1330–8; R. Quartararo, 'Imperial Defence in the Mediterranean on the Eve of the Ethiopian Crisis (July–October 1935)', *Historical Journal*, 20 (1977), pp. 190–1; M. J. Cohen, 'British Strategy in the Middle East in the Wake of the Abyssinian Crisis, 1936–39', in M. J. Cohen and M. Kolinsky (eds), *Britain and the Middle East in the 1930s: Security Problems, 1935–39* (London: Macmillan Press [now Palgrave Macmillan], 1992), pp. 21–40.
6. Cabinet minutes, 22 August 1935, PRO, CAB 23/82/42(35); Defence Policy and Requirements Sub-Committee meeting, 23 August 1935, PRO, CAB 16/136; COS minutes of the 149th meeting, 6 September 1935, PRO, CAB 53/5.
7. R. J. Young, *In Command of France: French Foreign Policy and Military Planning 1933–1940* (Cambridge, MA: Harvard University Press, 1978), pp. 110–4; A. P. Adamthwaite, *France and the Coming of the Second World War, 1936–1939* (London: Frank Cass, 1977), pp. 32–6; J.-B. Duroselle, *La décadence, 1932–1939* (Paris: Imprimerie Nationale, 1979), pp. 147–57; N. Jordan, *The Popular Front and Central Europe: the Dilemmas of French Impotence 1918–1940* (Cambridge: Cambridge University Press, 1992), pp. 33–5, 67–9 and 101–3; R. A. C. Parker, 'Great Britain, France and the Ethiopian Crisis 1935–1936', *English Historical Review*, lxxxix (1974), pp. 293–332.
8. *DBFP*, 2, xv, nos. 69, 81, 118, 305, 320, 374, pp. 81–2, 95–7, 144, 382, 402–3 and 476–7. See also W. Shorrock, *From Ally to Enemy: the Enigma of Fascist*

Italy in French Diplomacy, 1920–1940 (Kent, OH: Kent State University Press, 1988), pp. 143–58; R. Quartararo, *Roma tra Londra e Berlino: politica estera fascista dal 1930 al 1940* (Rome: Bonacci, 1980), pp. 246–58.

9. *Akten zur Deutschen Auswärtigen Politik, 1918–1945*, C, iv/ii, nos. 337, 485, 486, 525, pp. 697–9, 954–8 and 1022–4. See also E. Robertson, 'Hitler and Sanctions: Mussolini and the Rhineland', *European Studies Review*, 7 (1977), pp. 418–21; J. Petersen, *Hitler-Mussolini: Die Entstehung der Achse Berlin-Rom, 1933–1936* (Tübingen: Niemeyer, 1973), pp. 468–71.

10. Corbin to Flandin, 18 May 1936, Ministère des Affaires Etrangères, Paris [MAE], Eur 30–40, Italie, 303. See also M. Thomas, *Britain, France and Appeasement: Anglo-French Relations in the Popular Front Era* (Oxford: Berg, 1996), pp. 55–8; Shorrock, *From Ally to Enemy*, pp. 170–4 and 181–6.

11. Mémento, 14 April 1936, Service Historique de l'Armée de la Marine, Vincennes [SHM], 1BB2, 182; Durand-Viel to Piétri, 9 June 1936, SHM, 1BB2, 208; note au ministre, 6 July 1936, SHM, 1BB2, 184; R. J. Young, 'French Military Intelligence and the Franco-Italian Alliance, 1933–39', *Historical Journal*, 28 (1985), pp. 143–68; N. Jordan, 'Maurice Gamelin, Italy and the Eastern Alliances', *Journal of Strategic Studies*, 14 (December 1991), pp. 428–41.

12. Chatfield to Backhouse, 27 March 1936, Chatfield Papers, National Maritime Museum, Greenwich [NMM], CHAT 4/1; COS minutes of the 178th meeting, 16 June 1936, PRO, CAB 53/5; Cabinet minutes, 17 June 1936, PRO, CAB 23/84/42(36).

13. *DDF*, 2, ii, no. 332, p. 501.

14. L. Blum, *L'histoire jugera* (Montreal: Editions de l'Arbe, 1945), pp. 100–2; J. Jackson, *The Popular Front in France: Defending Democracy, 1934–38* (Cambridge: Cambridge University Press, 1988), pp. 42–51; C. Serrano, *L'enjeu espagnol: PCF et guerre d'Espagne* (Paris: Messidor/Editions Sociales, 1987), pp. 9–36.

15. J. E. Dreifort, *Yvon Delbos at the Quai d'Orsay: French Foreign Policy During the Popular Front* (Lawrence, KS: University Press of Kansas, 1973), pp. 38–44 and 151–6; Young, 'French Military Intelligence and the Franco-Italian Alliance', pp. 148–50 and 162–3; Jordan, 'Maurice Gamelin, Italy and the Eastern Alliances', pp. 435–6.

16. G. Stone, 'The European Great Powers and the Spanish Civil War, 1936–1939', in R. Boyce and E. M. Robertson (eds), *Paths to War: New Essays on the Origins of the Second World War* (London: Macmillan, 1989), pp. 212–17; Thomas, *Britain, France and Appeasement*, pp. 89–108.

17. 'Problems facing His Majesty's Government in the Mediterranean as a result of the Italo-League dispute', 12 June 1936, PRO, CAB 24/262/CP 165(36); 'Problems facing His Majesty's Government in the Mediterranean as a result of the Italo-League dispute', 19 June 1936, PRO, CAB 24/263/CP 174(36); 'Italian foreign policy in the Spanish Civil War' and 'Western Mediterranean: Situation arising from the Spanish Civil War', 31 August 1936, PRO, CAB 24/264/CP 233(36) and CP 234(36); Cabinet minutes, 2 September 1936, PRO, CAB 23/85/56(36).

18. Review of Imperial Defence, 22 February 1937, PRO, CAB 21/700; Cabinet minutes, 24 February 1937, PRO, CAB 23/87/9(37).

19. *DDF*, 2, iv, no. 395, pp. 686–7; Procès-verbal du séance de la CPDN, 15 February 1937, Service Historique de l'Armée de la Terre, Vincennes [SHAT], 2N23.

20. *DDF*, 2, v, nos. 152–4, pp. 244–7; Delbos to Corbin, 1 May 1937, MAE, Papiers d'Agents, Massigli, 93; Procès-verbal du séance de la CPDN, 9 July 1937, SHAT, 2N23.
21. Questions submitted by the Australian delegation, 31 May 1937, PRO, CAB 53/31/COS 590. See also S. W. Roskill, *Naval Policy between the Wars* (2 vols, London: Trustees of the National Maritime Museum, 1976), ii, p. 347.
22. Appreciation of the situation in the Far East, 14 June 1937, PRO, CAB 16/182/DP(P)5; Chatfield to Backhouse, 12 July 1937, NMM, CHT 4/1; DP(P) meeting, 15 July 1937, PRO, FO 371/21160/R5291/1/22; Hankey to Chamberlain, 19 July 1937, PRO, PREM 1/276; Hankey to Eden, 23 July 1937, PRO, FO 954/13; 'Anglo-Italian Relations', CID paper, 28 July 1937, PRO, CAB 4/26/CID 1346-B.
23. Chamberlain to Mussolini, 27 July 1937, Archivio Storico Diplomatico, Rome [ASD], De Felice, Grandi, 47/112; Mussolini to Chamberlain, 31 July 1937, PRO, PREM 1/276.
24. Franco to Mussolini, 3 August 1937, ASD, AG, US, 10; 'Processo verbale della riunione a Palazzo Venezia', 5 August 1937, ASD, AG, UC, 10, 46/1; 'Conversazione fra Cavagnari e Moreno', 7 August 1937, ASD, AG, US, 10; G. Giorgerini, *Da Matapan al Golfo Persico: la marina militare italiana dal fascismo alla Repubblica* (Milan: A. Mondadori, 1989), pp. 352–3; W. C. Frank, 'Naval Operations in the Spanish Civil War, 1936–39', *Naval War College Review* (Jan.–Feb. 1984), pp. 42–3; B. R. Sullivan, 'Fascist Italy's Military Involvement in the Spanish Civil War: a Review Essay', *Journal of Military History*, 59 (1995), p. 716.
25. G. Ciano, *L'Europa verso la catastrofe* (Verona: A. Mondadori, 1948), p. 210; B. Mussolini, *Opera Omnia*, xxviii (Florence: La Fenice, 1980), pp. 239–42; DDF, 2, vi, nos. 360, 365, 375, pp. 634–8, 648–9 and 658–60.
26. Ciano, *L'Europa verso la catastrofe*, pp. 206–9; Ingram to Eden, 27 August 1937, PRO, FO 371/21358/W16254/23/41; Crolla to Ciano, 23 August 1937, ASD, De Felice, Grandi, 50, 125/1; Thomas to Eden, 25 August 1937, PRO, FO 371/21179/R5810/419/22.
27. Pound to Admiralty, 15 August 1937, PRO, FO 371/21357/W5646/23/41; Vansittart minute, 16 August 1937, PRO, FO 371/21358/W15802/23/41; Notes of a meeting of Ministers, 17 August 1937, PRO, FO 371/21357/W 15727/23/41.
28. Eden memorandum, 30 August 1937, PRO, FO 371/21358/W16299/23/41; Eden memorandum, 1 September 1937, PRO, FO 371/21359/W16584/23/41; Eden memorandum, 2 September 1937, PRO, FO 371/21358/W16521/23/41; Nicolas-Barrelon to Gaudin de Villaine, 2 September 1937, SHM, 1BB7, 40; DNI memorandum, 6 September 1937, PRO, ADM 116/3917/M04827/37.
29. Franco note, 3 September 1937, ASD, AG, US, 95; Crolla to Ciano, 3 September 1937, ASD, De Felice, Grandi, 50, 125/1; G. Ciano, *Diario 1937–1943* (Rome: Rizzoli, 1990), p. 33; Ciano, *L'Europa verso la catastrofe*, p. 209; Ingram to Eden, 7 September 1937, PRO, FO 371/21404/W16755/16618/41.
30. P. Gretton, 'The Nyon Conference – the Naval Aspect', *English Historical Review*, xc (1975), pp. 103–12; W. C. Mills, 'The Nyon Conference: Neville Chamberlain, Anthony Eden, and the Appeasement of Italy in 1937', *International History Review*, 15 (1993), pp. 1–22.
31. Admiralty note, 2 September 1937, PRO, ADM 116/3917/M04776/37; Meeting held in Vansittart's room at the Foreign Office, 6 September 1937,

PRO, FO 371/21404/W16802/16618/41; Cabinet minutes, 8 September 1937, PRO, CAB 23/88/34(37), Bevan to Perth, 10 September 1937, PRO, ADM 116/3917/M05077/37.

32. Les minutes de la conférence de Nyon, 10–11 September 1937, SHM, 1BB2, 204/1; L'accord de Nyon, 13 September 1937, SHM, 1BB2, 204/1; Ciano to Eden and Delbos, 17 September 1937, Ufficio Storico della Marina Militare, Rome [USMM], 3309; Ingram to Eden, 19 September 1937, PRO, FO 371/21406/W17645/16618/41; Ciano, *Diario*, 13 September 1937, 21 September 1937, pp. 36, 39.

33. *DDF*, 2, vi, no. 465, pp. 814–17; DDF, 2, vii, nos. 54, 61, 88, 138, pp. 102–3, 117, 156–7 and 230–1; Mussolini, *Opera Omnia*, xxix, pp. 99–102.

34. Darlan note, 12 November 1937, SHM, 1BB2, 208/12; Campinchi to Daladier, 24 November 1937, SHAT, 2N24. See also R. M. Salerno, 'The French Navy and the Appeasement of Italy, 1937–9', *English Historical Review*, cxii (1997), pp. 73–80.

35. Darlan note, November 1937, SHM, 1BB2, 208/11; Campinchi to Daladier, 24 November 1937, SHAT, 2N24.

36. Gamelin note, 9 November 1937, SHAT, 1K224/9; Gamelin to Daladier, 28 November 1937, SHAT, 2N24; Procès-verbal du séance de la CPDN, 8 December 1937, SHAT, 2N24; DDF, 2, vii, no. 325, pp. 633–44.

37. Procès-verbal du séance de la CPDN, 8 December 1937, SHAT, 2N24; DDF, 2, vii, no. 325, pp. 633–44; Daladier memorandum, 22 December 1937, SHAT, 2N24; N. 2720/3-OS/EMAA, 27 December 1937, Service Historique de l'Armée de l'Air, Vincennes, 2B104; Young, 'French Military Intelligence', p. 150.

38. Chatfield to Backhouse, 8 October 1937, NMM, CHT 4/1; Cabinet minutes, 13 October 1937, PRO, CAB 23/89/37(37)5.

39. Phipps to Eden, 1 November 1937, Vansittart minute, 6 November 1937, PRO, FO 371/21162/R7531/1/22; Eden to Chamberlain, 3 November 1937, PRO, PREM 1/210; Hankey to Inskip, 2 November 1937, PRO, CAB 21/588; Hankey to Vansittart, 3 November 1937, PRO, CAB 21/588 (original emphasis).

40. Strang minute, 13 January 1938, PRO, FO 371/22418/R343/43/22; 'Combined plan for the defence of Egypt', 18 January 1938, PRO, CAB 21/579; 'Defence of Egypt', 14 February 1938, PRO, CAB 53/36/COS 686; 'Mediterranean, Middle East and North-East Africa appreciation', 21 February 1938, PRO, CAB 53/37/COS 691; Hore-Belisha to Inskip, 24 February 1938, PRO, CAB 21/580.

41. Perth to Eden, 16 February 1938, PRO, FO 371/22311/R1414/137/3; Perth to Eden, 17 February 1938, PRO, FO 371/22403/R1615/23/22; Halifax to Perth, 21 February 1938, PRO, FO 371/22403/R1610/23/22; Vansittart to Eden, 16 February 1938, PRO, CAB 21/579; Eden to Chamberlain, 17 February 1938, PRO, PREM 1/276; Cabinet minutes, 9 March 1938, PRO, CAB 23/92/11(38).

42. Procès-verbal du séance de la CPDN, 15 March 1938, SHAT, 2N25; Phipps to Halifax, 26 March 1938, Phipps Papers, Churchill Archives Centre, Cambridge, PHPP 1/20; Fraser to Phipps, 16 March 1938, PRO, FO 371/22338/R 3035/162/12; C. A. Micaud, *The French Right and Nazi Germany, 1933–39* (Durham NC: Duke University Press, 1943), pp. 156–8.

43. Procès-verbal du séance de la CPDN, 15 March 1938, SHAT, 2N25; Gamelin note N. 1082, 14 March 1938, MAE, P-40, Daladier, 1.

44. 2e Bureau Bulletin d'Études N. 51, 1 March 1938, SHM, 1BB2, 94; Bourrague to Charveriat, 3 March 1938, MAE, Eur 30–40, Italie, 281.

45. Blondel to Paul-Boncour, 20 March 1938, MAE, Eur 30–40, 272; Corbin to Paul-Boncour, 21 March 1938, MAE, Eur 30–40, 272; Paul-Boncour to Corbin, 22 March 1938, MAE, Eur 30–40, Italie, 272.

46. Cabinet minutes, 12 March 1938, PRO, CAB 23/92/12(38); Cabinet Foreign Policy Committee, 25th meeting, 15 March 1938, PRO, CAB 27/623; Neville to Hilda, 13 March 1938, Neville Chamberlain Papers, Birmingham University Library, NC 18/1/1041.

47. 'Situation in the event of war against Germany', 16 March 1938, PRO, CAB 53/36/COS 697; 'Military implications of German aggression against Czechoslovakia', 28 March 1938, PRO, CAB 53/37/COS 698 (Revise).

48. Perth to Halifax, 13 March 1938, PRO, FO 371/22315/R 2493/137/3; D. Dilks (ed.), *The Diaries of Sir Alexander Cadogan, 1938–1945* (New York: Putnam, 1972), pp. 60–6; Cabinet Foreign Policy Committee, 27th meeting, 21 March 1938, PRO, CAB 27/623; Cabinet minutes, 22 March 1938, PRO, CAB 23/93/15(38).

49. Perth to Halifax, 26 April 1938, PRO, CAB 21/562. See also D. C. Watt, 'Gli accordi mediterranei anglo-italiani del aprile 1938', *Rivista di studi politici internazionale*, 26 (1959).

5
The Making of the Anglo-French Alliance, 1938–39

Talbot Imlay

In the spring of 1939 the threat of war weighed heavily over Europe. In March, just six months after the Munich Conference, Germany destroyed what remained of Czechoslovakia, violently repudiating Hitler's assurances that the Sudetenland represented the limit of Germany's territorial ambitions in Europe. Soon afterwards the Germans began to threaten their eastern neighbours, particularly Poland. In April Italian troops invaded and annexed Albania, an apparent step towards Mussolini's oft-declared goal of a Mediterranean Empire. In this tense international situation, a Quai d'Orsay evaluation in June found comfort in the state of Anglo-French relations. The two countries, its author enthused, were 'perfectly in agreement' on the need to prevent or resist 'coups de force' in Europe.[1] If the conclusion is somewhat exaggerated, the satisfactory tone is understandable. For most of the period after 1918, Paris and London tangled over European politics, particularly the treatment of Germany.[2] A remarkable turnaround, however, occurred in the months following Munich as French and British policies converged on a shared resolve to resist future aggression in Europe, culminating in early 1939 in the creation of an alliance. Britain and France vowed to resist any attempt by Nazi Germany to expand its territory by force. Hitler would not achieve *Lebensraum* without a war.[3]

As a significant episode in the origins of the second world war, the making of the Anglo-French alliance has attracted a good deal of scholarly attention, which can be broadly divided into two tendencies. The first is to examine the policy of one country largely in isolation – sometimes France, more often Britain.[4] The second tends to place British policy or more generally Anglo-German relations at the centre of the story. It assumes that decisions made in London (and Berlin) dictated the course of events and what happened in Paris (or elsewhere) was of secondary importance.[5] With few exceptions, studies of British and French policies in relation to one another are missing.[6] This is unfortunate since juxtaposing the two offers important insights into the making of the Anglo-French alliance and the origins of the war.

A closer examination of the months preceding the alliance – and an examination of both British and French policies – highlights the critical role of France. Following Munich, French leaders considered and then rejected a retreat into isolation, in effect choosing to resist future German expansion in Europe. It is worth stressing that this decision preceded that of the British and was taken largely independently of them. If the British exerted little influence on French decisions, the opposite was not the case, which points to the role of misperception. Beginning in late 1938, fears of a French retreat, when combined with a 'war scare' triggered by reports of an impending German attack in western Europe, compelled the British to revise their foreign and defence policies. Signficantly, British leaders appear to have been largely ignorant of the French decision to resist Germany. Why this might be so points to the role of manipulation. Evidence suggests that French staff officers deliberately encouraged Whitehall's fears of a French retreat and of Germany's aggressive intentions in the west despite the questionable soundness of both claims. More surprising perhaps, there is also evidence that the British General Staff knowingly collaborated with their French counterparts in this effort.

The evolution of French policy begins with Munich, which inflicted a tremendous strategic blow. By dismembering Czechoslovakia, the agreement eliminated a powerful ally in Germany's rear.[7] Recognition of this fact prompted the French to reassess their strategic policy. Informing this process was the pressing question of what to do when, as expected, the Germans next challenged the status quo. This in turn raised the issue of eastern Europe and of France's remaining alliances with Poland and the Soviet Union, since it was assumed that Germany's immediate expansionist ambitions lay eastwards. Thus, at stake were questions of French resistance to German hegemony and France's role in Europe. Despite significant political and military support for a retreat from eastern Europe, the French rejected this option. In so doing, they committed themselves to a policy of resisting German expansion, if necessary by war.

Among French leaders a policy of retreat enjoyed the determined support of foreign minister Georges Bonnet. During the Czech crisis Bonnet had laboured tirelessly and sometimes deviously to keep France out of any war. Afterwards, this remained his overriding goal. Motivating him was a mix of genuine pacifism – a legacy of his trench experiences during the first world war – and a profound and highly politicized belief in his country's internal and external weakness. As he had explained to a journalist in April 1938:

> Let's not have any more heroics. We are not capable of them. . . . It is all very well to proclaim yourself the policemen of Europe, but for this you need more than cap guns, straw handcuffs and paper prisons. . . . France can no longer permit itself a blood bath such as that of 1914. Our demographic strength declines each year. Finally, the Popular Front placed the country in such a state that it would be wise for France to allow itself a period of convalescence. Any imprudence could be fatal.[8]

To avoid the disaster of war, Bonnet was convinced, the French had to abandon their great power pretensions and accommodate themselves to German expansion. This is not to say he was a defeatist. Rather Bonnet sought a peaceful and stable European order founded on a Franco-German (and perhaps British) arrangement whereby, in return for a free-hand in eastern Europe, Germany would leave France, and more generally western Europe, alone.

Donning the realist cloak, Bonnet argued after Munich that changed circumstances demanded new policies. As he told the British ambassador, this meant 'some revision' of French commitments in eastern Europe.[9] As self-styled realists, Quai d'Orsay officials found it difficult to disagree with the proposition that French policy must reflect the new realities of post-Munich Europe even if they resented Bonnet's penchant for private diplomacy. Even René Massigli, the outgoing political director and opponent of appeasement, admitted that Munich would usher in a 'period of withdrawal [*receuillement*]' for France. Other officials spoke of an 'adjustment' of France's eastern alliances.[10]

Together Bonnet and his officials worked to 'revise' these. While the latter prepared memoranda stressing the difficulties and disadvantages of France's ties with Eastern Europe, the foreign minister made sure these received wide circulation inside and outside the Quai d'Orsay.[11] Not content with only one poker in the fire, after Munich Bonnet also sought to improve relations directly with Germany. Following an unofficial German *demarche* in October, he eagerly entered into negotiations that produced a Franco-German Declaration of Non-Aggression, signed two months later in Paris.[12] Innocuous in wording, the declaration nevertheless prompted a flurry of rumours concerning private promises of a 'free hand' to Germany in eastern Europe. What exactly transpired is impossible to know for certain, but it matters little since Bonnet viewed the declaration more as a beginning than an end – as one step in a larger process of negotiating France's new role in a post-Munich Europe. Its purpose was both to sound out German intentions and to accustom French opinion to the idea of a Franco-German accommodation.[13]

Bonnet and the Quai d'Orsay could not alone determine France's course. Given the strategic stakes, a policy of retreat would need the support of French military chiefs. Interestingly, General Maurice Gamelin, chief of staff for national defence, initially endorsed a version of Bonnet's policy. Two weeks after Munich, he submitted a 'Note on the present situation' to Daladier with a covering letter drawing attention to the 'urgent nature of the questions with which it deals'. While hardly bereft of Gamelin's characteristic caution, the paper proposed nothing less than a fundamental recasting of French strategy.[14] He argued that Munich had resulted in a reversal of the strategic situation in central and eastern Europe that would likely prompt Germany to renew its *Drang nach Osten* (march to the east), because it was there that the Reich would find the vital raw materials it needed to defeat an enemy blockade. Significantly, Gamelin offered little hope of resisting German expansion. Neither Poland nor the Soviet Union could be relied upon, while Germany's growing relative strength meant that it could simultaneously wage war on several fronts against multiple enemies.

Given this bleak assessment of German intentions and capabilities, Gamelin proposed that France turn away from eastern Europe and 'concentrate its efforts on the Mediterranean'. While he did mention that this shift would allow France to maintain 'ties' to eastern Europe, this point contradicted his doubts about the feasibility of resisting German expansion. In fact, Gamelin's proposal amounted to the abandonment of eastern Europe and an eastern front as the French focused instead on defending themelves and their Mediterranean Empire. '[I]t is through the cohesion of its Empire,' he asserted in this regard, 'that she [France] will remain a great power'. France, in effect, would trade its traditional role as a European great power for the smaller, and safer, one of a Mediterranean power – a strategy similar to Bonnet's. Germany would be free to expand eastwards while Italy would become France's principal rival.

Gamelin's proposals possessed far-reaching strategic implications. Since the nineteenth century an eastern front had operated as an essential component of French strategy against Germany. An eastern front would help redress the imbalance of power caused by Germany's greater demographic and economic resources. At the same time, in an age of industrial war, it would deny Germany many of the critical raw materials, such as oil and tungsten, which were needed to defeat a blockade and wage a prolonged conflict. Strategic considerations explain both the alliance with Russia before 1914 and the series of military and political agreements signed in the 1920s with Poland, Rumania, Yugoslavia and Czechoslovakia.[15] Additional proof of an eastern front's hold on French strategy came in 1935 with the signing of a Franco-Soviet alliance despite the widespread distrust of communism in French political and military circles. As premier Edouard Herriot commented at the time, 'I consult the map. I see only one country, which can bring us the necessary counterweight and create a second front in case of war. That is the Soviet Union. . . .'[16]

To revise France's eastern alliances as Bonnet sought and Gamelin suggested – to abandon an eastern front – meant acquiescing in Germany's domination of the continent and France's eclipse as a great power. Recognizing the profound implications of Gamelin's 'Note', Daladier's military Cabinet asked for the views of the individual service chiefs. Significantly, Admiral François Darlan, the naval chief, General Emile Bührer, the chief of France's long-suffering colonial army, and General Joseph Vuillemin, chief of the air staff, all endorsed Gamelin's proposals.[17] More significantly, General Colson, the chief of the army staff, did not. In his response, Colson outlined two choices for France; either to pursue its traditional policy of a second front in eastern Europe or to retreat behind its borders and empire. Rejecting the latter, Colson warned that a French retreat from eastern Europe would allow Germany to gain the resources it needed to wage a long war while depriving France of the support of valuable military forces, particularly Poland's 50 divisions. Rather than retreat, Colson urged a diplomatic, economic and military effort to build an 'eastern bloc' from the Baltic to the Balkans capable of 'barring the path to the Drang nach Osten'. Without this bloc the French would be incapable of resisting German hegemony in Europe.

Prompted by Colson, Gamelin repudiated his earlier proposal. Forwarding the responses to Daladier's military cabinet, Gamelin singled out and endorsed Colson's response – that France 'cannot be content to retreat into itself and its empire, but must seek to reconstitute in Eastern Europe forces to resist Germanism [sic]'.[18] Never again did Gamelin speak of refocusing French strategy or of abandoning France's eastern allies. There are several reasons for this *volte-face*. In addition to clashing with Gamelin's understanding of France's great-power role, a reorientation of French strategy along the lines proposed risked leaving France alone against a more powerful Germany. Indeed, given the notion that reigned in staff circles of 'l'Allemagne éternelle', a Germany inherently bent on European dominance, there was every reason to discount the possibility of any long-term accommodation with Germany. The fact that 'France remained the only element of resistance on the continent', a general staff paper argued in January 1939, meant that Hitler would sooner or later seek its destruction.[19] For material and moral reasons France could not retreat from eastern Europe.

For Gamelin and the army staff, a reaffirmation of France's strategic interests in eastern Europe entailed resistance to German expansion, if necessary by force. Intelligence reports after Munich indicated that German leaders were unhappy with the status quo in the region.[20] Indeed, the conviction quickly grew in staff circles that Germany would soon seek to employ the same methods – propaganda, intimidation and force – that had succeeded so well during the Czech crisis. Gamelin accordingly reported to Daladier in late December that Hitler 'is determined to pursue the execution of his hegemonic program'. Equally to the point, Gamelin and the general staff were convinced that Germany would move eastwards, probably against Poland or Rumania, in the spring.[21] 'Expansion eastwards and security in the West' was how the military attaché in Berlin summarized prevailing views of German intentions in early 1939.[22] In the absence of hard evidence, staff officers reasoned that before attacking in the West the Germans would seek to gain control of the raw materials of central and eastern Europe. With Germany apparently bent on expansion in the east, the opposite of retreat was resistance.

The decision to oppose German expansion, when combined with Germany's superior demographic and industrial resources, made an eastern front more necessary than ever. France and Britain, Gamelin wrote to Daladier in January 1939, could 'envisage with sang-froid' a European war but only 'on condition of help from Eastern Europe'. In particular, he noted that the addition of Polish, Rumanian and Yugoslavian divisions would help offset the 'very marked superiority' that Germany and Italy enjoyed.[23] The question of an eastern front, moreover, inevitably raised that of its make-up and of the Soviet Union's role in particular. Dislike and distrust of the Soviet Union and Bolshevism made French staff officers reluctant to co-operate with Moscow – hence their refusal to conclude a military accord to complement the 1935 alliance. Prompted by the Deuxième Bureau, which underlined the

Soviet Union's potential military contribution to an eastern front, views began to change after Munich.[24] As early as December 1938 Gamelin observed that Europe's salvation rested partly 'in the hope of a renewal of Russian power . . .'.[25]

By early 1939 France's military leaders, led by Gamelin, recommitted themselves to an eastern front whose emerging keystone would be the Soviet Union. To defeat Bonnet, however, Gamelin needed the support of Premier Edouard Daladier – support which he received. Although a French retreat from eastern Europe enjoyed widespread support among the centre-right and right in French politics (as well as sections of the left), Daladier exploited Italy's ill-timed campaign of colonial demands in late 1938 to rally political support behind a policy of resistance. The widespread belief that the Germans supported, if they had not actually encouraged, the Italian action sapped confidence that Hitler's Germany would remain faithful to any accommodation. The result was a growing determination to resist not only Italian but also German expansion. A policy of 'retreat' or of 'renunciation,' Daladier declared in parliament in January 1939, would be 'disastrous for France's security'. Reiterating his refusal to consider Italian demands for French colonies in North Africa, he added, in an obvious reference to France's eastern alliances, that he would 'not accept anything which might hamper our ties with other countries or anything which runs the risk of weakening our mutual engagements [*solidarités*]. The value of these grows as the hour of danger approaches.'[26]

Together Daladier and Gamelin imposed a policy of resistance to German expansion based on a commitment to France's eastern alliances and the construction of an eastern front. Despite their doubts, the other services soon fell into line; even the air force, the most timid among them, rallied to an eastern front. The significance of this development is worth stressing. French policy from Munich to the Prague coup of March 1939 has often been described as '*attentiste*' – indecisive and uncertain.[27] Yet in fact a critical decision was taken during this period. By refusing to adopt a policy of retreat within France and its empire, by refusing to 'revise' their eastern alliances as Bonnet sought to do and as Gamelin had earlier suggested, the French effectively chose to resist further German expansion in Europe. This does not mean that they viewed war as inevitable. The possibility of deterrence remained and Daladier certainly sold a 'policy of firmness' to his political allies on these terms.[28] Several questions also remained unanswered, most notably that of France's concrete contribution to an eastern front. Nevertheless, the rejection of a French retreat certainly entailed the possibility, if not likelihood, of a European war. Indeed, a policy of retreat drew a good deal of its *raison d'être* from the belief that a Franco-German war was the only alternative.

What role did Britain play in French decisions during this period? Following Munich the prospects of substantial British military support for deterrence or, if necessary, for a European war appeared unlikely. Fully aware of the hostility in Britain to a continental commitment, French planners recognized that they could not rely upon British support on land. A general staff assessment in the mid-1930s, for example, noted that Britain's large-scale military intervention in 1914–18 was viewed as an exception never to be repeated.[29] To be sure, the French assumed that the British would eventually see reason, if only because Britain's own self-interest dictated opposition to Germany's hegemonic ambitions. But in late 1938, at the time of France's policy reassessment, pessimism on this score was more in evidence among French observers. Reports from London, for example, warned of the isolationist impulses in British policy. Typical were the naval attaché's comments in November:

> In sum, England presents itself as a state which is concentrating on itself, revising its position and conduct, and prepared even to abandon some of the principles upon which it has lived; and, while undergoing this introspection, it does not have time to consider the outside world with the same confidence it once had.[30]

Drawing the obvious conclusion from such reports, Daladier remarked to French military leaders in December that 'Britain will always think first of the safety of its own house'.[31]

As is well known, over the winter of 1938–39 the British revised their foreign and defence policies, strengthening a continental commitment. But if the French misjudged their ally, two points are worth emphasizing about decision-making in Paris. First, when French leaders considered and then rejected a policy of retreat from Europe, the future course of British policy remained unclear. Secondly, whatever their expectation of Britain, French planners fully recognized the limits of Britain's help. In a widely circulated report in November of that year, General Lelong, the military attaché in London, reminded his colleagues that Britain was in no state to intervene effectively on the continent and would not be for a long time. Even with the best of intentions, the British would need several years to field sizeable and well-equipped armed forces. 'As a result', Lelong concluded, 'it is upon us that the largest part of the effort of resistance will rest' – a conclusion that echoed previous staff appreciations during the 1930s.[32] Equally to the point, even after Britain's volte-face in early 1939 French planners doubted whether Britain – and still less the Empire – could or would make an effort at all comparable to that of 1914–18, the base-line for much of French strategic thinking. Years of observation fully apprised French planners of the political and economic constraints working on the British.[33]

These two points – the uncertainty surrounding future British policy and caution regarding Britain's present and ultimate contribution – suggest that arguments about the decisive influence of the British on French strategy are exaggerated.[34] France decided independently of Britain to resist future German expansion because French planners concluded that they had no choice. To allow Germany to gain control of Central and eastern Europe would only shift the balance of power further to France's disadvantage. This is not to say that the French dismissed Britain's potential contribution in a war. As a leading industrial and financial power with a global empire protected by the world's largest navy, Britain could offer valuable support. But its military contribution – present and projected – could not alone compensate for France's weakness *vis-à-vis* Germany. Indeed, it was precisely this weakness that forced French planners to renew their commitment to an eastern front.

Soon after Munich the French decided, largely independently of the British, to resist future German and Italian expansion in Europe. But what was Britain doing? Towards the end of 1938 British strategy appeared increasingly isolationist from Europe. The bases of defence policy, collectively known as 'limited liability', had been spelt out the year before by Thomas Inskip, the Minister for the Co-ordination of Defence, in his famous review. Approved by the Cabinet early in 1938, the review assigned priority in rearmament to the Royal Air Force and Royal Navy and confirmed the army's 'Cinderella' status by limiting the field force to two under-equipped divisions. Inskip and his colleagues hoped these priorities would not only conserve Britain's economic and financial resources, but also obviate the need to send a large army to the continent in wartime. With bitter memories of the carnage of 1914–18, Britain sought to limit its military contribution in another war largely to air and naval forces.[35]

By contrast, British foreign policy, caught between prime minister Neville Chamberlain's impatience to proceed with appeasement and the Foreign Office's caution, initially lacked clear direction. But this ambiguity decreased after Munich as Foreign Office officials undertook a major policy reassessment aimed at reducing Britain's European commitments. 'We simply cannot protect our own interests all over the world', wrote permanent under-secretary Sir Alexander Cadogan, 'and at the same time claim a preponderant voice in the ordering of affairs in continental Europe'.[36] The exercise resulted in the articulation of what Gladwynn Jebb, the Foreign Office's economic expert, termed a 'Defence of the West' policy based on the tacit division of Europe into blocs. In effect, the British would, with French help, build a barrier to German expansion in western Europe and the Mediterranean, leaving Germany free to expand its influence in central and eastern Europe.[37]

The policies of 'limited liability' and the 'Defence of the West' complemented each other. Britain's own security would be enhanced by strengthening its air and naval forces, while the security of western Europe, generally viewed as an area of vital national interest, would be safeguarded at minimal cost. Those who harboured doubts about Germany's ultimate intentions would be reassured, as would be those who feared for Britain's financial health under the pressure of mounting rearmament. The division of Europe into blocs offered grounds for a possible future settlement with Germany; in return for leaving western Europe alone, the Germans would be encouraged to direct their expansionist impulses eastwards. The apparent cynicism of such a bargain was not necessarily a deterrent. 'This policy is reminiscent of Machiavelli', Jebb admitted, 'but should not perhaps be dismissed for that reason alone'.[38] Although the British contemplated only economic and political – not military – expansion, this reservation stemmed as much from the belief that Germany could gain all it wanted by means short of war as it did from any carefully considered disapproval of the use of force. As Foreign Secretary Lord Halifax explained in October 1938: 'Henceforward we must count with German predominance in Central [and Eastern] Europe. Incidentally I have always felt myself that once Germany recovered her normal strength, this predominance was inevitable for obvious geographical and economic reasons.'[39]

Scholars have rightly questioned the wisdom of 'limited liability'. If the security of western Europe constituted a vital national interest, then the notion of rationing the means to defend the region appears dubious.[40] The fact that the viability of both policies depended on other countries, notably France, is also problematic. Without France and its army, the British simply lacked the means to defend western Europe. While this had arguably long been the case, Germany's growing strength and belligerence only reinforced this dependence. This situation makes the complacency of British officials towards the French after

Munich all the more striking. Indeed, Cadogan welcomed the evisceration of France's ally Czechoslovakia, believing that it would make the French more tractable. France, he remarked, 'has led us down the wrong path before now but perhaps, with the loss of her dominant military position on the continent, she may be expected to be more amenable'.[41] By this thinking, the weaker and more dependent the French, the more likely they would be to do Britain's bidding. While some officials questioned this logic, Halifax dismissed the suggestion that the French might 'contract out' of Europe, noting that it ignored the 'fundamental facts' underlying Franco-German relations.[42] Hostility between the two countries, he and others confidently assumed, remained too deep-seated to be overcome.

British complacency towards France, however, received several shocks beginning in December 1938. The first came from a series of reports by Colonel William Fraser, the military attaché in Paris. In his first report, Fraser warned that the French general staff expressed profound concern about the European balance of power in the wake of the Czech crisis. By removing Czechoslovakia from the military map of Europe, Munich eliminated France's strongest and most reliable continental ally, leaving the French to face a resurgent Germany, and perhaps Italy, alone. As Fraser explained in a subsequent report:

> To sum up . . . France to-day, with no allies to count on in Europe, finds herself faced by a greater Germany containing a population almost exactly double her own, and which will eventually be able, therefore, to mobilise two divisions for every one of hers, and having for an ally an Italy which is even now pursuing a hostile attitude towards her. . . . Prior to September, in virtue of her European alliances, France still considered that she was able to talk to Germany on equal terms; to-day she no longer thinks so.[43]

Given this unfavourable strategic picture, he argued, it was doubtful whether the French would actively resist further German expansion in eastern Europe. For the British, who feared being dragged into an unnecessary war in the region, this was arguably welcome news; but Fraser's reports also contained a far more disturbing suggestion – that the French might become so discouraged as to give Germany a free hand in western Europe. France, in short, might retreat within itself, leaving Britain to confront Germany alone.[44]

Fraser maintained that British policy decisively influenced the French, but he disagreed with the Foreign Office that this was a cause for complacency. According to the military attaché, there existed in every Frenchman a latent strain of anglophobia, which fuelled suspicions that the British intended to fight the next war to the last French soldier – suspicions seemingly confirmed by Britain's refusal to equip itself with an army capable of fighting on the continent. Unless the British revamped their defence policy and created a sizeable army, they could not count on French intervention in the event of a German attack on western Europe and on Britain in particular. As Fraser concluded: 'it becomes apparent that all French strategy must depend finally not only on friendship with Great Britain, but also on a knowledge of what Great Britain is prepared to do to help her on land'.[45]

Fraser's first convert was Sir Eric Phipps, the British ambassador in Paris. During the Czech crisis, the Foreign Office had criticized Phipps's reports for their excessive bias in favour of French appeasers. Afterwards, perhaps in an effort to appear more objective, he played down the influence of French appeasers, whom he characterized as wanting France 'to disinterest herself from Central Europe, sit down behind the Rhine and the Maginot Line, develop her empire, and make an agreement with Germany'. Dismissing these elements as a small minority in French politics, he assured Halifax in November that the French 'would fight like tigers to maintain their independence'.[46] But Phipps displayed far less confidence a month later. In his dispatch to London accompanying Fraser's first report, the ambassador underscored the importance of Britain's military effort to France and, echoing Fraser, warned that the French might lose heart if the British did not increase their potential military contribution, especially on land. '[I]t would be unwise too lightly to dismiss this possible tendency', he noted, 'with its danger to Great Britain in the event of an attack directed primarily against ourselves'.[47]

Fraser and Phipps's reports reached London at a time of shifting British perceptions of Germany's intentions. Any hope that Munich would usher in a period of prolonged peace quickly evaporated as German press attacks against Britain, bellicose speeches by Hitler, and the pogrom against the Jews in November 1938, poisoned Anglo-German relations. With public support for appeasement declining rapidly, Halifax informed the Cabinet that any further approach to Germany was for now 'out of the question', leaving Chamberlain to ruminate sadly on the existence of 'some fatality about Anglo-German relations which invariably blocks every effort to improve them'.[48] Soon afterwards rumours began to circulate that Hitler contemplated military action in the spring. Although it was initially thought that Germany would move eastwards, probably against the Ukraine, reports from various quarters suggested that an attack might come in the west, perhaps against Britain itself. While these reports were largely inaccurate, they produced a 'war scare' in Whitehall.[49] The belief that something had to be done became difficult to deny. 'All that can be said with practical certainty', Halifax informed the Cabinet, 'is that an "explosion" is likely to come in the comparative near future and that it is necessary for us to take immediate measures to guard against the possibility of its being directed against us'.[50]

Without the 'war scare' of early 1939, the Paris embassy reports would have created little impact on British policy. Coming when they did, however, the reports not only exacerbated fears of German intentions, but more importantly they decisively shaped Britain's response to these fears.[51] By underlining the need to reassure the French, the Paris reports prompted a series of decisions, which together gave British strategy a more continental orientation.

Foreign Office officials, who were the first to receive the Paris reports, reacted strongly. '[P]eople in this country forget all too easily . . .', wrote Sir Robert Vansittart, Cadogan's predecessor, 'that there are just as many Anglophobes in France as there are Francophobes in England. Indeed perhaps there are more.' In several memoranda over the next two months he argued that 'limited liability' would have to be scrapped in favour of a British Expeditionary Force (BEF) of around 30 divisions – considerably more than Fraser's suggested minimum of 20.[52] While Vansittart's colleagues displayed more caution, they too found it difficult to ignore Britain's strategic dependence on France. Referring to the possibility of a French retreat, Cadogan reluctantly admitted in January 1939 that 'the fact of the present situation must convince us that there is something in it'.[53] Halifax fully agreed; 'I am fully alive to the possible reactions of French policy', he remarked in early December. The same month he told the Committee of Imperial Defence (CID) that 'a time might come when the French would cease to be enthusiastic about their relations with Great Britain if they were left with the impression that it was they who must bear the brunt of the fighting and slaughter on land'.[54]

By early 1939, the combination of French irresolution and German resolve prompted the Foreign Office to advocate reversing the isolationist course of British strategy. Within the Foreign Policy Committee of the Cabinet Halifax pressed for staff talks with the French, arguing that they should be as comprehensive as possible and embrace 'every factor with which France and ourselves would be concerned' in the event of war. While admitting that the proposal constituted a 'big step forward and was almost tantamount to an Alliance . . .', Halifax nevertheless insisted that 'it was one which must be taken'.[55] The possibility of staff talks inevitably raised the issue of the BEF's size since the French would reject 'limited liability'. Although the Foreign Office initially opposed any expansion of the BEF, citing the lack of trained men and equipment, such practical considerations soon receded before the need to reassure the French. Accordingly, in January 1939 Halifax urged Cabinet ministers to agree to expand the BEF to six divisions.[56]

In revising Britain's foreign and defence policies the Foreign Office looked for and found allies among Britain's military advisors. Aware of Britain's military weakness and haunted by memories of 1914–18, the service chiefs of staff had long sought to avoid a formal military engagement to France that would tie Britain's hands. As recently as November 1938, the Chiefs of Staff Committee (COS) advised against extending Anglo-French staff talks beyond the current low-level contacts between service attachés. Any new arrangement, warned Air Marshal Newall, the chief of the air staff (CAS), would provide a 'definite commitment' to the French.[57] Yet, like Phipps, the COS soon changed their minds. Partly in response to a Foreign Office request to consider Fraser's reports 'as a matter of urgency,' the COS in early 1939 approved a series of papers by the Joint Planning Committee (JPC) that recommended among other things a limited expansion of the BEF and staff talks with the French.[58] A draft passage in one of the papers clearly marked the change in their thinking: 'We are now . . . entering into an entirely new and frank phase of our relations with the French on questions affecting the joint defence of the two countries. We are indeed taking them more closely into our confidence than even our own Dominions.'[59] No doubt the 'war scare' in early 1939 influenced the COS, but fears of a French retreat into isolation also played a key role since Britain needed France and its army to defend western Europe. Discussing the defence of Belgium, a major COS appreciation circulated in February remarked that 'any effective French support . . . is likely to be contingent on our intervention on land on the Continent'.[60] The presence of British troops, in other words, was necessary to ensure that France resisted a German attack in the West.

Together the Foreign Office and COS presented a formidable combination in support of revising British policy, but to accomplish their goal they needed to overcome Chamberlain's opposition. Viewing Munich as a first step in the pacification of European tensions, the prime minister was unmoved by French fears and concerns. On this point, he received powerful support from the Treasury. Holding fast to the elusive defence ration, the Treasury contended that since Britain could not afford to field a continental army, it made no sense to expend limited resources on the BEF.[61] The Treasury's efforts to delay a decision failed, however, largely because it possessed no answer to the danger posed by German resolve and French irresolution. Recognizing this, Chamberlain initially sought to reassure the French (and his domestic critics) with public statements of Britain's interest in the security of western Europe and of France in particular – a measure that conveniently avoided binding commitments. But more concrete measures soon proved necessary. In February 1939 the Cabinet agreed to open staff talks with the French and to expand the BEF to 19 divisions (six regular and 13 Territorial divisions). Although Chamberlain played down the significance of these decisions, they represented a marked shift in British military policy.[62] Announcing the government's decision in early March 1939, the Secretary of State for War, Leslie Hore-Belisha, remarked that if 'we are involved in a war our contribution and the ways in which we can make it will not be half-hearted nor based upon any theory of limited liability'.[63] The next month the government introduced conscription.

In the opening months of 1939 British strategy underwent significant revision. Soon after Munich mounting uncertainty surrounding German intentions and French resolve forced the British to commit themselves more fully to the defence of western Europe. 'Limited liability' was not dead; even those in favour of preparing the BEF for a continental role did not envisage an army on anything like the scale of the first world war. Nevertheless, a change had occurred. The question now was no longer whether an army would be sent but how large a one and when. The role of the French in this reversal is worth stressing. Fear of a French retreat into isolation gave concrete shape to the government's response to the 'war scare' of early 1939. Without this scare, British defence policy would probably have continued on the same lines as before by focusing on air and naval rearmament and leaving the military burden to France. The perceived need to ensure that the French actively participated in western Europe's defence eliminated this option.

The irony, of course, is that British leaders made decisions based on a misreading of French intentions (by early 1939 the French had rejected a policy of retreat) and of Britain's influence on French policy. Why were the British mistaken? One reason is neglect; during the interwar period British intelligence consistently failed to examine the French situation in any depth.[64] Widely held stereotypes of the French as unpredictable, impetuous and easily seduced by foolish proposals – all purportedly feminine characteristics – also played a contributing role. The French could not be trusted to reject a policy of retreat.[65] But popular stereotypes and neglect do not explain the whole story. Evidence suggests that the reports from the Paris embassy at the end of 1938 were also the product of manipulation.

If scholars have exaggerated Britain's role in French strategy, it is nevertheless true that French planners sought British political and military support. Initially, the French confidently assumed that rational argument and German bullying would persuade the British to ally with France, but they were soon forced to change tactics. In preparation for a meeting with British ministers in November 1938, Daladier ordered the creation of a massive dossier detailing the shifting balance of power in Germany's favour. With this evidence he expected to make his guests see reason.[66] As Daladier later noted, however, the meeting proved to be 'extremely disappointing' since Chamberlain and Halifax refused to consider either staff talks or the expansion of the BEF.[67]

However, rather than despair, the French altered their approach with Gamelin's staff taking the lead. Hoping to scare the British into action, high-ranking French staff officers, among them Colonel Petitbon, Gamelin's close aide, began to warn Colonel Fraser and his assistants that France might retreat into isolation if Britain remained indifferent to French needs.[68] While direct evidence that Gamelin orchestrated this campaign has not been found, circumstantial evidence suggests that he did. Staff officers such as Petitbon must have known that their warnings contradicted Gamelin's decision to resist German expansion. Also suggestive is the close accord between the advice offered by the French embassy in London and the revised arguments of staff officers, most notably Gamelin. Following Munich Lelong and Corbin recommended that the British be told bluntly that they would have to make good the loss of Czech military power to the European balance of power, since France alone could no longer carry the burden. The hint of blackmail is evident in Lelong's assessment forwarded to Daladier and Gamelin. 'The French Army', it read, 'constitutes the cover for the British Empire. Can it continue to play this role when confronted by the entire German Army (and perhaps the Italian Army)?'[69] Shortly thereafter an army staff paper explained that the British should be informed that, without substantial help, the French could only defend themselves and not the Low Countries and the Channel coast.[70] Interestingly, Gamelin modified a draft copy. Closely following Lelong's advice, the initial version referred to France's inability to serve as Britain's 'avant garde' on the continent, but on Gamelin's instructions, the final version dropped this vague reference in favour of a more precise – and threatening – one; that unless the British offered greater support, France would retreat into itself, abandoning Belgium and western Europe.[71] It was precisely this possibility that the British COS warned against in early 1939.

Robert Young has pointed to additional evidence that the French sought to manipulate British fears, notably French warnings in early 1939 that Germany's immediate ambitions lay in western Europe.[72] At the end of 1938, Gamelin informed Hore-Belisha, who was visiting Paris, that the Germans were likely to attack Holland in the spring. Similarly, Colonel Gauché, who in December 1938 indicated that Germany would move next against Poland or the Ukraine, warned Fraser in January 1939 of a possible German air offensive in the west coupled with an occupation of Holland.[73] These and other warnings, however, contradicted the belief of French planners that Germany would attack first in the east. The French general staff's manipulation, therefore, worked along two complementary lines. Having dangled the bogey of a French retreat that would leave Britain alone to face Germany, staff officers sharpened this danger by raising the possibility of a German advance in the west, a prospect that could be expected to alarm Whitehall far more than German expansion (peaceful or otherwise) in eastern Europe.

If the war scares that plagued Whitehall in early 1939 resulted partly from French misinformation, British staff officers also appear to have contributed. To understand the nature and significance of their efforts it is necessary to return to Munich. Unhappy with its subordinate role and convinced that Britain would eventually be compelled to send an army to Europe in the event of war, the general staff never fully embraced the strategy of 'limited liability'. Although the army, like the other two services, had long opposed a formal commitment to France, fearful of being tied to French coat-tails as in 1914, the general staff officers remained 'continentalist' in their strategic conceptions. The Czech crisis, which brought Europe to the brink of war, confirmed their belief that Britain had to possess an army capable of serving in Europe. Shocked that a minuscule and ill-equipped BEF might have been sent to the continent, staff officers emerged from the crisis determined to do something.[74] The recent crisis, an assessment declared in October 1938, had brought the question of the BEF 'into the foreground'. Repeating French arguments, it maintained that Munich, by eliminating Czechoslovakia and crippling an eastern front, upset the relative balance of power in Europe, leaving the French unable to defend western Europe alone.[75] The message was clear: Britain would have to help. Within the general staff, no one was more convinced of this than General Henry

Pownall, the wilful and energetic Director of Military Operations and Intelligence. The recent crisis, he intimated in October, has taught us that 'we must *expect* to have to send troops to help the French'.[76] Although Pownall said nothing about the BEF's projected size, and almost certainly did not envisage one on the scale of the British army in 1918, he clearly envisioned something considerably larger than the current force of two divisions.

The general staff's first step was to gain the backing of Hore-Belisha, a task which proved relatively easy despite the war minister's endorsement of 'limited liability' and his reputation as a political ally of Chamberlain. Interestingly, it appears that Hore-Belisha was himself concerned about French morale, having noted in November 1938 that 'France was finished'.[77] The next step was to win over the COS. Proceeding cautiously in presenting its case, the War Office sidestepped the issue of a new role for the BEF and instead stressed the need to raise the field force to a level where it could carry out its assigned missions, including the lowly one of continental warfare. In a paper presented to the COS in December 1938, Lord Gort, the Chief of the Imperial General Staff (CIGS), explained that unless 'adequate preparations' were taken in peacetime 'an unjustifiable and avoidable sacrifice' would be inevitable if the BEF were sent to Europe. In what was certainly an unintended irony, Gort echoed the arguments of military chiefs before 1914 when he reassured his colleagues that a larger force was unnecessary. By preventing a rapid German victory, 'an efficient and well-equipped British field force' would provide Britain and its allies with the time needed to mobilize their immense resources, thereby ensuring a long war.[78] Having laid the foundation, Hore-Belisha later that month submitted a paper to the CID requesting an additional £81 million to prepare a field force of four divisions for a counter-offensive role, to equip four territorial army divisions for modern warfare, and to create a two-division colonial army.[79]

From the outset, the air force strongly opposed the War Office's proposals. Wedded to the doctrine of strategic bombing, the air staff feared that a continental commitment would divert scarce financial and economic resources from the RAF's own expansion programmes. Rejecting any need for a BEF, the air staff argued that strategic bombing offered Britain the only means of winning a European war. As a staff paper explained in November:

[I]t is worth remembering that it is not enough to avoid losing a war. We have got to be able to win it. The Navy cannot win a war for us in less than a matter of years. We certainly cannot win it with an Army of four or five divisions. We do not know that we can win it in the air. But a powerful air striking force seems our only means of providing a backing of immediate force behind our policy that might be effective within a reasonable time.[80]

Thus behind the debate on the BEF and spending priorities lurked a struggle over British strategy. Outside the confines of the air ministry, however, the air staff preferred not to emphasize its strategic bombing plans, a prudent choice given the lack of bombers, trained crews and technical equipment needed to mount a sustained bombing campaign – a point the head of Bomber Command reluctantly conceded in May 1939.[81] Rather than discuss doctrine, the air staff, in contesting the War Office's arguments for a larger BEF, cited the danger of an 'unlimited commitment' to France. 'Once we were launched on land in support of the French in France it might well be impossible to turn off the tap', Newall told the COS in January 1939.[82] This argument worked in the past and could reasonably be expected to do so again.

Unfortunately for Newall, the general staff anticipated the air staff's response. Unwilling to rely on persuasion alone, in October 1938 Pownall drew Colonel Fraser and the French into his efforts to prepare the BEF for a continental role. He instructed Fraser to prompt the French to press the issue of the BEF's size during the visit of British ministers to Paris in November. The military attaché was to 'make hints, in the form of questions, that such questions [about the BEF] might be raised during the discussion'.[83] Having encouraged the French to protest, the general staff then pointed to the fragility of French resolve as a reason to strengthen the army. 'Henceforth', read a widely circulated general staff paper in January, 'France's survival as a European power is conditional on her being able to count on Britain's support in any contingency that may arise'.[84] Early in 1939 the War Office also began to warn that Germany might attack in the west rather than the east. This partly reflected the War Office's genuine uncertainty about German intentions, the result of ambiguous and confusing information. Nevertheless, an element of calculation is also evident, as warnings of a German move westwards contradicted general-staff and especially military-intelligence assumptions that the Germans would initially expand eastwards to acquire the resources needed to wage a long war.[85] The general staff, in any case, appeared to be more interested in encouraging fears than in gauging the accuracy of its information. Referring to reports of a German attack in the west, Pownall intimated in January 1939 that there was 'a distinct element of propaganda in it. The French know we regard the Low Countries as vital to our security and they are using that as a lever to put a bit of ginger into us. More power to them! It is having a most admirable effect.'[86]

Predictably, the air ministry remained unconvinced about the combined danger of a French retreat and a German attack on the west, and questioned the reliability of the army's information.[87] Fortunately for the army, however, it had more success in convincing the navy. Like the army, the navy was jealous of the air force's growing share of the defence budget. 'The Air Force has . . . become a political vote-catcher', Admiral Backhouse, chief of the naval staff, grumbled in November 1938, 'and no one dare say no to whatever they ask for'.[88] Exacerbating matters were unfavourable shifts in the balance of naval power caused by domestic and international constraints on naval expansion after 1919 and by mistaken staff assessments of the timing of a possible future war. With only ten capital ships projected to be in commission in 1939, the navy after Munich was stretched too thin to cope with Britain's potential challengers.[89] While naval planners had long counted on the wartime co-operation of the French *Marine Nationale*, especially in the Mediterranean, the widening gap between resources and commitments reinforced their dependence on France. The prospect of a French retreat into isolation accordingly horrified them. As Backhouse wrote in January 1939:

> If we were to tell France that we did not intend . . . to send more than a few divisions to her assistance could we be surprised if she gave up the unequal struggle and made the best terms she could with Germany and Italy rather than risk the loss of much more by defeat in war?[90]

Put simply, French demands would have to be met since the Admiralty could not risk war without the support of the French navy.

With the navy's support the army overrode air-force objections to its expansion proposals and steered the COS towards a continental commitment. With COS backing, the Foreign Office in early 1939 overcame the resistance of Chamberlain and the Treasury and reoriented British foreign policy towards an alliance with France.

By early 1939 the basis of the Anglo-French alliance had been laid. Discouraged by Munich, French leaders seriously considered a policy of retreat, which would give Germany a free hand in eastern Europe and allow France to focus on defending itself and its empire. Led by Gamelin, the French rejected this option, because Hitler's Germany could not be trusted and because a policy of retreat clashed with their understanding of France's great-power role. In rejecting a policy of retreat and recommitting themselves to their eastern allies, the French in effect decided to resist future German expansion. Britain did not play an important role in this decision. The French general staff decided to resist Germany at a time when the prospects of British help were at their lowest. Equally to the point, Britain's support, while welcome, could not compensate for French weakness *vis-à-vis* Germany. The French chose to resist German expansion because they believed they had no choice. To do nothing would allow Germany to turn against France at a later date when it was stronger.

The period between Munich and the Anglo-French alliance also produced significant changes to British policy. By February 1939 the isolationist course in British strategy had been reversed as the Cabinet decided to enter into an alliance with France, a step sealed by the request for staff talks and the decision to expand the BEF. Significantly, assessments of the French position played an important role in this evolution. Fear of a French retreat into isolation, when combined with mounting concern about Germany's aims, convinced the Foreign Office and COS that something had to be done to reassure Paris. French staff officers encouraged British fears by feeding Colonel Fraser and others misleading information about French irresolution and German resolve. It appears that British staff officers collaborated in this effort. If so, the French arguably got the better of the British. Pownall and his colleagues initially believed that the security of Britain and, more generally, of western Europe could largely be divorced from that of eastern Europe. That French planners did not accept this division can be seen from the growing importance they placed on an eastern front in their deliberations. Yet when they approached the British, French staff officers spoke only of western Europe. One can speculate that, realizing it was too much to ask the British to commit themselves to eastern Europe, the French chose to proceed in stages. Once the British accepted greater responsibility for the defence of western Europe, strategic logic would lead them to value eastern Europe as well. And, as it turned out, that is precisely what happened. Following the Prague coup in March 1939, the British and French not only issued guarantees to Poland, Romania, Greece and Turkey, but in order to make these guarantees militarily viable, they also pursued a Soviet alliance. In the last few months of peace, France and Britain strove to construct an eastern front against Germany – a strategy long embraced by the French.

All this draws attention to the critical role of France in the making of the Anglo-French alliance and the origins of the second world war. The importance of the decision to resist German (and Italian) expansion in Europe, taken by Daladier at Gamelin's prompting, cannot be exaggerated. In its absence, subsequent decisions in London would have mattered little, since the British lacked the means to defend Europe. If the French had opted for a policy of retreat into isolation, it is difficult to see how the British could not have followed suit. The French decision, taken without a guarantee of British support, indicates that Britain's influence on French strategy can be overstated. Contrary to much of the existing literature, the answer to the question of 'how war came' in September 1939 is to be found at least as much in Paris as in London – and perhaps more.

Notes

1. 'Note. Rapports franco-britanniques', Sous-Direction d'Europe, 3 June 1939, Papiers 1940, Reconstitution Foucques Duparc, Archives du Ministère des Affaires Etrangères (MAE), Paris: vol. 33.
2. For a schematic but still useful view, see A. Wolfers, *Britain and France between the Wars* (New York: Harcourt, Brace and Co., 1940) and W. M. Jordan, *Great Britain, France and the German Problem, 1919–1939* (London: Oxford University Press, 1943). For a more nuanced view, especially for the 1920s, see S. Shuker, *The End of French Predominance in Europe* (Chapel Hill, NC: University of North Carolina Press, 1976); J. Bariéty, *Les relations franco-allemandes après la Première Guerre Mondiale, 1920–1925* (Paris: Publications de la Sorbonne, 1977); and M. Trachtenberg, *Reparations in World Politics* (New York: Columbia University Press, 1980).
3. G. L. Weinberg, *The Foreign Policy of Hitler's Germany: Starting World War II, 1937–1939* (Chicago: University of Chicago Press, 1980), pp. 534–627.
4. Examples on the British side are R. A. C. Parker, *Chamberlain and Appeasement: British Policy and the Origins of the Second World War* (Basingstoke: Macmillan Press [now Palgrave Macmillan], 1993); J. Charmley, *Chamberlain and the Lost Peace* (London: Hodder and Stoughton, 1989). For the French, see R. J. Young, *In Command of France: French Foreign and Defence Policy, 1933–1940* (Cambridge, MA: Harvard University Press, 1978); J.-B. Duroselle, *La décadence 1932–1939* (Paris: Imprimerie Nationale, 1979); M. S. Alexander, *The Republic in Danger: General Maurice Gamelin and the Politics of French Defence, 1933–1940* (Cambridge: Cambridge University Press, 1992); E. du Réau, *Edouard Daladier 1884–1970* (Paris: Fayard, 1993).
5. Good examples are D. C. Watt, *How War Came: the Immediate Origins of the Second World War, 1938–1939* (London: Heinemann, 1989) who writes that '[t]he war which was to break Europe into two . . . was in the beginning fun-

damentally a war between the British and German people'; W. Murray, *The Change in the European Balance of Power, 1938–1939: the Path to Ruin* (Princeton, NJ: Princeton University Press, 1984), for whom Allied policy invariably means British policy; and R. Rosencrance and Z. Steiner, 'British Grand Strategy and the Origins of World War II', in R. Rosencrance and A. A. Stein (eds), *The Domestic Bases of Grand Strategy* (Ithaca, NY: Cornell University Press, 1993), pp. 124–53.

6. Exceptions for a slightly earlier period in the 1930s include N. Rostow, *Anglo-French Relations, 1934–1936* (London: Macmillan, 1984) and M. Thomas, *Britain, France and Appeasement: Anglo-French Relations in the Popular Front Era* (Oxford: Berg, 1996).

7. The Czechs had 30 well-armed and trained divisions. French intelligence estimated that it would take as many as 60 divisions to defeat the Czechs. See 'Note sur une action offensive pour soutenir la Tchéco-slovaquie', CSG memorandum [1938], Service Historique de l'Armée de Terre, Vincennes (SHAT), 7N3434/3, and 'Note succincte sur l'armée tchécoslovaque,' [1938], SHAT, 1N90/3. Also see M. Hauner, 'La Tchécoslovaquie en tant que facteur militaire', *Revue des Etudes Slaves*, 52 (1979), pp. 178–92. For a dissenting view, see P. Jackson, 'French Military Intelligence and Czechoslovakia, 1938', *Diplomacy and Statecraft*, 5 (1994), pp. 81–106.

8. P. Lazareff, *De Munich à Vichy* (New York: Brentano's, 1944), pp. 32–3. For Bonnet in general, see A. Adamthwaite, *France and the Coming of the Second World War, 1936–1939* (London: Frank Cass, 1977), pp. 264–79; Duroselle, *La décadence*, pp. 381–8; C. Barbier, 'Das französische Außenministerium und die diplomatische Aktivität vom Münchener Abkommen bis zur Kriegserklärung' in K. Hildebrand et al., *1939 An der Schwelle zum Weltkrieg* (Berlin: W. de Gruyter, 1990), pp. 43–54; H. F. Bellstadt, *Apaisement oder Krieg: Frankreichs Außenminister Georges Bonnet und die deutsch-französische Erklärung vom 6. Dezember 1938* (Bonn: Bouvier, 1993), pp. 33–85.

9. Phipps to Foreign Office, 12 October 1938, PRO FO 371/216121/C12161/1050/17. Also see his comments in Archives de l'Assemblée Nationale, Paris [AAN], Commission des affaires étrangères, 16ème carton, vol. 7, 6 October 1938.

10. Massigli is in Réunion hebdomadaire, 5 October 1938, SHAT 7N2525. For 'adjustment', see 'Note', by Rochat, 30 December 1938, MAE, Papiers 1940, Hoppenot, vol. 5. For 'realism' among Quai d'Orsay officials, see the comments in J. Chauvel, *Commentaire. I: De Vienne à Alger (1938–1944)* (Paris: Fayard, 1971), pp. 57–8.

11. For Quai d'Orsay officials, see 'Le Pacte franco-soviétique', January 1939, MAE, Papiers 1940, Cabinet Bonnet, vol. 16; and 'Note sur les accords franco-polonais', 28 December 1938, MAE, Papiers 1940, Cabinet Bonnet, vol. 10. For circulated dispatches see 'Note. Rapport franco-polonais', 19 November 1938, MAE, Papiers 1940, Cabinet Bonnet, vol. 10, a copy of which is in Archives Nationale, Paris (AN), Papiers Daladier, 2DA4/3/a.

12. Bellstadt, *Apaisement oder Krieg*, pp. 33–42. Also see Bonnet to François-Poncet, 13 October 1938, AN, Papiers André François-Poncet, 462/AP/23.

13. See the editorial in *Le Temps*, a newspaper reputed to be close to the Quai d'Orsay. 'Bulletin du jour', 7 December 1938. For the controversy over a 'free hand', see Bellstedt, *Apaisement oder Krieg*, pp. 16–27.

14. 'Note sur la situation actuelle', 12 October 1938, SHAT 5N579/1; reproduced in Documents Diplomatiques Français [DDF], 2ème série, tome XII, no. 286. The best study of Gamelin is Alexander, *The Republic in Danger*; also see P. le Goyet, *Le mystère Gamelin* (Paris: Presses de la Cité, 1975).

15. For France's eastern alliances, see P. Wandycz, *France and her Eastern Allies, 1919–1925* (Minneapolis, MN: University of Minnesota Press, 1962) and *The Twilight of French Eastern Alliances, 1926–1939: French-Czechoslovak-Polish Relations from Locarno to the Remilitarization of the Rhineland* (Princeton, NJ: Princeton University Press, 1988).

16. Cited in W. E. Scott, *Alliance Against Hitler: the Origins of the Franco-Soviet Pact* (Durham, NC: Duke University Press, 1962), p. 239.

17. For Darlan, see 'La Situation actuelle de la politique militaire de la France', 17 October 1938, Service Historique de la Marine, Vincennes (SHM), 1BB²171; for Bührer, see Bührer to Gamelin, 19 October 1938, SHAT 5N579/17; and for Vuillemin, Vuillemin to Gamelin, 25 October 1938, SHAT, 5N579/1 and 17.

18. 'Note sur la situation actuelle', 26 October 1938, signed by Colson and enclosed in a note from Gamelin to Daladier, 26 October 1938, SHAT, 2N224/1. N. Jordan, in citing the 12 October Note in isolation, mistakenly argues that Gamelin remained committed to a retreat from eastern Europe in 1938–39. See *The Popular Front and Central Europe*, pp. 289–91.

19. 'Le Problème militaire français', January 1939, SHAT 7N2524/1.

20. 'Note sur le développement des forces terrestres allemandes', 30 November 1938, SHAT, 7N2676 (emphasis in original); also see 'Au 1er Janvier 1939', undated, SHAT, 7N and 'Principaux renseignements . . .', 4 February 1939, SHAT, 7N2151.

21. Gamelin to Daladier, 27 December 1938, SHAT, 1N43/3/6.

22. Didelet to Ministre de la Guerre, 10 January 1939, SHAT, 7N2602/2. Also see 'Compte-rendu de renseignement', 22 December 1938, Gauché, SHAT, 1N47/3/2; P. Jackson, *France and the German Menace, 1933–1939* (Oxford: Oxford University Press, 2000), pp. 314–25.

23. Gamelin to Daladier, 7 January 1939, SHAT, 2N224/1.

24. For the Deuxième Bureau see 'Considérations sur la constitution d'un bloc oriental', by Gauché, 28 December 1939, SHAT, 7N2522/3. This copy contains marginalia by Gamelin. And see 'Compte-rendu de renseignement', 22 December 1938, 1N47/3/2.

25. Gamelin to Daladier, 3 December 1938, SHAT 5N579/1/17.

26. Journal Officiel, Chambre des Députés, 1939, 26 January 1939, p. 248. Also see his comments in Archives du Senat, Paris [AS], Sous-Commission de la Défense Nationale, 27 January 1939.

27. R. Young, 'The Aftermath of Munich: the Course of French Diplomacy, October 1938 to March 1939', *French Historical Studies*, 8 (1973), pp. 305–22; E. du Réau, 'Enjeux stratégiques et rédeploiement diplomatique français: novembre 1938–septembre 1939', *Relations internationales*, 35 (1983), pp. 319–35; and Y. Lacaze, *La France et Munich* (Berne: Peter Lang, 1992), pp. 277–8.

28. See for example Daladier's speech to the Radical Party's Executive Committee on 15 January. 'Le Comité éxécutif radical-socialiste réuni hier . . .', in *L'Ere nouvelle*, 16 January 1939, pp. 1–2.

29. 'Note sur les relations militaires franco-britanniques', [mid-1930s], SHAT 7N3438/1. From London, Corbin remarked simply that the word 'alliance' exercises 'a veritable terror' on British minds. See Corbin to Leger, 2 July 1936, MAE, Papiers 1940, Leger, vol. 12.
30. 'Compte-rendu de renseignement', 3 November 1938, SHM, 1BB⁷ 42. Corbin agreed. See Corbin to MAE, 21 December 1938, MAE, Europe-1930–40, Grande-Bretagne, vol. 266.
31. CSDN meeting, 5 December 1938, SHAT, 2N20.
32. For Lelong, see 'Etude sur la participation de l'Angleterre dans l'éventualité d'une action commune franco-britannique en cas de guerre', 9 November 1938, SHAT, 7N2815. A copy can be found in Daladier's papers. For general staff appreciations, see 'Note sur l'appui éventuel de la Grande-Bretagne', EMA, 9 January 1935, SHAT, 7N3438/1; and 'Note sur l'appui militaire de la Grande-Bretagne', EMA, 2 May 1935, SHAT, 7N2840/1.
33. For example, see Gamelin to Daladier, 15 April 1939, SHAT, 5N579/2/17.
34. The classic statement is F. Bédarida, 'La "gouvernante anglaise"', in R. Rémond and J. Bourdin, (eds), *Edouard Daladier. Chef du gouvernement* (Paris: FNSP, 1977), pp. 228–40.
35. British defence policy is well covered in M. Howard, *The Continental Commitment* (London: Maurice Temple Smith, 1972), pp. 113–17; P. Dennis, *Decision by Default: Conscription and British Defence, 1919–1939* (London: Duke University Press, 1972), pp. 109–225; N. H. Gibbs, *Grand Strategy, I: Rearmament Policy* (London: HMSO, 1976), pp. 491–528; B. J. Bond, *British Military Policy between the Two World Wars* (Oxford: Oxford University Press, 1980), pp. 253–70.
36. Cadogan to Halifax, 15 October 1938, cover letter for paper dated 14 October, Public Record Office, Kew (PRO): FO 371/21659/C14471/42/18. Also see D. Lammers, 'From Whitehall after Munich: the Foreign Office and the Future Course of British Policy', *Historical Journal*, XVI (1973), 831–56. But see Z. Steiner who stresses the confused and undecided nature of Foreign Office officials following Munich: 'Evaluation des rapports de force en Europe occidentale en 1938: le point de vue du Foreign Office', in R. Frank and R. Girault (eds), *La Puissance en Europe 1938–1940* (Paris: Publications de la Sorbonne, 1984), pp. 55–71.
37. For Jebb, see 'Preliminary Outline of Suggested Paper on Policy', [late October 1938], PRO, FO 371/21659/C14471/42/18. The other Foreign Office papers are in this file.
38. 'Preliminary outline of a suggested paper on policy', PRO, FO 371/216589/C14471/42/18.
39. Halifax to Lord Francis Scott, 18 October 1938, PRO, FO 800/328.
40. See especially Howard, *The Continental Commitment*, pp. 128 and 144–6; Murray, *The Change in the European Balance of Power*, passim; Bond, *British Military Policy*, pp. 259–60.
41. Paper dated 15 October 1938, PRO, FO 371/21659/C14471/42/18.
42. Oliver Harvey, one of Halifax's advisors, questioned British complacency regarding France. See Harvey to Halifax, 27 October 1938, FO 800/311; Halifax to Phipps, 1 November 1938, PRO, FO 800/311.
43. Fraser to Phipps, 5 and 22 December 1938, PRO, FO 371/22915/C1503/130/17 and FO 371/21597/C15175/36/17.

44. Fraser to Phipps, 4 January 1939, PRO FO 371/22915/C20/15/18.
45. Fraser to Phipps, 22 December 1938, PRO FO 371/22915/C1503/130/17.
46. Phipps to Halifax, 18 November 1938, PRO, CAB 21/971; Phipps to Halifax, 7 November 1938, PRO, FO 800/311. For Phipps in general, see D. C. Watt, 'Chamberlain's Ambassadors', in M.L. Dockrill and B. McKercher (eds), *Diplomacy and World Power: Studies in British Foreign Policy, 1890–1950* (Cambridge: Cambridge University Press, 1996), pp. 157–62; J. Herman, *The Paris Embassy of Sir Eric Phipps: Anglo-French Relations and the Foreign Office, 1937–1939* (Brighton, UK: Sussex Academic Press, 1998).
47. Phipps to Halifax, 7 December 1938, PRO FO 371/21597/C15175/36/17.
48. Halifax is in Cabinet minutes, 16 November 1938, PRO, CAB 23/96; Chamberlain is in Neville to Ida Chamberlain, 13 November 1938, Neville Chamberlain Papers, Birmingham University Library, NC 18/1/1076. One sign of declining support for appeasement is the warning from the Conservative Research Department in November 1938 against calling a general election precisely because one of the main issues would be the government's foreign policy. See Clarke to Director (CRD), 28 November 1938, Conservative Party Archive, Bodleian Library, Oxford, CRD 1/7/34.
49. The literature on the war scare is extensive. See Watt, *How War Came*, pp. 99–107; W. K. Wark, *The Ultimate Enemy: British Intelligence and Nazi Germany, 1933–1939* (Ithaca, NY: Cornell University Press, 1985), pp. 38–60; S. Aster, *1939: the Making of the Second World War* (London, 1977), pp. 38–60; M. S. Alexander, 'Les réactions à la menace stratégique allemande en Europe occidentale: la Grande Bretagne, la Belgique et le 'cas Hollande', décembre 1938–février 1939', *Cahiers d'histoire de la Seconde Guerre Mondiale*, 7 (1982), pp. 5–38; C. Andrew, *Secret Service: the Making of the British Intelligence Community* (New York: Viking, 1985), pp. 412–17.
50. The dossier is in PRO, CAB 27/627. For Halifax, see Cabinet minutes, 25 January 1939, annex, PRO, CAB 23/97.
51. Most scholars largely ignore the influence of France on British policy during this period. Exceptions are M. Dockrill, *British Establishment Perspectives on France, 1936–40* (Basingstoke: Macmillan Press [now Palgrave Macmillan], 1999), pp. 67–128; and C. A. MacDonald, 'Britain, France and the April Crisis of 1939', *European Studies Review*, 2 (1972), pp. 151–69.
52. Vansittart's initial comments are in a minute, 19 December 1938, Vansittart papers, Churchill College Archives Centre, Cambridge, VNST, 2/39. For his memoranda, see, PRO, FO 371/22922; December 1938, C358/282/17/2; 21 January 1939, C940/281/17; and 7 February 1939, C1978/281/17.
53. Cadogan minute, 27 January 1939, PRO, FO 371/22922/C1983/281/17. Also see the comments of William Strang, another high-ranking official, in Strang minute, 9 February 1939, PRO, FO 371/22915/C1503/130/17 and 'Military relations between the United Kingdom and the three Western Powers (France, Belgium, Netherlands)', by Strang, 16 January 1939, C880/130/17.
54. Halifax minute, 31 December 1938, PRO, FO 371/21597/C15514/36/17; CID, minutes of the 341st meeting, 15 December 1938, PRO, CAB 2/8.
55. FPC meetings, 26 January 1939 and 1 February 1939, PRO, CAB 27/624 and CAB 23/97/(39)3.
56. FPC meeting, 23 January 1939, PRO, CAB 27/624.

57. Newall to Ismay, 19 October 1938; 'Staff Conversations with France', 18 November 1938, PRO, CAB 53/42/COS 789 and 795. For COS aversion to a continental commitment, see D. C. Watt, *Too Serious a Business: European Armed Forces and the Approach to the Second World War* (London: Temple Smith, 1975), pp. 129–31; C. Barnett, *The Collapse of British Power* (London: Eyre Methuen Ltd, 1972), chapter 5; and Howard, *The Continental Commitment*, pp. 102–03.

58. For the Foreign Office request, see FO to Ismay, 4 January 1939, PRO, CAB 21/510. For the reports see, 'German aggression against Holland', 25 January 1939; 'The Strategic position of France in a European war', 1 February 1939; 'Staff conversations with France and Belgium', 6 February 1939, all in PRO, CAB 53/44/COS 830, 833, and 838.

59. 'Staff conversations with the French', 28 February 1939, PRO, CAB 55/15/JP 361.

60. 'European Appreciation, 1939–40', February 1939, PRO, CAB 53/45/COS 843.

61. Note on WO memorandum, [October 31 or 1 November 1938], PRO, T 161/1071/S42580/3; Simon to Wood, 25 January 1939, PRO, AIR 8/250.

62. For Chamberlain, see the minutes of meeting at 10 Downing Street, 10 February 1939, PRO, CAB 21/511.

63. Cited in P. Dennis, *The Territorial Army, 1906–1940* (Woodbridge, Suffolk: Royal Historical Society, 1987), pp. 237–8.

64. M. S. Alexander and W. J. Philpott, 'The Entente Cordiale and the Next War: Anglo-French Views on Future Military Cooperation, 1928–39', *Intelligence and National Security*, 13 (1998), pp. 53–84. More generally on mutual perceptions, see P. M. H. Bell, *France and Britain 1900–1940* (London: Longman, 1996), *passim*.

65. See the suggestive studies by J. F. V. Keiger, 'La perception de la puissance française par le Foreign Office', in P. Milza and R. Poidevin (eds), *La Puissance française à la 'Belle Epoque': Mythe ou réalité?* (Paris: Institut d'histoire du temps présent, 1992), pp. 176–84; F. Costigiliola, 'L'image de la France aux Etats-Unis', in R. Frank (ed.), *Images et imaginaire dans les relations internationales depuis 1938* (Paris: CNRS, 1994), pp. 93–109; E. Weber, 'Of Stereotypes and of the French', *Journal of Contemporary History*, 25 (1990), pp. 169–203.

66. The dossier is in AN, Papiers Daladier, 2DA4/3/b.

67. Daladier post-war ms note, AN, Papiers Daladier, 2DA4/3/b.

68. In addition to Fraser's reports, cited earlier, see War Office to Strang, 17 November 1938, containing extracts of a letter from Fraser, 18 October 1938, PRO, FO 371/21592/C14067/13/17.

69. 'Etude sur la participation de l'Angleterre dans l'éventualité d'une action commune franco-britannique en cas de guerre', 9 November 1938, SHAT, 7N2815. For Corbin, see Corbin to MAE, 8 November 1938, MAE, Europe 1930–1940, Grande-Bretagne, vol. 291.

70. 'Note concernant les demandes à présenter au Gouvernement Britannique relatives à l'action militaire terrestre', 23 November 1938, AN, Papiers Daladier, 2DA4/3/b.

71. Gamelin's copy with changes is in SHAT, 7N3438/3/3.

72. Young, *In Command of France*, pp. 222–3.

73. For Gamelin, see Notes on visit to France, 31 December 1938–3 January 1939, Hore-Belisha Papers, Churchill College Archives Centre, Cambridge, HOBE 5/45. For Gauché, see Fraser to Phipps, 18 January 1939, enclosed in Phipps to Foreign Office, 19 January 1939, PRO, FO 371/22961/C835/15/18.

74. The shock of staff officers is apparent in the diaries of General Edmund Ironside, who would become CIGS in September 1939. See Ironside Diaries, 1938, vol. 3, 3 September 1938, pp. 263–5; and 22 September 1938, p. 311, Trinity College Library, University of Toronto [hereafter TCUT]. I am grateful to Professor Wesley Wark for this information.

75. 'The role of the army in the light of the Czechoslovakian crisis', general staff paper, October 1938, PRO, CAB 21/510.

76. Pownall diary, 3 October 1938, B. J. Bond (ed.), *Chief of Staff: the Diaries of Lt. General Sir Henry Pownall* (2 vols, London: Leo Cooper, 1974), *i*, p. 164.

77. Ironside Diaries, 1938, vol. 4, 5 November 1938. TCUT. Also see notes on a meeting with General Herring, 31 December 1938–3 January 1939, HOBE 5/45.

78. 'Present policy in the light of recent developments', by Gort, 2 December 1938, PRO, CAB 21/510/COS 811. For pre-1914 planning, see S. R. Williamson, *The Politics of Grand Strategy: Britain and France Prepare for War, 1904–1914* (Cambridge, MA: Harvard University Press, 1969), pp. 167–204.

79. 'The state of preparedness of the army in relation to its role', by Hore-Belisha, 12 December 1938, PRO, CAB 53/43/1498-B.

80. 'The situation of the bomber force in relation to the principle of parity', air staff paper, 2 November 1938, PRO, AIR 8/246. By 1938 strategic bombing doctrine was already threatened by the Cabinet pressure to shift priority in air rearmament from bombers to fighters. See Newall to Simon, 7 November 1938, PRO, AIR 8/250.

81. Ludlow-Hewitt to under-secretary of state of air ministry, 25 May 1939, PRO, AIR 6/58. Also see M. Smith, *British Air Strategy Between the Wars* (Oxford: Oxford University Press, 1984), pp. 277–78.

82. COS 268th meeting, 18 January 1939, PRO, CAB 53/10. Also see CID, minutes of the 341st meeting, 15 December 1938, PRO, CAB 2/8; COS 265th meeting, 21 December 1938, PRO, CAB 53/10.

83. Pownall diary, 24 October 1938, Bond, *Chief of Staff*, *i*, pp. 167–8.

84. 'Note on Germany's present position and future aims', 7 January 1939, PRO, WO 190/748. Also see Beaumont-Nesbitt to Strang, 18 January 1939, PRO, FO 371/22915/C671/130/17.

85. For example, see War Office to Strang, 28 February 1939, which includes 'Note on German Military Situation', PRO, FO 371/22958/C2450/13/18. Also see Beaumont-Nesbitt to Strang, 12 January 1939, FO 371/22961/C718/15/18. For the Secret Service, see 'Compte-rendu de mission à Londres les 30 et 31 janvier et le 1er février 1939,' undated, SHAT, Archives récupérées de la Russie, 503/250.

86. Pownall diary, 23 January 1939, Bond, *Chief of Staff*, *i*, pp. 183–4.

87. For air staff doubts, see Slessor to CAS via DCAS, 24 January 1939, PRO, AIR 8/235.

88. Backhouse to Vice-Admiral Meyrick, 21 November 1938, PRO, ADM 205/3.

89. See S. Roskill, *Naval Policy Between the Wars, vol II: the Period of Reluctant Rearmament, 1930–1939* (London: Collins, 1976), p. 432; J. A. Maiolo, *The Royal Navy and Nazi Germany, 1933–39* (Basingstoke: Macmillan Press [now Palgrave Macmillan], 1998), pp. 132–59.

90. Backhouse to Ismay, 16 January 1939, PRO, CAB 21/511. For the navy's interest in co-operation in the Mediterranean, see Bridges to Cadogan, 25 November 1938, PRO, CAB 104/76.

6
Intelligence in Anglo-French Relations before the Outbreak of the Second World War

Peter Jackson and Joseph A. Maiolo

Before the outbreak of war in 1939 French and British strategic inter-ests converged over the growing threat of fascist revisionism in Europe. Although the two states pursued 'conflicting strategies of peace', leaders in both states understood the ultimate importance of co-operation to the future of Europe.[1] Yet efforts towards co-operation on both sides were often stymied by mutual incomprehension and even suspicion. Between the British and the French there existed profound political, cul-tural and geo-strategic differences that were difficult to overcome during the 1930s. A look at the role of intelligence in Franco-British relations sheds new light on the obstacles that stood in the way of effective co-operation between the wars.

There was no systematic collaboration in intelligence matters until the very eve of war. For French soldiers and statesmen the hope was that, quite apart from their practical utility, intelligence exchanges were an initial step towards a full-blown military alliance with the British. This was precisely what British policy-makers wished to avoid for most of the period in question. As a result the British defence establishment was extremely reluctant to pool its intelligence resources with those of France. But this reluctance created other problems for policy-makers on both sides of the channel. In particular, the French worried about Britain's willingness and ability to participate in another continental land war. Indeed, persistent uncertainty about British intentions was a major factor in French strategy and diplomacy in the pre-war decade. On the British side, Whitehall's unwillingness to enter into a closer rela-tionship with the French led to constant uncertainty about the fighting power of Britain's most important ally. As international tensions mounted after 1935, British policy-makers faced a sharpening dilemma. Acquiring the necessary information about French military intentions and capabilities meant increased co-operation with France's military establishment. This 'intelligence trap' was a constant problem for British strategic planning up to and beyond the outbreak of war in 1939. In this sense, the question of intelligence collaboration paralleled the larger pattern of political and military relations between the two states. In yet another such parallel, true co-operation was undertaken too late and without sufficient commitment.

The organization of intelligence in Britain and France

The organizational structures of the French and British intelligence communities significantly conditioned prospects for co-operation. Permanent, professional intelligence agencies were established in Britain and France in the late-nineteenth century to meet the increasing demand for information about the military capacities of foreign powers. Between the wars these agencies were still comparatively small and lacked the bureaucratic influence to set their own agenda for co-operation with other states. Moreover, the near-monopoly of the military services over intelligence activity in France added to the obstacles to systematic collaboration. Official and political opinion in Britain opposed any on-going co-operation with the French military.

During the 1930s the only permanent foreign intelligence agencies in France were the Deuxième Bureaux of the army, the navy and the air-force general staffs.[2] These were charged with providing their various staffs and ministries with up to date assessments of the strategic situation. The army Deuxième Bureau was by far the largest and best funded. It also produced the most comprehensive studies of international political and military issues. The Deuxième Bureaux of the naval and air staff tended to focus more narrowly on foreign sea and air power respectively. There was no intelligence agency charged specifically with reporting on economic and industrial issues. This task was instead the responsibility of the Secrétariat Général of the Conseil Supérieur de la Défense Nationale, the body charged with planning France's mobilization for war.

France's chief secret service, the Service de Renseignements [SR], was formally attached to the army Deuxième Bureau. The SR was funded by the war ministry (reorganized as the ministry of national defence in 1936) and its commanding officer was responsible both to the army high command and to the minister of war. Its responsibilities included both the management of agent networks (human intelligence) and the interception and analysis of foreign telegrams and radio traffic. Secret intelligence was not the exclusive preserve of the army, the naval staff also operating a secret service. But this agency was comparatively tiny and chronically under-funded. Most secret intelligence-gathering abroad was undertaken by the army SR. Through the SR the army also played an important role in French counter-intelligence. The SR offices on the Avenue de Tourville in Paris also included a counter-intelligence section, the Section de Centralisation des Renseignements [SCR]. This unit acted with the Sûreté Générale (after 1936 the Sûreté Nationale) and the Paris Préfecture de Police to combat foreign espionage and revolutionary subversion.[3]

The military thus dominated intelligence activity in France. The French foreign ministry did not possess its own secret intelligence service. It did operate a code-breaking service of its own, the Cabinet Noir, but this co-operated only sporadically with the SR signals intelligence unit. The Quai d'Orsay did, however, receive a steady flow of secret intelligence through daily briefings with SR officers. And the SR, in turn, depended on foreign ministry co-operation to gather intelligence outside of France.

While the focus of French intelligence services was unquestionably Germany, intelligence officers were posted in all capitals where France possessed embassies or important legations. Among the most important and prolific of these were military, naval and air attachés. These service attachés were responsible for producing wide-ranging reports on the political, economic and military situation in the states to which they were posted. These reports were based predominantly on open sources. Service attachés in London, who additionally functioned as liaison officers between the French and British military establishments, were central to the intelligence-sharing and staff conversations that occurred in the 1930s.[4] Of the various French attachés posted in London during the 1930s, the most important was unquestionably military attaché Albert Lelong. Assigned to the London embassy in 1936 at the express request of General Maurice Gamelin, chief of the French army general staff, Lelong cultivated excellent relations with the British General Staff. His frequent and well-informed reports on British political and military affairs reached the French army high command and the government.[5]

Relations between French attachés and their British hosts were generally very good.[6] French secret intelligence work against Britain, conversely, was very circumscribed between the wars. The SR did not post one of its officers to London. It does appear to have had one *correspon-dant isolé* in Britain, but this agent focused on gathering intelligence on Germany.[7] A study was prepared on the prospects for gathering secret intelligence in Britain in October 1932. In this report the SR noted that the Special Commissioner of the Sûreté Générale in Calais, who travelled to London frequently to liaise with the French embassy about counter-espionage, was also involved 'on occasion' in 'proper intelligence work'. His information was based on 'numerous contacts with hotel personnel in London'. These sources, the report noted, 'could be extremely useful in the case the SR should decide to open a post at Calais in order to gather intelligence in Great Britain'. Such a post would focus on collecting information about Germany, it was added, 'unless new instructions were received'. No evidence has turned up that this project was ever put into operation.[8]

Another potential source of secret information on British policy was signals intelligence. Between the wars both the *cabinet noir* (the code-breaking unit within the French foreign ministry) and the *service d'é-coutes* (the SR signals intelligence section) successfully decrypted a large volume of foreign diplomatic correspondence, including that of Britain, Germany and Italy. From 1918 through to the mid-1920s French signals intelligence succeeded in breaking high-grade British diplomatic ciphers.[9] By the 1930s, however, this source appears to have dried up. The available archival evidence suggests that by the early 1930s neither diplomatic nor military code-breakers were able to crack the highest-grade British ciphers. French cryptanalysts had access only to the 'R' code, a low-grade Foreign Office cipher used for transmissions that were not highly sensitive. Signals intelligence could provide little information on high policy in London.[10]

The synthesis and analysis of incoming intelligence was performed by the analytical sections of the three services' Deuxième Bureaux. The assessments produced by these sections normally travelled through the machinery of the general staff and high command before reaching civilian authorities at the service ministries. The important exception to this rule were the reports of army, naval and air attachés, which were also forwarded directly to the respective war, air or *marine* ministers as a matter of routine. Apart from these reports, it was very rare even for senior intelligence officers to have direct access to civilian decision-makers. Intelligence reached these *décideurs* primarily through high-ranking military officials.[11]

One important feature of the French intelligence community during this period, which has direct relevance to intelligence co-operation with

Britain, was the absence of any permanent inter-departmental committee charged with co-ordinating army, air and naval intelligence work.
Although various information-sharing arrangements were introduced at
times during the 1930s, there was no permanent organ responsible for
producing overall assessments. Such a body might have provided intelligence with a measure of independence within the French government
bureaucracy in the same way that the Joint Intelligence Committee
secured a voice for British intelligence during the Second World War.
Instead, France's intelligence services remained in relative isolation
within the service general staffs. Systematic co-operation with French
intelligence would therefore mean collaboration with the French
military.

In Britain a range of agencies belonging to different departments were
responsible for the collection, analysis and dissemination of intelligence. Political intelligence was the preserve of the Foreign Office.
Intelligence on military issues was the responsibility of the Military
Intelligence Directorate at the War Office, assessments of foreign maritime power were the purview of the Naval Intelligence Directorate at
the Admiralty, and estimates of the situation in the air were prepared
by the Air Intelligence Directorate at the air ministry. Assessments of
the industrial and overall economic situation were prepared by the
Industrial Intelligence Centre [IIC], which was constituted as a sub-
committee to the Committee of Imperial Defence. Although these
various intelligence agencies shared the common task of building up an
accurate image of the international military situation, 'they approached
their work with an extreme individualism'.[12] There was insufficient
information-sharing and general co-operation between army, naval
and air intelligence, and the Foreign Office jealously guarded its near
monopoly over political intelligence. This was in contrast to the situation in France, where there was both daily liaison and systematic
exchanges of assessments between the three service intelligence departments and the Quai d'Orsay.

There were important distinctions between French and British intelligence machinery. The most important was that in Britain secret intelligence was controlled by the Foreign Office. The Secret Intelligence
Service [SIS] and the British signals intelligence agency, the Government
Codes & Ciphers School [GC&CS], were attached to the Foreign Office.
SIS and GC&CS collected raw intelligence for the foreign ministry and
the intelligence directories. Secret information was integrated into the
policy process primarily through the analyses prepared by these agencies. Direct contact between the head of SIS, Admiral Hugh Sinclair, or

his deputy, General Stewart Menzies, and political leaders was probably even more rare in Britain than it was in France.[13]

Another key difference was that there was a trend towards greater centralization in Britain. In 1919 British signals intelligence had been amalgamated into the GC&CS. In France, conversely, the code-breaking departments at the Quai d'Orsay and at the ministry of war worked independently and with insufficient co-ordination throughout the inter-war period.[14] The first measures aimed at centralizing the British intelligence community as a whole were made in the mid-1930s with the formation of first the Inter-Service Intelligence Committee and then in 1936 its successor, the Joint Intelligence Sub-Committee [JIC] of the Chiefs of Staff Committee. Initially the JIC was assigned the rather narrow remit of preparing studies of specific military issues for the Chiefs of Staff Joint-Planning Sub-Committee. Through to the summer of 1939 it remained 'on the periphery' of Whitehall policy-making. This changed in July of that year when the JIC assumed responsibility for the assessment of all available political and military intelligence and its chairmanship passed to a Foreign Office official. From this point forward Britain possessed the only intelligence machinery in the world capable of 'all source analysis'.[15]

British secret intelligence gathering in France appears to have been limited to the activities of the SIS officers posted to the Paris embassy as passport-control officers. The SIS station chiefs in Paris during the 1930s were first Maurice Jeffes and then, from late 1937, Commander Wilfred 'Biffy' Dunderdale. The chief responsibility of the SIS station, which would have been performed with the co-operation of the SR, was doubtless to gather information on left-wing revolutionary organizations operating in western Europe. But the station would also have been responsible for gathering information and preparing reports on the situation inside France.[16]

Something that bears emphasis is that the size, organization and location of the intelligence services within the British and French official bureaucracies made an 'intelligence alliance' all but impossible. When compared to the intelligence machinery that emerged in Britain and the United States during the second world war, the inter-war intelligence communities were small, lacked institutional independence and were thus unable to establish regular liaison outside the normal channels of diplomatic and military contact. In France the intelligence services were so firmly embedded within the military apparatus that systematic co-operation between SIS and the Deuxième Bureau implied on-going staff conversations. This was anathema to most of Britain's political and military leadership, and so systematic intelligence liaison had to wait until war with Germany appeared close.

The British intelligence trap

The British were severely limited in their understanding of French capabilities and strategic interest. After all, Nazi Germany was the chief target and had first call on the resources available to British intelligence. The prime sources on the French armed services were the service attachés and, for the most part, these attachés could only report on what their hosts allowed them to see. The French were always willing to open up to the British, but at a price. The British were therefore caught in an intelligence trap: London could not obtain information by covert means nor could it exchange information with Paris for fear of being lured into an unwanted military commitment. The consequences of this intelligence trap emerged clearly in early 1938. In preparation for the arrival of French ministers to London in April 1938, the deputy secretary of the Committee of Imperial Defence discovered to his great dismay that one report frankly admitted that the Germans and Italians were better informed about the French army than were the British. He complained that 'it is intolerable that we should not have the same means of obtaining information about the French army as have the Germans and Italians, and that we should have to rely on "surmise" '.[17]

The consequences of the intelligence trap were even more striking when it came to evaluations of French air power. British fears of a 'French air menace' had helped to shape overall strategic policy in the early 1920s. The late 1920s were a period of stagnation for French military aviation. In 1932, however, evidence of its revival actually raised concerns about the security of the British Isles and led to an intensification of diplomatic efforts to abolish bombing. That year, French air-force officers courted the British air attaché with a special invitation to secret air exercises. His report of a public exhibition of new airframes and aero-engines added to the impression that France was resolved to regain its position as the dominant air power on the continent.[18] But this impression was short-lived. In 1933–34, despite the Armée de l'Air achieving independent status within the French defence establishment, the attaché had little of substance to report, particularly concerning technical and industrial matters.[19] This state of affairs changed dramatically after Hitler announced the Luftwaffe's existence to the world in March 1935 and claimed that it had already achieved parity with Britain's Royal Air Force. The British now had to ponder a question vital to their own safety: was the French air force powerful enough to deter Hitler? In August of that year Pierre Laval assured Anthony Eden personally that the Armée de l'Air was second to none. But this failed to impress the Foreign Office, which had already received worrying contraindications from 'confidential sources'. Over the next three years a steady stream of information would reach Whitehall that exposed a huge gulf between what various French politicians said about French air strength and what the British were prepared to believe. Complaining of a want of French 'frankness' the Foreign Office's Central Department turned to the air ministry and the IIC for more reliable information.[20]

The assessments the Foreign Office received were not comforting. Rather than making a positive contribution to European security by deterrence, French weakness in the air was becoming a significant destabilizing factor. An IIC report to ministers in October 1935 predicted that

> French aircraft factories, which at the moment appear to be behind both Germany and Great Britain in matters of design, will not be in a position to re-equip the French air force with really satisfactory types of aircraft for some years to come.[21]

Qualitatively, the problem was the over-development of prototypes to the point of obsolescence. This was exacerbated by a doctrinal tension between proponents of an independent and large-scale bombing role for the air force and advocates of making close support for ground operations the first priority in French air doctrine. With some exceptions (most notably the Morane 405 fighter) this debate resulted in poor multi-purpose designs unsuitable for either role. Quantitatively, the problem was the fragmented and artisanal state of France's aircraft industry, which had coped badly with the transition to modern mass production of all-metal airframes.[22] Further studies by the IIC and the Air Ministry in 1936 confirmed the breadth and depth of large-scale industrial failure.[23] But establishing the big picture was not the challenge; the real difficulty was instead obtaining accurate information on monthly aircraft production in order to project the future air balance. As the deputy director of air intelligence explained in late 1936: 'France has been particularly difficult to assess owing to a lack of information on the progress of the creation of certain new [squadrons], which appears to be considerably behind and also owing to the delayed and uncertain deliveries of new aircraft'.[24]

It was against this background that the air ministry and Foreign Office initially welcomed the reappointment of Pierre Cot as French air minister and the nationalization and centralization of the aircraft industry introduced by France's Popular Front government during the autumn of 1936. The IIC interpreted this as 'less a political than a practical step' that was necessary to restore the productive capacities of the aero-industry in France.[25] In early 1937 Group Captain Douglas Colyer, the British air attaché, praised Cot for his energy and sense of direction. He went as far as to predict that the coming years would see 'the French air force established as a much improved instrument of war and as an adversary not lightly to be reckoned with'.[26] Indeed Pierre Cot had hoped to transform the Armée de l'air into a powerful strategic bombing force, designed to win a coalition war with Britain and Russia against Germany and Italy. His efforts at rationalization laid the foundations for the marked revival of French aircraft production in 1939. But the initial dislocation and the rapid plunge in aircraft output caused by these radical measures left him vulnerable to political attacks. To defend his position, Cot inflated the performance of the French aircraft industry and the size of the air force in public and before various parliamentary committees. At the same time, he manipulated intelligence on the growth of the Luftwaffe.[27] This politicization damaged not only French air policy, but also Anglo-French relations. London lost faith in Cot's ability and veracity.

In the second half of 1937, lacking reliable sources, the Foreign Office and the air ministry found it impossible to arrive at accurate output figures. But the air ministry knew enough to label information from Paris as 'misleading'. Estimates of monthly output handed to the Foreign Office in this period ranged from 25 [as claimed by Cot's political opponents] to 90 [IIC estimate] and 125 [Air Ministry estimate].[28] Anything claimed by Cot was dismissed out of hand. In reaction to a July 1937 analysis, which described the virtual collapse of French aircraft production, Vansittart called Cot 'a remarkable liar'. The deputy director of air intelligence agreed.[29] What troubled the Foreign Office was the possibility that the situation might actually be worse than it appeared. Equally vexing was uncertainty over how France was perceived by potential enemies. The British ambassador in Paris commented with alarm at the tendency of German and Italian diplomats to denigrate French military strength and national resolve. German or Italian calculations based on the weakness of French air power posed a clear threat to peace. 'The trouble is that however strong France may really be,' lamented one Foreign Office official, 'the outward and visible signs which she at present displays are those of weakness rather than strength'.[30]

Consequently, in early September 1937, the Foreign Office urgently required information pertaining to the following questions:

> (a) whether the Air Ministry are getting all the information they can about the French air force, so as to be really aware of the true value of their potential allies (b) whether we can do anything to make the French Government put an end to the muddle.

In response to the first question, Chamberlain advocated a full and frank exchange of information about the state of British and French aircraft production at a meeting with premier Camille Chautemps in November 1937. In respect to the second question, he offered technical assistance to help develop aircraft production in France.[31] The way in which Whitehall struggled with the first question is our primary concern as it illustrates the difficulties it had in breaking free of the intelligence trap *vis-à-vis* France.

Clearly, the available overt and covert sources had proved wanting. Yet what was the solution? A formal exchange between air staffs offered one way out, which would also help to ensure the supply of accurate first-hand intelligence; but this could only be done on a reciprocal basis. As the British foreign secretary, Anthony Eden, argued,

> it has to be remembered of course that if we ask the French about the progress of their air force they will also ask questions about ours, but I see no harm in this. After all we have undertaken to defend France if the latter is the victim of unprovoked aggression, and France has given a similar undertaking towards us. In the circumstances it is rather silly that we should not now exchange information fully and frankly.[32]

Such arguments, calculated to advance the policy of wider staff conversations, raised hackles in Whitehall. The issue divided the foreign secretary and his officials on the one hand, who supported close *entente* relations, and certain members of the Cabinet and the chiefs of staff on the other, who feared that talks would saddle Britain with a commitment to the defence of France and jeopardize a détente with Berlin. In this case, however, the intelligence dilemma on French air armaments and production proved to be too important to be shelved any longer despite the fear of the French initiating staff conversations by the back door. Although the Cabinet rejected the Foreign Office's calls for full staff talks, Eden's proposal did result in limited technical exchanges via the air attachés, which began in February 1938.[33]

The deadlock over staff talks is not only significant because it inhibited the formal acquisition of knowledge about Britain's chief ally, but also because it resulted in impressionistic assessments of French power in the debate over British policy. Advocates of close *entente* co-operation underscored French strengths and France's value as an ally. Critics of this policy stressed French weakness and unreliability. It was at this level that a range of assumptions about the French national character helped to shape attitudes towards the entente. As Michael Dockrill has illustrated in his fine study of British attitudes towards France, there was substantial sympathy for Germany and antipathy towards France among Britain's elites during this period. Even within the Foreign Office, which had the reputation of being more sympathetic to France than the rest of the British establishment, there was considerable incomprehension and frustration.[34]

Foreign Office proponents of closer ties with France knew that evidence of French feebleness made the case against the *entente* difficult to overturn with strategic logic. In late 1937 Eden cautioned against exaggerating French weakness in relation to the Axis and stressed that 'the French Air Force and the French Navy are today at least equal and in the case of the latter superior to the respective Italian forces.'[35] A few weeks later he wrote privately to Chamberlain attacking the 'tendency among some of our colleagues to under-estimate the strength of France. The recurrent political crises in that country seem to them evidence of fundamental weakness. I am myself convinced, however, and Phipps and others better qualified than I to express an opinion share that conviction, the French army is absolutely sound. . . .'[36]

The contradictions in British attitudes towards France are obvious. Part of the problem was that the French political spectrum was broader than the British, with less common ground between left and right; and the far left was much stronger and played a more central role in mainstream politics in France than it did in Britain. But the fact that British anxieties were exaggerated should not obscure the fact that within the British 'official mind' there existed deep-seated apprehensions regarding France's political stability. In the summer of 1936, for instance, foreign secretary Anthony Eden wrote that France appeared to be 'growing more "red"'.[37] Later that year the Cabinet secretary, Maurice Hankey, judged that France was 'inoculated with the virus of communism, which is at present rattling the body politics, delaying much needed rearmament and causing acute internal dissension. . . . In her present state she is not a very desirable ally.' Likewise the chairman of the Chiefs of Staff Committee (COS), Admiral Chatfield, considered that 'France, our only real support, is unreliable politically and militarily, especially the former'.[38] The British found themselves caught in an intelligence trap. These impressionistic and skewed assessments reveal just how scarce real knowledge of French capabilities and staying power was in policy formation. In March 1938, prime minister Neville Chamberlain and his ministers recognized the fact that they 'could not afford to see France destroyed'. At the same time, the foreign secretary, Lord Halifax, explained the only lever the British had on French action in Europe was to keep Paris 'guessing' about what Britain would do in the event of war.[39] Ironically enough, in their strategic assessments of the one continental state which they could not afford to see 'destroyed', it was the British who were doing all the 'guessing'.

Sporadic co-operation until 1939

It would be misleading, however, to conclude from Britain's reluctance to co-operate systematically with French that no co-operation took place at all. There were, for example, exchanges concerning the situation in Europe, with the French usually providing the British with more information than they received in return. There was also extensive ad hoc co-operation between intelligence officials outside of Europe. From Tangier to Shanghai the security services of the world's two largest empires collaborated on a wide-range of issues from gun-running to drug smuggling to combating the ubiquitous Comintern. This collaboration continued throughout the inter-war period. But, until the spring of 1939, this co-operation was not systematic nor institutionalized.[40] While there were informal meetings between top-ranking intelligence officials, and also extensive unofficial collaboration 'in the field', official co-operation was limited to informal exchanges of information.

Franco-British intelligence co-operation was undertaken primarily through service attachés, British secret-service officers in Paris and French Sûreté commissioners in Calais and Bordeaux. Among these, military attachés were the most important. Lelong, for example, regularly discussed wider European military and political issues with British officials and prepared detailed reports on their views for his superiors in Paris. In October 1937, for example, British general staff officers returning from the Wehrmacht manoeuvres (to which the French military attaché in Berlin had been granted very limited access) shared their impressions of German military effectiveness with Lelong.[41]

Beaumount-Nesbitt, the British military attaché, fulfilled the same role in France. Service attachés were also the logical conduit for the exchange of more detailed intelligence on questions such as the strength of the German army and the rate of German weapons production. The attachés were perhaps even more important since they served as the first point of contact when the French and British defence establishments consulted with one another during periods of crisis. When full-blown staff conversations began in the spring of 1939 the service attachés in London and Paris were central to this process.[42]

If attachés were the most prolific channel for information-sharing, secret intelligence officials were responsible for exchanging more sensitive information. Unfortunately, the available archival evidence gives no indication of how frequently high-ranking British and French secret-service officers met between 1933 and mid-1936. From June 1936 onward, however, the diary of SR chief Colonel Louis Rivet provides a valuable picture of the frequency of high-level intelligence liaison. It indicates that Rivet travelled once to London in February 1937 for three days, where he had several meetings with both French and British officials. It also reveals that Menzies made three separate two-day visits to Paris, in October 1936, October 1937 and January 1939.[43] There are, in total, twenty-three separate references to meetings with representatives from British intelligence between June 1936 and March 1939. The majority of interviews were between the SR and officials from MI5. Significantly, security concerns appear to have taken precedence over secret-intelligence co-operation at this juncture.[44]

Contacts with the SIS station were probably more frequent. The passport-control office would have served as the conduit through which secret intelligence on issues ranging from revolutionary movements to the German army was exchanged between the SR-SCR in Paris and MI5-SIS in London. According to Paul Paillole, who worked in the German section of the SCR during the mid- to late-1930s, SIS station chief 'Biffy' Dunderdale was a frequent visitor to the offices of the SR on the Avenue Tourville. Yet there are very few allusions to the activities of either Dunderdale or his predecessor Jeffes in the French primary sources. Rivet recorded only two meetings with Jeffes and only one meeting with Dunderdale between June 1936 and March 1939.[45]

The third mechanism of security liaison with the British services were the Special Commissioners of the Sûreté based in Calais and Bordeaux, the two main points of entry for both human and commercial traffic with Great Britain in the years between the wars. Both commissioners were accredited to the French embassy in London and worked in co-operation with MI5. While the activities of these two officials, including the specifics of their relations with both MI5 in London and the SCR in Paris, remain unclear, the available evidence suggests that co-operation, even in the realms of counter-espionage and counter-subversion, was not systematic.[46]

Significantly, the chief impetus for intelligence co-operation between Britain and France for most of the inter-war period appears to have been British anxieties concerning communist subversion in France. The conviction that French society was inherently unstable and therefore particularly vulnerable to communism reached its zenith in the mid-1930s with the advent of Popular Front movements in Europe. In the spring and summer of 1936 Popular Front governments were elected in France and Spain. Shortly thereafter civil war broke out in Spain and France was paralysed by a wave of strikes. The British ambassador in Paris spoke of the possible 'Sovietisation' of Britain's most powerful ally on the continent, a source of deep concern to officials in Whitehall.[47]

British overtures for security and counter-intelligence collaboration with France should be interpreted within this context. In keeping with the general character of intelligence liaison during this period, these overtures were only semi-official. In April 1935 Menzies (no doubt under Sinclair's orders) wrote a personal note to Rivet's predecessor as SR chief, Lt Colonel Henri Roux, about prospects for increased collaboration against Comintern activity. He warned Roux that, because the attention of both the British and French secret services was focused increasingly on Germany, 'we run the risk of losing sight of the growth of other movements which could suddenly, and to our surprise, assume crucial importance'. He reminded his French colleague that, when they had last met, he had warned of the 'danger' that would arise as a result of the transfer of the Comintern's western European headquarters from Berlin to Paris after the Nazi seizure of power. In a passage that provides rare insight into the mindset of Britain's intelligence leadership, he warned that

> I am convinced that we would be taking a terrible risk if we do not keep a careful watch over the machinations of an organisation whose intentions are, in the final analysis, indubitably just as dangerous as those of our neighbours to the north.

The Comintern 'section for anti-British activities in India' was 'without any doubt' based in Paris. 'We have proof,' Menzies added, 'that the revolutionary activity of industrial workers here is controlled by instructions from various international committees in Paris'. He concluded by urging that:

> We must find some method of closer collaboration in order to acquire a more complete knowledge of this movement so that when the moment comes – and come it surely will – we will be in a position to advise our respective authorities as to the best methods to combat this enemy that resides in our midst.[48]

Despite the ever-increasing threat posed by Nazi rearmament, British intelligence remained deeply preoccupied with left-wing activities in Europe. The extent to which this preoccupation influenced assessments of the Nazi threat remains an open question. Yet it seems clear that it did lead to a greater willingness to share sensitive information with French intelligence.

Rivet responded to this missive by requesting whatever details the British had concerning Comintern activities in France. Menzies obliged by forwarding a 'Schedule of the principal revolutionary organisations operating from France but under the direct control of Moscow'. This report, most probably compiled by SIS counter-intelligence 'Section V' in co-operation with MI5, provided intelligence on the structure, location and activities of various Comintern or Comintern-sponsored organizations in Paris. It also included a list of 'key men' working for the Comintern in Paris. Menzies went so far as to suggest that 'it is possible that you may, now or later, find it advantageous in your own and our interests to pursue a more energetic policy' towards the foreign nationals on this list. The most prominent of these were Comintern leaders Willi Munzenburg and Otto Katz (both of whom were already under constant surveillance by the SCR).[49] The fragmentary nature of French intelligence records from this period makes it impossible to say how this information was used or what intelligence was sent to London in exchange. It does however reveal the importance attached to counter-subversion by the Whitehall establishment.

The Spanish conflict was another issue over which there was communion of views between British and French intelligence. French intelligence officials, like the majority of the French defence establishment, opposed all forms of intervention in the Spanish imbroglio.[50] There was a fairly regular exchange of views between French and British service attachés posted to Spain during the civil war. The reports on the war compiled by the French military attaché, Lt Colonel Henri Morel, often include accounts of conversations with various British officials in Spain.

Menzies visited Paris in October 1937 to exchange views over the civil war in Spain.[51] These exchanges in some ways parallelled Franco-British co-operation over the problematic question of non-intervention. The British government was willing to make common cause with France in order to ensure that the French adopted a policy line similar to its own.[52]

The report prepared for the high command by Rivet after Menzies' visit in October reveals the considerable restraints on secret-intelligence sharing at this stage. Menzies had requested information on the German army, on Italian activities in the Mediterranean, on the war in Spain, and on the climate of opinion in France regarding intervention in Spain. According to Rivet, '[t]he intelligence furnished to Colonel Menzies did not go beyond the level of practical exchanges between the SR and the [Secret] Intelligence Service'. This was because 'only the high command has the authority to furnish the [British] general staff with this information'. Consequently, 'the SR limited itself to summary responses' to questions concerning Germany, Italy and Spain. Intelligence on these issues was no doubt being withheld in the hopes of drawing the British into staff conversations. 'If necessary,' Rivet observed, 'more detailed responses can be communicated to the [S]IS, with the permission of the general staff'. He added that '. . . it would doubtless make sense to provide fuller information, given the common interest in these issues shared by the French and British staffs'.[53] The hope was that this interest would be recognized in London.

There was also co-operation in the attack on the Enigma enciphering machine used by the German ministry of defence, armed services and police forces to ensure the security of their communications. In order to decrypt these messages it was necessary to work out the settings of code-wheels. Intercepting and deciphering Enigma communications proved impossible for both French and British code-breakers during the 1930s.[54] A glimmer of hope appeared when the SR recruited Hans-Thilo Schmidt in 1931. Schmidt was a German who worked in the cipher branch of the German defence ministry, and whose brother, Rudolph Schmidt, was a rising star within the Reichswehr general staff. Over the course of the next nine years, in addition to selling the SR high-grade intelligence on German intentions, Schmidt also provided an instruction manual and regular collections of the daily key settings for the Enigma machine. These documents were examined by both SR and foreign ministry crypanalysts, who were unable to solve the Enigma puzzle. Major Gustave Bertrand, the head of SR signals intelligence, decided to cast his net wider and in December 1931 copies of the documents were forwarded to the British GC&CS through the SIS station in Paris. But the British were also unable to make much headway with the documents provided by Schmidt, and informed Bertrand that more precise and information was needed to break into German Engima traffic. Bertrand then tried the Biuro Szyfrów of the Polish general staff. Polish code-breakers exercised greater patience with the material than their French and British counterparts. Thanks mainly to a steady flow of documents from Schmidt, and the efforts of a brilliant young mathematician named Marian Rejewski, the Poles were eventually able to solve the problem of the wiring of the code-wheels. A replica of the Enigma machine was reconstructed along with a 'cryptographic Bombe'. Using these machines the Poles were able to decrypt Enigma traffic from 1933 through to mid-1938. But they revealed the secret of their success neither to the French nor the British.[55]

At the 'official' level, reciprocity and friendliness usually governed the Franco-British relationship. High-level visits took place; at least ten British army officers served annually in French units; the military attaché had privileged access to the French general staff; and three service attachés could inspect French weapons in production – at least those not on the 'secret list' – and they had better access to French manoeuvres than other foreign observers.[56] This all provided first-hand if largely impressionistic intelligence.[57] But official channels have a serious limitation; they are open to image management. More often than not, British officers saw what the French wanted them to see because, as Martin Alexander has shown, Gamelin and the rest of the French establishment were keen to manipulate British impressions of French power. Special treatment was therefore more a means of encouraging *entente* solidarity than an expression of that solidarity. As a result British statesmen and strategists, reluctant to be drawn into a military commitment to France but unable to fully penetrate beyond the image to the reality of French power, were caught in an intelligence trap: in an increasingly hostile world, France could not be a prime intelligence target, and yet high-level staff talks with a full and frank exchange of information (as opposed to the limited, low level talks of 1935–7) were always a step too far.

Worse still, as mentioned above, intelligence offered by the French was greeted with scepticism in London given the propensity of the Deuxième Bureau to inflate estimates either to protect the French defence budget or to convince the British of an imminent threat to European security. Although there were important exceptions, a few examples of the negative impact of French behaviour will suffice. In 1932, French secret documents supplied by the French prime minister were of more interest to MI3 for the insight gained into the 'meagre' French sources rather than as evidence of illegal German rearmament.[58] In 1933–4, French reports of assembled U-boats were correctly judged by the Admiralty to be wrong.[59] In 1934, the War Office and Foreign Office concluded that French figures for German army strength were 'exaggerated' as were French anxieties that Germany would be ready for the offensive by 1935.[60] Credibility, so swiftly squandered, recovers very slowly. Although there were some exchanges about Germany and Italy, a trade in high-quality intelligence that might have generated a virtuous cycle of formal and regular co-operation did not develop, partly because of the longstanding British fear that sensitive information would invariably be leaked to the press by the French. Chamberlain, for example, articulated the widespread belief that France 'never can keep a secret for more than half an hour'.[61]

Yet intelligence exchanges with France became steadily more important to the British services as Germany emerged as a clear and increasingly imminent threat to British interests. While French defence planning had concentrated on Germany almost since 1919, Britain's strategic priorities were more diffuse. The German threat did not become an overwhelming priority until the late-1930s. Consequently, British intelligence lacked sources of its own inside Germany when the Nazi regime introduced its massive rearmament programmes after 1933. The occasional pooling of information and exchange of impressions of foreign military power was therefore a constant feature in relations between French and British military intelligence during the 1930s. While French assessments of the situation in Germany were treated with scepticism, they were also frequently integrated into British strategic assessments. According to Sir Harry Hinsley, it was common practice for the British military intelligence [MI] to defer to French appreciations of the state of the German army. In the autumn of 1933, for example, the army Deuxième Bureau sent the British MI a strategic estimate which predicted that Germany would be ready for war by 1938. This judgement was adopted by the CIGS during the Defence Requirements Committee enquiry in November 1933 and thus played a significant role in Britain's longer-term strategic calculations.[62] In addition, information from French air intelligence was central to early British assessments of German air rearmament. In May 1934 the air-force Deuxième Bureau forwarded a report on the pace of Germany's clandestine air build-up which predicted that the Reich would possess a force of 500 first-line military aircraft by the summer of 1934. This estimate served as a basis for RAF calculations of the future air balance.[63]

A more pessimistic estimate, which predicted a first-line Luftwaffe of 1300 planes by 1936, was given to the British air attaché the following October. This appreciation agreed with intelligence obtained by the Foreign Office and contributed to a more alarmist view of German air power that was to play an important role in Whitehall thinking through to the summer of 1939.[64]

The War Office and the French army general staff continued to exchange views periodically through to the summer of 1938. But these exchanges were never made a matter of routine even during the conversations that took place between the British and French service staffs between 1935 and late 1938. Despite persistent French efforts, intelligence-pooling on German and Italian intentions and capabilities proceeded only intermittently on an *ad hoc* basis. The lone partial exception to this trend was collaboration between the French and British air staffs. This development was stimulated by the increasing anxiety with which both French and British statesmen viewed the situation in the air. In February 1937 the British and French air ministries formally agreed to exchange intelligence on the Luftwaffe and eventually extended this arrangement to sharing information on potential bombing targets in Germany. Once again, the need for information that only the French were in a position to provide led Whitehall to enter into a closer relationship with the French armed services than it would have liked. The arrangement was thus carefully circumscribed. The British air ministry made clear that these contacts were strictly limited to an exchange of technical information and did not imply a larger political commitment to provide automatic air assistance to France in the event of war.[65]

The case of the relationship between British and French naval intelligence provides an excellent illustration of this pattern of intermittent and uneven information-sharing. The regular exchange of naval information was established at the Washington Naval Conference in 1921–22 and reinforced by the subsequent London Naval Conference in 1930. According to the system states would provide other signatories with information about the specifications of their warships as well as details of their naval construction programmes. This system constituted the chief source of information on foreign naval power for both Britain and France through to the mid-1930s. However, as war with Italy in the Mediterranean became a distinct possibility during the autumn of 1935, the British Admiralty became suddenly desperate for full French co-operation. The Laval government initially hesitated to provide immediate and unstinting support to Britain because it had just forged a military alliance with Italy. These hesitations enraged officials in London who were characteristically convinced that they had a clearer grasp of France's interests than did the French themselves.[66] The French government eventually bowed to British pressure, however, backing international sanctions against Italy and entering into staff conversations in view of a possible war in the Mediterranean. An important component to these talks was a very extensive regime of information exchange which covered the disposition of Italian warships, the strength of Italy's coastal defences, the capacities of its naval installations, its fuel supplies, the location and size of its airfields and even the activities of its wireless and telegraph stations. These measures, which included the exchange of intelligence liaison officers, continued throughout the crisis. It constituted potentially the first step towards an integrated system of intelligence exchange.[67]

For the British, however, memories of 1914 and a reluctance to be drawn further down the road towards a continental commitment proved stronger than the need to co-operate. In April 1936 this system was scaled back at the insistence of the Admiralty to a monthly exchange of information on the disposition of warships. After civil war erupted in Spain the French attempted to revive a fuller programme of intelligence exchange. The deputy chief of staff of the French navy, Admiral François Darlan, travelled to London in early August 1936. The prime motive of this voyage was to initiate fuller collaboration between the two navies against the possibility of German and especially Italian action in the Mediterranean in support of General Franco. This was anathema to both political and naval circles in London. Darlan was refused an audience with the First Lord of the Admiralty, Samuel Hoare, and the Cabinet Secretary, Maurice Hankey. He was then forced to visit the Admiralty in plain clothes, without any formal introduction. Darlan's proposals for the immediate establishment of an 'extensive programme of intelligence exchange on the international situation' received a very frosty reception from naval chief of staff Admiral Ernle Chatfield.[68]

Another effort to bolster intelligence co-operation was made by French naval chief of staff Admiral Georges Durand-Viel the following November. Durand-Viel advised the British naval attaché in Paris that German, Italian and Soviet intervention in Spain might lead to 'incidents in the Mediterranean that would require a co-ordinated Franco-British response'. Intelligence-sharing would be a crucial prerequisite to such co-ordination. Chatfield rebuffed this request, remarking that 'the British naval staff could not collaborate more closely with the

French naval staff without reference to higher political authority'. Commenting on this exchange, an Admiralty staff officer noted: 'The French staffs, true to their traditional policy of trying to tempt us with an alliance or understanding, were always keener on staff talks than the British.'[69] Over the next two years, the Admiralty led the opposition to enhanced intelligence exchanges (or any other form of conversation) with the French. Chatfield and the naval staff consistently opposed British involvement in any war before the Admiralty's rearmament programme bore fruit. In May 1938 Captain Victor Dankwerts, head of the Royal Navy's planning division, advised that only 'a very meagre exchange of information' should be forwarded to the French staff.[70] Admiralty planners took it for granted that once the *Marine* had completed its first task of escorting colonial troops safely to metropolitan France, its heavy units would become available to fit into the Royal Navy's plans with very limited pre-war preparation.[71] Not until the spring of 1939 was intelligence co-operation re-established between the two navies on the scale that had prevailed during the Ethiopian crisis.

To sum up, intelligence co-operation against common threats down to the summer of 1938 was not negligible. There were episodes of fairly extensive intelligence-sharing. But the course of these exchanges was determined by the political context of Franco-British relations. The French search for a more substantial commitment led to a greater willingness among the intelligence services to pool their resources with those of Great Britain. British policy-makers, conversely, wished to avoid such a commitment while at the same time acquiring whatever information they could about both French and Axis military preparedness. They also wished to shore up the French government against the perceived threat of left-wing subversion. These considerations determined the extent of intelligence collaboration. The British intelligence services co-operated with the French only sporadically and over these specific issues. Accordingly, permanent mechanisms or standing procedures designed to facilitate effective collaboration did not emerge. The limited nature of this co-operation becomes more apparent when it is compared to French intelligence relationships with other European states. The Deuxième Bureau collaborated far more closely with Polish, Czechoslovak, Belgian and even Italian military intelligence than it did with the British services.[72] The development of anything close to an 'intelligence alliance' would only be possible when Britain made the all-important political commitment of comprehensive staff conversations in the spring of 1939.

To the eve of war

If the level of intelligence co-operation through to the summer of 1938 was circumscribed, by the outbreak of war France and Britain had established wide-ranging procedures that extended from the co-ordination of both counter- and signals intelligence work to the pooling of information gleaned from prisoners of war. Yet these arrangements remained hampered by a stubborn reluctance to accept fully the need for comprehensive intelligence collaboration.

The catalyst for enhanced co-operation was the radicalization of Hitler's policies in the spring and summer of 1938. Successive crises delivered a serious challenge to the policy of appeasement and led to close collaboration between the French and British military establishments. During these crises the War Office gradually moved toward establishing the regular exchange of situation updates with the Deuxième Bureau through the military attachés in London and Paris. Lelong was summoned to the War Office for consultations after the purge of the German high command in February, the Anschluss in March and the May crisis. After each of these consultations he prepared a lengthy summary of British views for both Daladier and the army general staff.[73]

The volume of information exchanges increased dramatically as war threatened over Czechoslovakia the following summer, beginning in mid-August when Lelong produced three reports entitled 'Intelligence on Germany', based on information communicated to him at the War Office. The French general staff adopted the same procedure with the British military attaché in Paris, Colonel William Fraser.[74] By early September he was forwarding 'Information Bulletins from the War Office' every day in addition to constant updates on the political and military situation in Britain. The information bulletins consisted primarily of reports on German mobilization measures and troop movements. These were compared and contrasted with the more voluminous and comprehensive intelligence on activity in Germany collected along the French frontier, which was summarized and communicated to the War Office through Fraser in Paris.[75] The threat of war had provided a much-needed stimulus to intelligence-sharing.

But once this threat diminished so too did the flow of intelligence back and forth across the English Channel. From October to December 1938 the summaries of intelligence from the War Office ceased. They did not resume until more rumours of another German move eastward began to surface in the middle of December. Reporting on the British response to the earliest of these rumours, Lelong identified 'clear hardening of opinion towards the Axis' in both official and popular opinion, as well as a 'strong current of sympathy for France'. On 15 December he judged that '[a]t last one sees a widespread recognition of the need for close Franco-British collaboration in the face of further aggression.' In late December he relayed intelligence received by the British that pointed to a decline in Hitler's popularity.[76] On 4 January 1939 he met Beaumount-Nesbitt, now head of the MID, to discuss the state of the German army. The MID had calculated that Germany could field an army of 95 divisions after mobilization and sought the views of the Deuxième Bureau on this.[77]

From early January onward intelligence from the War Office became a regular feature in Lelong's reporting. At the same time, there was a corresponding increase in information exchanges between the French and British air staffs. An interesting and important aspect of these shared assessments was their basic agreement on a range of issues relating to Germany's strategic position. The most important of these were: first, that the German economy was in great difficulty; and, second, that popular morale was in decline. These perceptions, probably exaggerated, underpinned the long-war strategy that was designed during the Franco-British staff talks on the eve of war.[78]

British interest in French information was intensified in mid-January by rumours of a possible German move against the Low Countries. This provided the French soldiers and statesmen with an opportunity to drive home the need for greatly enhanced military collaboration. In the aftermath of Munich most French intelligence sources rightly indicated that Germany was preparing for another eastward move. By early 1939 these preparations were correctly identified as directed against what remained of Czechoslovakia. Yet the information forwarded to London by both the army general staff and the Quai d'Orsay pointed to a German attack in the west either through Belgium and Holland or through Switzerland. In a meeting with Fraser, army Deuxième Bureau chief Colonel Maurice Gauché stressed the difficulties France faced in preventing Germany from overrunning Belgium. He also warned of the danger that German submarine and air bases in the Low Countries would pose to a Franco-British coalition.[79] Daladier, too, expressed great concern to British Ambassador Eric Phipps over the possibility of a German offensive.[80] After receiving an alarmed note from the Foreign Office in late January, the Quai d'Orsay responded that:

The French government has received analogous information to that of His Majesty. Although it has yet to be confirmed, this information suggests that a German action, if initially oriented toward eastern Europe, could be directed either suddenly or in conjunction with Italian ambitions, toward the west, that is to say Great Britain, France, Belgium, the Netherlands and Switzerland.[81]

Significantly, however, there is no evidence that rumours of a German attack in the west were taken seriously by French intelligence during this period. Indeed, the Deuxième Bureau's focus on eastern Europe persisted down to the outbreak of war. Rivet's diary contains no reference whatsoever to a possible German invasion of the Low Countries in early 1939. The SIS station chief in Paris, who was in close contact with both Rivet and Gauché, reported correctly that French intelligence was 'entirely calm' and discounted rumours of impending German attacks in the west.[82]

The tactic succeeded brilliantly – despite SIS misgivings.[83] French information concerning German ground- and air-offensive intentions in the west corresponded with the disinformation emanating from the Abwehr and was received with great alarm by civilian decision-makers in London. Lord Halifax became convinced that war with Germany was imminent. He advised the foreign policy sub-committee of the Cabinet that Britain needed to revise its continental policy to prevent Germany from overrunning Holland and Belgium and establishing air bases within easy striking distance of England. The only way this could be accomplished was to enter into the close military relationship with France that British policy had steadfastly refused to consider since 1919. The Cabinet approved this decision, and on 29 January Britain proposed detailed staff conversations and joint military planning based on the hypothesis of war between and Anglo-French coalition and the Axis.[84] France thus obtained the continental military commitment from Britain it had sought since 1919.

On the surface, this episode appears to underline both the possibilities and the dangers that are inherent in intelligence-sharing. The exchange of information, particularly secret information, provides a tempting opportunity for manipulating the perceptions of other states. What is perhaps most interesting about this case, however, is that, in addition to exposing French duplicity, it also illustrates the enhanced co-operation that had developed between the British and French general staffs during the summer of 1938. Indeed the impetus for the French disinformation campaign appears to have come from London. The previous October British army chief of staff Sir Henry Pownall, frustrated by the Chamberlain government's refusal to recognize the need for a powerful continental army, instructed Fraser to 'have a nice chat' with Gamelin's chief of staff and to suggest that France intensify its pressure on London for a truly substantial BEF. The French responded with exaggerated reports of a German invasion in the west.[85]

The British proposal of staff conversations was the necessary stimulus to expanded co-operation between the intelligence services. The question came up during the first round of staff talks in early April. The French delegation raised the question of establishing a firm arrangement regarding intelligence-sharing. In its report on these meetings the British delegation asked the CIGS for 'authority to agree in the next stage of our conversations to the fullest exchange in time of peace of all forms of Service Intelligence, and to discuss arrangements whereby information can be exchanged in war with a minimum of delay'.[86] Two days later the JIC was ordered to prepare a study of ways and means to best organize the exchange of service intelligence. The resulting 'Note on the subject of the exchange of service intelligence' reflected the differing attitudes towards intelligence co-operation with France within the three services. The Admiralty was least enthusiastic about establishing closer ties with the naval Deuxième Bureau in Paris. The JIC noted that the intelligence exchange which had been on-going since the previous summer was considered sufficient by the Naval Intelligence Division and that no further measures were necessary. The air staff exhibited a much greater interest in increasing the level of information exchange with the French air force. It was observed that, while air-ministry intelligence was in close touch with the French air staff, these contacts had been limited primarily to an exchange of information about likely objectives of air attack. The JIC noted that these exchanges would now be expanded to 'an exchange of subjects covering a much wider field'. Particular importance was attached by the JIC to establishing mechanisms for the swift transmission of intelligence on Axis air-force deployment in the event of increased international tension. It was the Military Intelligence division of the War Office, however, that seems to have grasped the need for a truly joint intelligence effort against Germany. The MI representatives advocated that both British and French intelligence prepare studies of Axis military forces, war-making potential and political intentions. These would be exchanged and then serve as the basis for a conference between MI and Deuxième Bureau officials.[87] This suggestion by the MI was of singular importance. It marked the first step toward a possible system of jointly prepared assessments and thus the true co-ordination of the French and British intelligence efforts. Such a system was never achieved. But the principle of joint assessments is now considered absolutely central to effective co-operation and is a defining characteristic of the subsequent Anglo-American intelligence relationship.

The British commitment to France also appears to have stimulated increased collaboration between British and French secret intelligence. On 30 January 1939, only hours after Britain had extended a formal offer of staff conversations to France, deputy secret-service chief Commandant Malraison and the head of counter-intelligence, Captain Guy Schlesser, visited London to consult with their opposite numbers at SIS and MI5. The report produced by Schlesser upon his return to Paris paints a generally favourable picture of the state of British intelligence and the prospects for collaboration. At this meeting Colonel Vernon Kell advised Schlesser that '[Soviet] activity in England is non-existent, both in terms of intelligence and political subversion'. The real danger was instead the activity of German espionage, particularly in western Europe.[88]

From this meeting emerged perhaps the first major effort to co-ordinate French and British secret-intelligence operations in Europe since 1919. During their conference with Malraison and Schlesser in February, Menzies and Kell both expressed unhappiness with the situation in Holland. Schlesser agreed that 'German intelligence and counter-intelligence operates with confidence in Holland, where they benefit from the tolerance, and sometimes even the goodwill, of the local police'. Schlesser described the SIS station chief in The Hague, Major Richard Stevens, as 'an agent of remarkable finesse' who had 'recruited a team of twenty reliable agents' within the Dutch police. With the approval of Menzies, Stevens offered to place these agents at the disposal of the SR in Holland in exchange for access to the French network of spies run by the large intelligence post at Lille. The British further suggested reinforced surveillance of Germany's frontier with the Low Countries. Menzies proposed that SIS would cover the Dutch-German frontier if the SR would assume responsibility for Germany's borders with Luxembourg and Belgium.[89] On 24 February Stevens travelled down to Paris to meet with Rivet and the station chief at Lille in order to arrange the details of secret-service collaboration in Holland.[90] A lack of evidence makes it difficult to evaluate the results of this collaboration. What is clear, however, is that access to French agents did not prevent Stevens from being taken in by an elaborate intelligence plant set up by the *Sicherheitsdienst* (the security service of the German SS) in the autumn of 1939 – the notorious 'Venlo affair'.[91]

Relatively close collaboration probably continued in the domain of human intelligence from the outbreak of war until the fall of France in June 1940. Unfortunately, the fragmentary nature of the available documents makes it impossible to confirm this. Conversely, it is now possible to trace the outlines of an emerging Franco-British 'intelligence alliance' in the realm of signals intelligence. Indeed by far the most important co-operation between the two intelligence services, along with Polish intelligence, concerned the continued attack on the Enigma machine. A conference was eventually convened between Polish, French and British code-breakers in Poland in July 1939. Here the Poles revealed their previous success against the Enigma machine and offered to share their technology and methods with the French and the British. On 16 August two reconstructed Enigma machines along with two 'crypto-graphic bombes' arrived in Paris. Biffy Dunderdale was presented with one of each, which he personally escorted across the channel. A decisive step towards cracking the Enigma puzzle was thus taken.[92]

Co-operation did not end here. French and British cryptanalysts worked closely together, drawing on combined resources far greater than those available to the Poles. As work by Martin Thomas has shown, success against the Enigma was achieved in an atmosphere of very close 'working partnership' between Bletchley Park in Britain and PC Bruno in France. A Franco-British committee on telecommunications was established to link the French Inspection-Générale Technique des Trans-missions de la Défense Nationale with the British Wireless Telegraphy Board. This new committee was responsible primarily for co-ordinating the interception and distribution of German wireless traffic between British and French listening stations. Relations between the British and French signals-intelligence communities improved further during the Phoney War. By the spring of 1940 Enigma messages intercepted and decrypted in Britain were being forwarded immediately both to PC Bruno and to the general staff of the French army in the field. Similarly, intercepts decrypted by the French were forwarded directly to Bletchley Park.[93] Collaboration regarding the attack on the Enigma cipher was both intimate and on-going. Signals-intelligence co-operation between the British and French secret services survived the fall of France and lasted well into the Vichy period. It constituted perhaps the most impor-tant and durable aspect of the Franco-British intelligence alliance.

There was also extensive collaboration between the British and French authorities responsible for censorship, postal interception and the inter-rogation of prisoners of war. Censorship liaison officers were exchanged between the British Postal and Telegraphic Censorship Bureau and the

French Service des Contrôles des Correspondences. Arrangements were made to co-ordinate the interception of Axis and neutral state mail at the various postal and telegraph stations in Britain, France and in their imperial territories.[94] Arrangements for the systematic exchange of intelligence drawn from German prisoners were also hammered out on the eve of war – an important source of information on both the deployment of the Wehrmacht and the political and economic situation inside Germany.[95]

Collaboration in both the gathering and assessment of information was also a feature of a Franco-British committee established in May 1939 to co-ordinate planning for economic warfare against the Axis. Weeks later two separate French missions were established in London to co-ordinate purchases from neutral states of raw materials vital to the German war effort. These were forerunners of the 26-member Mission Française en Angleterre de Guerre Economique, which was an inter-departmental liaison mission to the British ministry of economic warfare. The synthesis and analysis of industrial, financial and commercial intelligence was a central activity of the officials on these committees.[96]

Despite the evolution of systematic information-sharing, steps towards joint assessment and greater secret-service co-operation, reflex attitudes of rivalry and mistrust set clear limits on the extent of institutionalized collaboration. The JIC paper on intelligence co-operation discussed above stressed, for example, that 'in peacetime no revelation should take place of secret methods of obtaining information and in particular of cryptography'. When issuing this edict, the JIC appears to have been unaware of existing co-operation between the SR and SIS in France. Its prescription regarding cryptography was also superseded by close collaboration in the attack on Enigma. But it does reveal Whitehall's deep-seated hesitancy in regard to security co-operation with France at this juncture. It is therefore not surprising that machinery for joint assessment of all intelligence by French and British analysts was never established. And there were also limits to signals-intelligence co-operation. Despite the progress made in the joint effort against the German cipher, both sides held back much information concerning their work against neutral states, as well as their successes against each other's ciphers.[97] Even as late as July 1939, amid intensive planning for a joint war effort, the JIC remained opposed to anything like an 'intelligence alliance', concluding that 'it is advisable to hand over as little as possible [to the French], provided that the maintenance of good relations is not prejudiced'.[98]

Conclusion

Undoubtedly Franco-British intelligence co-operation was nothing like the Anglo-American relationship both during and after the second world war. There were exchanges of information back and forth; for the most part, however, this consisted of the British sharing information they had acquired on communist subversion in France and the French providing intelligence on the growth of Germany's military power. There were no permanent French analysts in London or British analysts in Paris. Nor was there any attempt at joint assessment. Yet it is also important to remember that there were few precedents for the systematic sharing of secret information during peacetime. While France had already enjoyed a close intelligence relationship with Poland and particularly with Czechoslovakia, the institutional memories of co-operation in 1914–18, combined with the extensive nature of Franco-British war planning in the spring and summer of 1939, provided the foundations for the closest intelligence relationship to date. The mechanisms that were in place by the time war broke out in September 1939 were by far the most extensive peacetime intelligence-sharing arrangements in history.

In both Britain and France intelligence-sharing was subordinate to foreign policy. Indeed the foregoing analysis illuminates the hesitations and limitations that characterized Britain's commitment to the *entente* throughout the pre-war decade. Because British policy-makers misread the political situation in Europe, especially the prospects for reaching an agreement with Nazi Germany, they also misjudged the need to forge closer links with the French policy machine in general and the intelligence services in particular. Worse, they found themselves caught in an intelligence trap. Had the JIC or joint military planners issued full and systematic appraisals of France's strategic situation, had foreign-policy makers discussed the impact on France of Britain's German policy, then intelligence *might* have had the opportunity to inform policy-making by throwing the French strategic predicament into sharper relief. Even so, it is doubtful whether the Chamberlain government would have altered course. Britain's policy towards France was determined by its policy towards Germany. The imperative to avoid war and corresponding hopes for appeasement overrode Foreign Office arguments that co-operation with France was essential. Knowledge of France's military posture and strategic plans was not a priority until the Chamberlain government's commitment to appeasement wavered in the spring of 1939. The same is true of arguments for a 'full and frank exchange' with

France's intelligence community. Consequently, extensive and systematic pooling of information was not formalized until planning for war began in earnest in April 1939.

Notes

1. A. Wolfers, *Britain and France between Two Wars: Conflicting Strategies of Peace since Versailles* (New York: Harcourt, Brace and Co., 1940).
2. Where not otherwise stated, the following section on the organization of French intelligence is drawn from P. Jackson, *France and the Nazi Menace: Intelligence and Policy Making, 1933–1939* (Oxford: Oxford University Press, 2000), pp. 11–44.
3. 'Etude: Coopération directe pour certains départements particulièrement touchés par les questions de la Défense Nationale', no date but *circa* 1934, Service Historique de l'Armée de Terre [SHAT], Archives Récupérées de la Russie [ARR], 1388. Counter-intelligence in France was dismantled after the Dreyfus affair of the 1890s and only re-established during the first world war. On the fortunes of military intelligence from 1871 to 1918 see D. Porch, *The French Secret Services: From the Dreyfus Affair to the Gulf War* (Basingstoke: Macmillan [now Palgrave Macmillan], 1995) pp. 54–118 and O. Forcade, 'Renseignement et histoire militaire: Etat des lieux', in P. Lacoste (ed.) *Le Renseignement à la française* (Paris: Economica, 1998), pp. 49–78.
4. On the role of the attaché see M. Vaïsse, 'L'Évolution de la fonction d'attaché militaire en France au XXe siècle', *Relations Internationales*, 32 (1982), pp. 507–24; M. Alexander, 'Perspectives on Intra-Alliance Intelligence', *Intelligence and National Security*, 13 (1998), pp. 4–7.
5. For more on Lelong's career and role see M. S. Alexander, *The Republic in Danger: General Maurice Gamelin and the Politics of French Defence, 1933–1940* (Cambridge: Cambridge University Press, 1992), pp. 47 and 266–78.
6. M. S. Alexander and W. J. Philpott, 'The Entente Cordiale and the Next War: Anglo-French Views on a Future Military Co-operation, 1928–39', *Intelligence and National Security*, 13 (1998), pp. 659–60 and 675.
7. 'Liste des posts SR en temps de paix', 1925, SHAT 7N2486/1, and 'Comptes-rendus du renseignements' (for 1939), SHAT 7N2570/1.
8. 'Note sur les relations en Angleterre', 15 October 1932, SHAT, ARR, 152/1428.
9. C. Andrew, 'Déchiffrement et diplomatie: le cabinet noir du Quai d'Orsay sous la Troisième République', *Relations Internationales*, 5 (1976), esp. pp. 59–63.
10. Transcripts of British 'R' intercepts (labelled 'chiffre alla' by the *cabinet noir*) are in Ministère des Affaires Etrangères [MAE], Collection de Télégrammes Interceptés, Vols. 1–2. We are grateful to David Alvarez for bringing this document to our attention and to John Ferris for information on British ciphers during this period.
11. Rivet met with Daladier only five times during his tenure as secret-intelligence chief. He considered this contact manifestly insufficient. For his views see 'Rapports du SR avec le ministre', 1941, in *Fonds Paillole*, SHAT, 1K545/1/3. See also P. Jackson, 'La politisation du renseignement en France,

1933–1939', in G.-H. Soutou, J. Frémeaux and O. Forcade (eds), *L'Exploitation du renseignement* (Paris: Economica, 2001), pp. 63–82.

12. W. K. Wark, *The Ultimate Enemy: British Intelligence and Nazi Germany, 1933–39* (New York: Columbia University Press, 1986), p. 20. Discussion of the organization of pre-war British intelligence is drawn from this study and F. H. Hinsley et. al., *British Intelligence and the Second World War: its Influence on Strategy and Operations, Vol. I,* (London: HMSO, 1979), pp. 3–43 and C. Andrew, *Secret Service: the Making of the British Intelligence Community* (London: Heinemann, 1985), pp. 481–626.

13. Christopher Andrew judges that Sinclair 'had the ear' of Chamberlain in 1938–39, but there is no evidence of face-to-face meetings. Secret intelligence reached Chamberlain instead through either foreign secretary Lord Halifax or permanent under-secretary Alexander Cadogan. See Andrew, *Secret Service*, pp. 560–6 and 580–1.

14. Jackson, *France and the Nazi Menace*, pp. 30–1; Andrew, 'Déchiffrement et diplomatie', pp. 60–4.

15. Hinsley, *British Intelligence*, pp. 36–40; Andrew, *Secret Service*, pp. 591–2; E. Thomas, 'The evolution of the JIC system up to and during World War II', in C. Andrew and J. Noakes (eds), *Intelligence and International Relations* (Exeter: Exeter University Press, 1987), pp. 221–34. On the concept of 'all-source analysis' see M. Herman, *Intelligence Power in Peace and War* (Cambridge: Cambridge University Press, 1996), pp. 101–13.

16. Unfortunately, the present state of the British archives makes it impossible to describe the activities of the SIS with any certainty. See Andrew, *Secret Service*, p. 416.

17. Phipps to Halifax, 24 April 1938, and Phipps to Ismay, 26 March 1938, Public Record Office, Kew [PRO], CAB 21/554.

18. Foreign Office, minute on air attaché report, 20 December 1932, PRO, FO 371/16373/W13892/1446/17. See J. Ferris, 'The Theory of a French Air Menace', *Journal of Strategic Studies*, 10 (1987), pp. 61–83.

19. See the air attaché's annual reports 1933–35, 12 January 1934, 28 January 1935 and January 1936, PRO, FO 371/17660/C371/317/17, FO 371/18803/C809/809/17, and FO 371/198743/C375/375/17.

20. Laval, to Eden, and FO impressions in Central Department minutes, August 1935, PRO, FO 371/18800/C5821/227/17; Foreign Office-air ministry correspondence, 26 April 1934, PRO, FO 371/17653/C2653/85/17.

21. Foreign Office comment on 'The French Air Force', CID paper no. 1195-B, October 1935, PRO, FO 371/18800/C6985/227/17.

22. Assessment in air ministry 'Intelligence Summary' of January 1936, pp. 10–11, PRO, AIR 2/210.

23. 'Clearly the French are in a serious mess over their air rearmament', noted one Foreign Office official on reading 'The French Air Force in regard to expansion and re-equipment', IIC memorandum, CID Paper No. 1247-B, 15 July 1936, PRO, FO 371/19871/C5391/172/17.

24. Wing Commander R. V. Goddard, 30 November 1936, PRO, AIR 9/76/IIA/1/61/77.

25. 'France: Nationalisation of the armaments industry', IIC memorandum, ICF/62/F/2, 19 August 1936, PRO, FO371/19871/C6300/172/17; 'France: Nationalisation of the aircraft industry', IIC memorandum, ICF/62/2, 12

November 1936, PRO, FO 371/19870/C8511/140/17; Alexander, *Republic In Danger*, p. 67.

26. Air attaché's annual report, 30 January 1937, PRO, FO 371/20697/C1903/1903/17.

27. On this question see Jackson, *France and the Nazi Menace*, pp. 191–202 and 232–41.

28. Foreign Office minutes, 'French aircraft production', 16–22 November 1937, PRO, FO 371/20696/C7848/822/17.

29. Vansittart, 19 July 1937, PRO, FO 371/20694/C3571/C4601/C4989/122/17; Group Captain Buss to Foreign Office, 6 September 1937, PRO, FO 371/20694 C6346/122/17.

30. On Foreign Office apprehension that the appearance of French weakness presented Germany and Italy with a temptation, see J. Herman, *The Paris Embassy of Sir Eric Phipps: Anglo-French Relations and the Foreign Office* (Brighton: Sussex University Press, 1998), pp. 36, 58 and 61–2.

31. Rumbold and other Foreign Office minutes, 6 September to 7 October 1937, PRO, FO 371/20694/C6346/122/17; M. Thomas, *Britain, France and Appeasement: Anglo-French Relations in the Popular Front Era* (Oxford: Berg, 1996), pp. 164–7.

32. Eden minute, 28 November 1937, PRO, FO 371/20694/C8434/122/17.

33. M. Dockrill, *British Establishment Perspectives on France, 1936–40* (Basingstoke: Macmillan Press [now Palgrave Macmillan], 1999), pp. 91–5; Thomas, *Britain, France and Appeasement*, pp. 164–6.

34. Dockrill, *British Perspectives, passim*.

35. Eden, minute, 7 October 1937, PRO, FO 371/20694/C6346/122/17.

36. Eden to Chamberlain, January 1938 PRO, FO 371/21593/C362/G; Dockrill, *British Perspectives*, pp. 90–1.

37. Eden minute, 25 August 1936, PRO, FO 371/19858/C5939/1/17.

38. Dockrill, *British Perspectives*, p. 53.

39. 'The situation in Europe – Possible measures to avert German action in Czechoslovakia', Foreign Policy Committee paper, 18 March 1938, PRO, CAB 23/623/FP(36).

40. On imperial intelligence co-operation see the superbly researched study by M. Miller, *Shanghai on the Métro: Spies, Intrigue and the French between the Wars* (Berkeley: University of California Press, 1994), esp. pp. 3, 112–13, 132 and 139.

41. 'Impressions rapportées des manoeuvres allemandes', 19 October 1937, SHAT, 7N2513. Also cited in Alexander and Philpott, 'Entente Cordiale', p. 68.

42. Alexander and Philpott, 'Entente Cordiale,' pp. 65–72.

43. *Carnets Rivet*, entries for 10, 12, 13 February 1937 [Rivet in London] and 14 October 1936, 19–20 October 1937 and 17–18 January 1939 [Menzies in Paris].

44. *Carnets Rivet*, entries for 7 May 1937, 28 February 1938, 26 October 1938, 16 November 1938. See J. Curry, *The Security Service 1908–1945: the Official History* (Kew: Public Record Office, 1999), pp. 138 and 161, and Andrew, *Secret Service*, p. 508.

45. References to meetings with Jeffes in *Carnets Rivet*, 11 March 1937 and 23 February 1938. Rivet appears to have first met Dunderdale on 14 October 1938 (although the two also lunched together while the latter was in Poland

in late 1936). There are also two mentions of a British intelligence officer referred to as 'Dolinoff' in these diaries, who cannot be identified.

46. 'Poste d'Etudes externes', n.d. and 'Notes sure les relations en Angleterre', 15 October 1932, SHAT, ARR, 152/1428.

47. Phipps cited in Herman, *Paris Embassy*, p. 29.

48. 'Compte-rendu: très secret et personnel', translation of letter from 'le colonel "M"' to Roux, 8 April 1935, SHAT, ARR, 67/2192.

49. Menzies to Roux, 4 June 1935, SHAT, ARR, 67/2192. On Munzenburg and Katz see P. Broué, *Histoire de l'Internationale Communiste, 1919–1943* (Paris: Fayard, 1997), pp. 1024 and 1054–55; C. Andrew and O. Gordievsky, *KGB: the Inside Story of its Foreign Operations from Lenin to Gorbachev* (London: Hodder and Stoughton, 1990), pp. 146–59; T. Wolton, *Le grande recrutement* (Paris: Broché, 1997), *passim*.

50. On this issue see J. M. Parilla, *Las fuerzas armadas francesas ante la guerra civil Española, 1936–1939* (Madrid: Colección Ediciones Ejército, 1987) and P. Jackson, 'Stratégie et idéologie: le haut commandement français et la guerre civile espagnole', *Guerres Mondiales et Conflits Contemporaines*, 198 (2001), pp. 66–81.

51. 'Compte-rendu', 22 October 1937 and *Carnets Rivet*, 19 October 1937, SHAT, ARR, 702/208. Col. Morel's reports are in SHAT 7N2754-2756.

52. For recent discussion of non-intervention see E. Moradiellos, 'The Allies and the Spanish Civil War', in S. Balfour and P. Preston (eds), *Spain and the Great Powers in the Twentieth Century* (London: Routledge, 1999), pp. 96–126; M. Habeck, 'The Spanish Civil War and the Origins of the Second World War', in G. Martel (ed.), *The Origins of the Second World War Reconsidered* (London: Routledge, 2nd edn, 1999), pp. 204–223; G. Stone, 'Britain, France and the Spanish Problem, 1936–1939', in D. Richardson and G. Stone (eds), *Decisions and Diplomacy: Essays in Twentieth Century International History* (London: Routledge, 1995), pp. 129–52.

53. 'Compte-rendu', 22 October 1937, SHAT, ARR, 702/208.

54. On this question see D. Kahn, *Seizing the Enigma: the Race to Break the German U-Boat Codes* (London: Souvenier, 1992), pp. 31–44.

55. The above paragraph is drawn from *Fonds Paillole*, SHAT, 1K545/11/17/19 and 12/2/2; G. Bloch, *"Enigma" avant "Ultra" (1930–1940)* (Paris: privately published, 1988); Kahn, *Seizing the Enigma*, 31–67; F. H. Hinsley et al., 'The Polish, French and British Contributions to the Breaking of the Enigma: a Revised Account', in *British Intelligence and the Second World War: Vol. IV, part 2* (London: HMSO, 1988), pp. 945–959; G. Bertrand, *Enigma: ou la plus grande énigme de la guerre* (Paris: Plon, 1975), pp. 11–78, and J. Stengers, 'Enigma, the French, the Poles and the British, 1931–1940', in C. Andrew and D. Dilks (eds), *The Missing Dimension: Governments and Intelligence Communities in the Twentieth Century* (London: Macmillan, 1984), pp. 126–37.

56. Britain and France operated procedures whereby contractors were responsible for not exposing technical secrets to foreign attachés. See for instance the report of the British air attaché on a visit in January 1936 to the Hotchkiss works. The attaché and some visiting RAF officers were permitted to see France's new 25-mm aircraft gun but 'this gun was on the Secret List and could not, therefore, be shown to us in any detail'. Report of 28 January 1936, PRO, AIR 2/1713 S37596.

57. See Alexander and Philpott, 'Entente Cordiale', pp. 53–84.
58. MI3 estimate, 27 June 1932, PRO, WO 190/150/MI3/812.
59. Naval attaché report, 6 November 1933, PRO, FO371/16755/C9831/6165/18; J. Maiolo, *The Royal Navy and Nazi Germany 1933–39* (Basingstoke: Macmillan Press [now Palgrave Macmillan], 1998), p. 30.
60. See the minutes about a military attaché reported of 21 June 1934 in PRO, FO 371/17653/C3827/85/17 and the War Office reply to the Foreign Office, 5 July 1934, PRO, WO190/262/C958/85/17. War Office intelligence indicated that the Germans might be ready for the offensive by 1938.
61. Cited in K. Feiling, *The Life of Neville Chamberlain* (London: Macmillan, 1946), p. 323; Alexander and Philpott, 'Entente Cordiale', pp. 62 and 68; B. Bond, *Chief of Staff: the Diaries of Lt. Gen. Sir Henry Pownall* (2 vols, London: Leo Cooper, 1972), *i*, pp. 134–6 and 142–4.
62. MI memorandum on the German military situation, 11 November 1933, PRO, WO 190/230.
63. Wark, *Ultimate Enemy*, pp. 37–8.
64. Jackson, *France and the Nazi Menace*, pp. 124–5; Wark, *Ultimate Enemy*, pp. 42–3.
65. On this question see P. Fridenson and J. Lecuir, *La France et la Grande Bretagne face aux problèmes aériens (1935–1939)* (Vincennes: Service Historique de l'Armée de l'Air, 1976), pp. 111–36 and Thomas, *Britain, France and Appeasement*, pp. 165–6 and 174.
66. On Anglo-French relations during the crisis see R. A. C. Parker, 'France, Britain and the Ethiopian Crisis, 1935–1936', *English Historical Review*, lxxxix (1974), pp. 269–97; N. Rostow, *Anglo-French Relations, 1934–36* (New York: St Martin's Press, 1984), pp. 214–32; J. B. Duroselle, *Politique étrangère de la France: la décadence* (Paris: Imprimerie Nationale, 1979), pp. 143–52.
67. 'Anglo-French naval staff collaboration 1936–1939', n.d., but certainly written in the spring of 1939, PRO, ADM 223/487.
68. The French account of this meeting, 'Entretiens franco-britanniques du 5 août 1936', is in *Documents Diplomatiques Français* [DDF] 2ème série, tome III, no. 87.
69. 'Anglo-French naval staff collaboration, 1936–1939', (see note 67 above).
70. Maiolo, *Royal Navy and Nazi Germany*, p. 154.
71. In the aftermath of the 1935 Abyssinian crisis, the Admiralty prepared a common code to issue to the French in the event of naval co-operation; 'Confidential communications with possible allies', Naval Intelligence Division memorandum, 1 June 1938, PRO, ADM 1/9894.
72. On relations between French intelligence and other intelligence services see the voluminous documentation in SHAT, 7N2681 and ARR, 152/14781–14783. See also R. J. Young, 'French Military Intelligence and the Franco-Italian Alliance', *Historical Journal*, 28 (1985), pp. 147–53 and M. Alexander, 'In Lieu of Alliance: the French General Staff's Secret Co-operation with Neutral Belgium, 1936–1940', *Journal of Strategic Studies*, 13 (1991), pp. 413–27.
73. See the Lelong reports for 27 January, 10 and 17 February, 25 and 26 May and 2 June 1938, SHAT, 7N2814/2.
74. 'Renseignements sur l'Allemagne', 11, 17 and 22 August 1938, SHAT, 7N2815. See also a letter from Lelong to Deuxième Bureau chief Col. Maurice Gauché of 29 July 1938 in the same carton.

75. See, for example, the 'Bulletins' forwarded to Paris by Lelong beginning on 8 September 1938 and continuing through to the end of the month in SHAT, 7N2815. On French intelligence collection during the Czechoslovak crisis see Jackson, *France and the Nazi Menace*, pp. 257–64.
76. Lelong reports of 14, 15 and 28 December 1938, SHAT, 7N2815.
77. 'Renseignements militaires sur l'Allemagne', 5 January 1939, SHAT, 7N2816.
78. Wark, *Ultimate Enemy*, pp. 170–87 and 211–24; Jackson, *France and the Nazi Menace*, pp. 350–87.
79. P. Jackson, 'Intelligence and the End of Appeasement', in R. Boyce (ed.), *French Foreign and Defence Policy, 1918–1940: the Decline and Fall of a Great Power* (London: Routledge, 1998), pp. 248–9.
80. Phipps to London, 29 January 1939, *Documents on British Foreign Policy*, 3rd Series, IV, no. 94.
81. Draft communication to the British Embassy, 30 January 1939, MAE, *Papiers 1940: Rochat*, 18.
82. *Carnets Rivet*, tome II, entries for January and February 1939 and Andrew, *Secret Service*, p. 584. On the Abwehr and disinformation see D. C. Watt, *How War Came: the Immediate Origins of the Second World War, 1938–1939* (New York: Heinemann, 1989), pp. 100–7.
83. Menzies discounted rumours of a German offensive in the west in the meeting with Schlesser in London on 31 January 1939: 'Compte-rendu de mission à Londres', 2 Febuary 1939, SHAT, ARR, 503/250.
84. 'Aide-mémoire du gouvernement britannique', 29 January 1939, DDF, 2ème série, XIII, no. 454. For the analysis of the Political Directorate, 30 January 1939, see *ibid.*, no. 460.
85. T. Imlay, 'How to Win a War: Franco-British Planning for War against Germany, 1938–1940', PhD dissertation, Yale University, 1997, pp. 150–1.
86. 'Staff conversations with the French', Strategical Appreciation Sub-Committee memorandum, 11 April 1939, PRO, AIR 9/114/AFC 7.
87. 'Note on the subject of the exchange of service intelligence between French and British staffs', JIC minutes, 21 April 1939, and 'Exchange of intelligence between French and British staffs', JIC memorandum, 18 April 1939, PRO, CAB 56/3/AFC[J]35 and JIC 9.
88. 'Compte-rendu de mission à Londres les 30 & 31 janvier 1939', 1 February 1939, and 'Prévisions britanniques', 19 Febuary 1939, SHAT, ARR 503/250 and 251.
89. 'Compte-rendu de mission à Londres . . .', *ibid.*
90. *Carnets Rivet*, 24 February 1939.
91. It is clear that several of Stevens' agents were double agents working for German intelligence. See Andrew, *Secret Service*, pp. 608–17.
92. Hinsley, 'The Polish, French and British Contribution to Breaking the Enigma', pp. 949–59, and Kahn, *Seizing the Enigma*, pp. 77–81.
93. The information in the preceding paragraph is drawn from M. Thomas, 'France in British Signals Intelligence, 1939–1945', *French History*, 14 (2000), pp. 41–55.
94. *Ibid.*, pp. 44–9.
95. K. Fedorowich, 'Axis Prisoners of War as Sources for British Military Intelligence, 1939–42', *Intelligence and National Security*, 14 (1999), pp. 156–78; Thomas, 'France in British Signals Intelligence', pp. 47–8.

96. 'Note on the co-operation of the French mission with the MEW', Ministry of Economic Warfare memorandum, 15 September 1939, PRO, FO 837/391. 'La Guerre économique', undated, MAE, *Papiers Reynaud*, I. On economic warfare in Franco-British Strategy see W. N. Medlicott, *The Economic Blockade* (London: HMSO, 1952), pp. 36–7 and 133–6 and M. A. Reussner, *Les conversations franco-britanniques d'Ètat-Major, 1935–1939* (Vincennes: Service Historique de la Marine, 1969), pp. 213–41.
97. Thomas, 'France in British Signals Intelligence', p. 49.
98. Minutes of the 30th meeting of the Joint Intelligence Committee, 7 July 1939, PRO, CAB 56/1.

7
Imperial Defence or Diversionary Attack? Anglo-French Strategic Planning in the Near East, 1936–40

Martin Thomas

From the escalation of the Abyssinian crisis in 1935 until the authorities in French-controlled Syria and Lebanon declared their loyalty to the Vichy government in July 1940, the eastern Mediterranean and its Near East margins were a focal point of Anglo-French defence co-operation. From Egypt in the south through the western arc of the Middle East to Turkey and Greece in the north, British and French imperial and strategic interests were entwined. The western powers confronted similar problems across the region. The signature of an Anglo-Egyptian treaty of alliance on 26 August 1936 was echoed some weeks later by the long-delayed conclusion of French draft treaties promising full self-government in their Levant mandates. In both cases, faltering implementation of treaty pledges caused bitter dispute. The outbreak of the Arab revolt in Palestine fed nationalist dissent in Syria, and the neighbouring British and French mandatory administrations were hard-pressed to maintain imperial control between 1936 and 1939. Yet, by 1939, the presence of substantial British and French military forces in Egypt, Palestine and the Levant territories – albeit substantially devoted to imperial policing during the preceding three years – presented an opportunity for limited operations against the Axis powers mounted from the Middle East. The key to any such assault was to secure the active involvement of Turkey. The prospects for this seemed good. Having joined the western powers' 'peace front' in May, on 19 October 1939 the Turkish government signed a joint treaty of alliance with Britain and France.

Anglo-French defence co-operation in the eastern Mediterranean and Near East region in the years 1936–40 developed in four key areas. First, the two powers' security interests converged in the light of the heightened Italian menace in 1936. Second, their imperial policing requirements in Palestine and the Levant states were also broadly similar, and necessitated closer Anglo-French security contacts and political-intelligence exchanges. Third, the British and French fostered regional collaboration with Turkey, their major Balkan ally in 1939. Finally, both powers examined the prospects for joint offensive operations based upon the projection of an expeditionary force into the Balkans and the capture of Italian air and naval bases in the Dodecanese islands.

What emerges from an examination of these developments is that, despite common security problems and similar regional interests, British and French strategic co-operation was stunted by Britain's reluctance to abandon the appeasement of Italy. Detailed Anglo-French defence planning in the Near East, conducted from April 1939, was characterized by improvised proposals constrained by the more pressing requirements of the western front. The Turkish government was acutely aware of this. The consolidation of the 'peace front' in 1939 was undermined by Turkey's legitimate doubts about the capacity and commitment of its western allies who were themselves torn between the potential benefits of a diversionary Near Eastern attack and the imperatives of continental and imperial defence.

Eastern Mediterranean security after the Abyssinian crisis

The Italian invasion of Ethiopia in October 1935 challenged Britain's regional supremacy in the eastern Mediterranean, north-east Africa and the Red Sea. French sea and air communications with Morocco and Algeria were similarly threatened. Retaliatory French attacks against Italian Libya were planned from Tunisia and the key French North African naval base at Bizerta. Admiral William Fisher, Commander-in-Chief of Britain's Mediterranean fleet, and Major-General George Weir, General Officer Commanding (GOC) in Egypt, also proposed offensive operations including Fleet Air Arm attacks from Malta against Italian bases and a pre-emptive strike by mobile forces in Egypt against eastern Libya. But in Paris and London the political will to confront Italian aggression was lacking; with Cabinet agreement the British Admiralty and the service chiefs put a brake upon joint strategic planning and the active enforcement of limited sanctions.[1] The build-up of Italian forces in Libya and Ethiopia posed obvious threats to the security of Egypt and the Sudan, heightening Egyptian demands for a firmer British defence commitment in 1936. Besides its intrinsic damage to Britain's imperial prestige, it was recognized that any failure to satisfy Egyptian needs might provoke a backlash against Britain's unilateral control over the

Suez Canal zone and the eastern Mediterranean fleet base at Alexandria. The Egyptian royal family and Wafdist premier Mustafa al-Nahhas considered military concessions within the Anglo-Egyptian treaty conditional upon assured British supremacy in the region.[2]

The requirement to strengthen Britain's Mediterranean fleet, both to meet the Italian naval and air threat and to make a show of policing League of Nations sanctions, exposed the over-extension of Britain's naval power and the limited defences of its key eastern Mediterranean bases, Alexandria above all.[3] The service chiefs only completed a comprehensive Suez Canal Defence Plan in early October 1935. As Steven Morewood has clarified, the requirement to keep this plan secret (its details were not released to the Egyptian government), and the expectation that additional restrictions upon Suez traffic would escalate Anglo-Italian tension, hindered the consolidation of fixed defences within the Canal zone during 1936.[4] The additional concentration of Mediterranean fleet units in Egyptian waters from August 1935 provided greater protection for Suez and kept key vessels beyond the range of Italian short-range bombers. But Alexandria could not cope with this additional shipping; the third cruiser squadron was forced to use Haifa as an overflow base, and both ports lacked adequate anti-aircraft defences. Although in March 1936 the Committee of Imperial Defence (CID) approved a reconsideration of expenditure upon British Mediterranean ports to meet the danger of Italian bombardment, in the short term Malta and Gibraltar took priority over eastern Mediterranean bases.[5]

The French, too, enjoyed local naval superiority during the Abyssinian crisis but worried about their exposure to surprise attack. With five cruiser squadrons and a flotilla of 12 destroyers operating out of Toulon by November 1935, the French naval presence in the northwest Mediterranean was powerful.[6] But the concentration of shipping in Toulon and Bizerta, which also accommodated over 90 per cent of the French Mediterranean fleet's fuel oil and petroleum stores, raised obvious fears of air attack even though these bases had stronger anti-aircraft protection than their British equivalents in Malta and Egypt. Horrified by the Anglo-German Naval Agreement in June, the French naval staff had also moved forces from the Mediterranean to Brest and was reluctant to see its newest battlecruisers, *Dunkerque* and *Strasbourg* (built to counter Germany's *Panzerschiffe* 'pocket' battleships), squandered in any encounter with the Italian fleet. With the outbreak of the Ethiopian war, chief of naval staff Admiral Georges Durand-Viel had to reverse re-equipment priorities to increase harbour defences in

Mediterranean ports at the expense of France's Atlantic bases.[7] Just as British and French politicians and diplomats sometimes worked at cross-purposes during the Abyssinian crisis, so, too, defence co-operation in the Mediterranean was limited by mutual distrust. In October 1935 the British Mediterranean fleet command at Malta reacted with dismay to French reluctance to begin offensive planning until Marine Nationale reserves, of which there was a chronic shortage, were mobilized.[8] After further talks with Admiral Georges Robert on Christmas day, the First Sea Lord, Admiral Sir Ernle Chatfield, was disappointed to learn that the French fleet's priority was to protect troop transports from Morocco and Algeria. Meanwhile, the British authorities policing sanctions at the southern end of the Red Sea found that the limits they imposed upon the refuelling of Italian vessels at Aden were negated by the French port authorities at Djibouti who were prepared to meet Italian requests for additional fuel and stores.[9]

Admiral Durand-Viel admitted to British naval attaché Hammill that he dreaded a bilateral Anglo-Italian accord modelled on the Anglo-German Naval Agreement. While the British and French Admiralties exchanged intelligence regarding fleet dispositions and Italian shipping movements, both sides remained cagey about their longer-term planning.[10] In January 1936 Durand-Viel and Robert agreed that up to two flotillas of French submarines might be sent to work alongside British units east of the line between Cap Bon and Marettimo island off western Sicily which marked the boundary between the French and British Mediterranean commands. However, by the time sanctions were abandoned in June 1936, the French naval planning staff remained lukewarm towards closer co-operation. Durand-Viel's successor, Admiral Jean-François Darlan, even worried that an Anglo-French naval partnership would make it harder to secure adequate rearmament funding from the Assemblée.[11]

Nonetheless, it was an inescapable truth that Italian expansionism would force British and French defence planners closer together within the Mediterranean theatre. Quite apart from the Italian naval and air threat in 1935–36, intensified fascist radio propaganda, principally directed from an Arab-language broadcast centre at Bari, stirred nationalist sentiment against Britain and France throughout their Arab territories. Additional fascist broadcasts to Malta played upon Maltese fears of bombardment.[12] For the bureaucrats and commanders who administered the British empire in the Middle East, confronting Italy in any future war became a lasting preoccupation. This set them at odds with Baldwin's Cabinet for whom the appeasement of Italy remained an

important objective. The service chiefs were anxious for talks with Rome
to succeed and still entertained plans for the temporary evacuation of
the Mediterranean *in extremis*.[13] But delays to the military re-equipment
programme in the Mediterranean theatre were dangerous, particularly
as it was generally accepted that Mussolini would be an opportunist
aggressor most likely to strike if he detected a failure of British resolve.
To French irritation, immediately after the Anglo-Italian Gentlemen's
Agreement in early 1937 the British government pursued *détente* with
Italy while slowing down the modernization of Mediterranean defences
at Valletta and Alexandria.[14] This policy disturbed ambassador Sir Miles
Lampson in Cairo who warned in April 1937 that further concessions
to Italy, especially *de jure* recognition of its Abyssinian conquest, would
undermine Britain's standing in Egypt, Saudi Arabia and Turkey.[15] Still,
the British effort to achieve a comprehensive regional settlement with
Italy continued into 1938 although it was frustrated in practice by
flagrant Italian intervention in the Spanish Civil War and Mussolini's
underlying determination to challenge British and French predominance in North Africa. As before, defensive preparations in the eastern
Mediterranean were curbed by the requirements of British diplomacy in
Rome; the prospect of talks with the Italians being used repeatedly to
cut expenditure on fixed installations in Egypt, Palestine and Cyprus.[16]

Having been tantalized by military and air force collaboration with
Italy in the six months following the Rome agreements in January 1935,
during the following year France moved decisively from détente towards
confrontation with Italy. The foreign ministry's Levant directorate had
hoped to capitalize upon the Rome agreements to settle outstanding
Franco-Italian imperial rivalries in North Africa, Syria, Arabia, the Red
Sea and Somaliland, and to shut down the invidious Bari broadcast-
ing station. But from 1936 onwards any resumption of such dialogue
required a prior French recognition of Italy's conquest of Abyssinia
plus French acquiescence in Italy's support for General Franco.[17] This
was unacceptable to Léon Blum's Popular Front administration during
1936–37. However, the desire for a renewed Franco-Italian partnership
in southern Europe persisted across a broad section of the French right,
within the departments of the Alpes Maritimes where cultural and
familial ties with Italy were strongest, and amongst senior officials inside
Edouard Daladier's war ministry and at the French embassy in Rome.[18]
This indulgence towards Italy was further stimulated by the smoke-
screen created by officials in Rome. Italian diplomats and service ministry staff matched warnings that any escalation of sanctions or closure
of Suez would provoke immediate retaliation with assurances that

the 1935 Rome agreements could easily be restored.[19] But those more directly concerned with Mediterranean defence such as Darlan, air minister Pierre Cot, minister of colonies Marius Moutet and Daladier himself, accepted the challenge of Franco-Italian rivalry. For the French navy in particular, this was nothing new. Since the Washington Conference in 1921–22 and the London Naval Treaty in 1930 there had been an ongoing Franco-Italian naval race in the Mediterranean.[20]

Since Anglo-French naval planning during the Abyssinian crisis firmly established that the Royal Navy would take primary responsibility for maritime communications in the eastern Mediterranean, at first glance one could overlook the importance that Darlan's naval staff attached to strategic planning in this theatre. The direct French naval contribution in the eastern Mediterranean during 1938–40 was confined to the Levant cruiser squadron. But concomitant French plans for naval operations against Italy in the western Mediterranean and on the eastern margins of French North Africa bore the imprint of Darlan and Daladier's contingency planning.[21] If, as Daladier feared, Italy should decide to risk a Mediterranean confrontation, attacks against Italian targets in the eastern Mediterranean were vitally important, despite the relative insignificance of French naval and air forces in the region. In essence, the Anglo-French-Turkish actions against the Italian Dodecanese eventually planned in 1939–40 were the counterpart to French-directed assaults against Libya co-ordinated from French North Africa.[22]

Mounting French enthusiasm for aggressive operations in the eastern Mediterranean reflected the fact that the Levant mandates were less exposed to external attack than British Egypt. There was no need for fixed Syrian defences akin to Britain's detailed Suez Canal Defence Plan. The French Levant garrison was unlikely to face Turkish, Soviet or Italian invasion. Britain's local problems were altogether more severe. In August 1937 Chatfield warned Fisher's successor as Mediterranean fleet commander, Admiral Sir Dudley Pound, that long-term naval operations in the eastern Mediterranean against Italy might be undermined by the abrupt defeat of British land forces in Egypt.[23] Over the autumn and winter of 1937–38 intelligence on Italian reinforcement of Libya, some of it relayed by the French war ministry's intelligence service, was closely monitored by the service chiefs whose plan for the defence of Egypt was still far from completion, with neither fighters nor anti-aircraft defences yet dispatched to protect Alexandria. The result was a stream of CID memoranda pleading for reinforcements and warning of the conflict between Mediterranean and Far Eastern imperial defence needs.[24] The French naval authorities were more fortunate. There were no French overseas Dominions requiring protection from Japan. Nor did the French ever contemplate an equivalent to Britain's Singapore strategy of Far Eastern reinforcement, a scheme which, if implemented, would denude the Mediterranean fleet of its striking power.[25] Not surprisingly, by January 1938 Pound, Weir and Lampson were all strongly opposed to the dispatch of a Main Fleet to Singapore, a view strengthened in 1937 as Britain extended its commitments to Greece and Turkey.[26] Chatfield and Duff Cooper, Secretary of State for War, had already impressed upon the Cabinet during the Far Eastern crisis in late 1937 that a token reinforcement of Singapore, based upon two battleships drawn from the Mediterranean, was not strategically sound. In subsequent months, the service chiefs repeatedly emphasized the dilemmas of imperial over-extension to their ministerial masters.[27]

As talks with Mussolini figured ever larger in Chamberlain's thinking, in February 1938 the British Chiefs of Staff Committee (COS) reviewed the strategic position and prospects in the eastern Mediterranean. Again, their report carried a mixed message. Britain was 'immensely stronger' than Italy financially and economically. This was confirmed by a November 1937 Industrial Intelligence Centre report which revealed Italy's continued dependence upon liquid fuel imports, the country's precarious financial position and outlays for Italian operations in Spain having prevented the replenishment of stocks over the preceding year. But the COS cautioned that Italy's strategic advantage lay in the combination of surprise with the ability to concentrate strong forces in a confined area. Britain's eastern Mediterranean port defences remained incomplete, the Egyptian garrison was stretched by the requirements of local policing and the Arab revolt in Palestine, and it remained hard to assess the likely effectiveness of Italian air attacks upon British shipping (although these were generally over-estimated). There were insufficient docking and repair facilities at Alexandria to cope with warships seriously damaged while serving in the eastern Mediterranean, and peacetime reinforcement of the Middle East garrisons to offset the risk of Italian air attacks on British troop ships seemed essential. Despite Cabinet approval, in March 1938, of an additional army brigade for the defence of Egypt, the requirements of RAF expansion for home defence took precedence over an increased Middle East reserve. In sum, the COS considered closer Mediterranean co-operation with France, Turkey and possibly the Soviet Union the best means to overcome British material shortages.[28] Since France relied upon Syria and Iraq for over 50 per cent of its crude oil and some 40 per cent of its liquid fuel imports, the rationale for closer Mediterranean collaboration was easily proved. In May 1936 the Quai d'Orsay's Levant division reminded the French service chiefs that British goodwill was the sole guarantee of French oil supplies. And in February 1938 General Charles Huntziger, supreme commander in the Levant, predicted a doubling in the volume of oil supplies piped to the Syrian coast over the coming decade.[29]

This seemingly unequivocal conclusion suited the evolution of strategic thinking in Paris where Blum's brief return to office immediately after the Anschluss in March 1938 stimulated a re-assessment of France's military options. In late March the Conseil Supérieur de la Guerre reviewed the global strategic outlook. Chiefly concerned with the threat to Czechoslovakia, the military planners also reinforced Daladier's personal conviction that Mussolini would seize upon war in Europe to pursue Italian aggrandisement in the Mediterranean theatre. Yet while the service chiefs on both sides of the Channel shared common assumptions about the Italian threat, Chamberlain's tenacious courtship of Italy during 1938–39 still retarded joint strategic planning in the Mediterranean.[30]

Imperial policing, 1936–39

Between 1936 and 1939 British and French imperial policing in the Middle East was dominated by the conjunction of Arab revolt against the scale of Jewish immigration into Palestine with the efforts made by both powers to renegotiate the basis for their continued presence in Egypt, Syria and Lebanon. Britain and France would not cede sovereign control until their primordial security requirements were met. Inevitably, this cemented the link between wider strategic planning in the Near East and deteriorating political relations with Arab nationalist parties. Preparations for war in the eastern Mediterranean and Near East undermined the process of imperial reform and so complicated problems of internal order. Throughout, the nagging problem of Palestine diminished Arab respect for western imperial rule and formed a yardstick for nationalist assessments of British intentions. In February 1939 the COS Joint Intelligence Committee noted that Palestine remained the single issue around which widespread Arab opposition to British imperial control might coalesce.[31] Syria and Lebanon were also touched by the Palestine revolt. There were strong ties between the urban notables and wealthy elites of the Levant region, and Syrian Arabism and nationalist protest provided key models for Palestinian leaders. After the rebellion began in spring 1936, Syria's commerce suffered, Arab refugees fled into southern Lebanon, and Damascus became a key refuge for Palestinian rebel leaders closely aligned with Syria's National Bloc. In Lebanon especially, press campaigns and Arab propaganda alleging widespread British and Jewish atrocities in Palestine generated hostility to Britain which even transcended the Muslim-Maronite Christian divide in Beirut.[32]

The increased tension across Palestine and the French Levant produced contrasting responses from the imperial authorities on the spot and the metropolitan governments in London and Paris. Locally, the mounting challenges to their political control promoted closer co-operation between the High Commission administrations in Jerusalem and Damascus. But the façade of a solid imperial power front concealed grave French reservations about British plans for a Palestine partition and corresponding British criticisms of the putative independence treaties with Syria and Lebanon. Both at the metropolitan centre and within the Middle Eastern territories themselves, a vein of Anglo-French imperial rivalry and mutual suspicion persisted beneath the outward displays of solidarity. Nourished in the 1920s by British support for the Hashemite dynasty, the disputed claim to Mosul, protracted negotiations over frontier demarcation and French allegations of equivocal British security co-operation while the Syrian revolt was at its peak in 1925–27, *entente* across the Middle East was a fragile reed. As the French naval command at Beirut noted wryly in October 1936, Britain's Middle Eastern authorities always handled local problems with an eye to strategic interest. Furthermore, both the Quai d'Orsay's Levant division and the High Commission in Beirut saw a British hand in the growth of pan-Arabist sentiment in Syria, Transjordan and Palestine, and feared that a British-directed Arab confederation might be the intended result.[33] As British officials realized, the contrast between Palestine's likely fate under partition and the greater success of the other Arab mandates – Iraq and Syria – in edging towards full independence inevitably fed popular criticism of British rule. Anticipating the government's abandonment of partition 12 months later, in November 1937 Anthony Eden, the foreign secretary, angered the Colonial Office by suggesting a reconsideration of the Peel Commission's recommendations because of their adverse effects upon British standing within the Middle East, something Italian propaganda was quick to exploit.[34] In the circumstances, successive French governments were relatively mild in their criticisms of the Palestine situation.

Since the peace settlement imposed in the Middle East by Britain and France was less an attempt to contain Ottoman power than a struggle between the peace-makers for regional control – particularly over a so-called *Syrie intégrale* – the development of Anglo-French co-operation in the 1930s was more surprising than its previous absence.[35] This improvement in *entente* relations in the Middle East was driven by the shared experience of colonial disorder, although the growing preoccupation with German and Italian power undoubtedly played its part. The Syrian revolt of the mid-1920s, and still more so the protracted and expensive pacification which followed it, suggested that the management of inter-communal relations within the French Levant was scarcely easier than Britain's hopeless quest to reconcile its mandatory obligations to the Arab majority in Palestine with its notional commitment to a Jewish national home.[36] A snapshot of the work of French security forces in Syria during September 1937, for example, reveals troops struggling to contain violence between Christians, Arabs and Kurds in upper Jazira; keeping Syrian, Alawite and Turkish rioters apart in Alexandretta; and policing the collection of taxes in the Jabal Druze.[37] In Syria, Lebanon and Palestine, the requirements of long-term imperial policing fired military interest in the development of local strategic facilities; 900 metres of additional docking capacity in Beirut harbour, the construction of additional military airfields in the Syrian interior, and greater recourse to locally raised troop levies to ease the pressure of policing upon regular Armée d'Afrique regiments, all stemmed from the Syrian revolt and added to French military potential within the region.[38] On the British side, for General Sir John Dill, GOC in Palestine in 1936–37, insufficient manpower frustrated his plans to conduct a more vigorous counter-insurgency against Palestinian rebels. Additional facilities enabling him to call forward reinforcements more effectively were central to his preferred strategy to restore order.[39] By 1936 the completion of the port of Haifa and the possibility that a revised treaty settlement with Egypt might compel the Middle East command to relocate its major strategic reserve to Palestine also concentrated the minds of strategic planners in Whitehall.

Within France and Britain, attachment to the Middle East mandates as vital strategic assets increased in direct proportion to the growing risk of a European conflict.[40] The Anglo-Egyptian treaty stipulated that in war British and Egyptian army units were to work together, the Egyptians assuming wider defensive responsibilities to allow British troops greater freedom to operate against the Italians in Libya and East Africa. In fact, the Egyptian government was not kept abreast of British strategy or the details of the Suez Canal Defence Plan – the War Office military mission sent to train Egyptian army cadres was in its infancy, and ambassador Lampson doubted Egyptian loyalty. In similar vein, within Syria and Lebanon French-trained paramilitary *troupes spéciales* were assigned a broad internal security role in order to permit the French Levant army to serve as a Balkan expeditionary force. A Franco-Syrian military convention agreed as part of the bilateral treaty negotiations in September 1936 laid down detailed arrangements for the gradual transfer of local security tasks to Syrian troops once French strategic requirements were met.[41] In both cases, increased Arab opposition to British and French policy complicated strategic planning. In August 1937 the British service chiefs warned that the increased demands of imperial policing in Palestine might undermine plans to reinforce Egypt with troops sent from India. As disorders in Palestine peaked during 1937–38, British security forces lost the battle to re-impose control. They were hidebound by the Cabinet's refusal to admit the seriousness of the local situation by imposing martial law, a reluctance nurtured by fear of international criticism. Only from May 1938, with the adoption of more sophisticated counter-insurgency techniques by GOC Lieutenant-General Sir Robert Haining and Captain Orde Wingate's Special Night Squads, did the military balance gradually shift in British favour.[42] As 1939 dawned, Lampson and the Middle East command were convinced that Egyptian co-operation in war required a convincing British show of strength in the Canal Zone and the Red Sea. Cabinet divisions over the reinforcement of Egypt during the final week of the Czech crisis in September 1938 could hardly have made a favourable impression. Above all, it was vital to settle the Palestine question 'in such a way as to avoid [the] danger of its being a drain in wartime and our being faced with a hostile block of Arab countries'.[43]

As British and French rule was severely challenged, so security, intelligence and cross-border co-operation between imperial authorities grew almost by default. By 1934 the Zionist land purchases co-ordinated by the Jewish National Fund, which so inflamed Arab protests in Palestine, threatened to spill over into French territory, forcing Comte de Martel's Levant High Commission to proscribe any Zionist purchase of Syrian land.[44] This problem illustrated the obvious potential for Arab opposition to Jewish settlement in Palestine to affect both political conditions in the French Mandates and imperial relations with Britain. As the Palestine revolt escalated, from 1937 officers of the French garrison in Syria and the British-led Transjordan frontier force co-operated in the maintenance of frontier security. Once war broke out this cross-border collaboration was extended to prevent British or French deserters from seeking refuge outside their own territory.[45]

These low-level contacts typified the relatively amicable co-existence between the British and French authorities in the Middle East in the late 1930s. Although security co-operation remained a touchy issue – not least because so many key Palestinian leaders, including the Mufti of Jerusalem, had fled to Syria and Lebanon – the intense local rivalry of the 1920s had abated.[46] French confinement of Palestinian leaders contrasted with Britain's earlier refusal to extradite Syrian rebels from Palestine and Jordan. By December 1938 the Levant high command was in a position to relay precise lists of its anticipated raw material and foodstuff purchases from Palestine and Egypt in the event of war.[47] However, until 1939, the missing element was any serious discussion of joint strategic planning. If anything, during the first three months of 1939 the British and French governments regarded joint military talks on a Syria-Palestine defence scheme as politically inexpedient. As Arab-Jewish negotiations got under way in London in early February, the future of the Palestine mandate inevitably dominated Arab politics, particularly within Egypt, Iraq and Syria. The tight restrictions upon Jewish immigration set within the White Paper on Palestine in May confirmed British sensitivity to Arab opinion. This was not an opportune moment to advertise an Anglo-French commitment to exploit Arab territory in a war against the Axis. Equally, the French Chamber of Deputies' ultimate refusal to ratify the Franco-Syrian treaty cast a long shadow over domestic politics in the Syrian Mandate where separatist movements in the Alawite and Jabal Druze regions were already a major concern. Fearful of Damascene reaction, the Beirut High Commission refused British requests in January 1939 for the extradition of two Palestinian rebel leaders, justifying this decision by reference to the volatility of Franco-Syrian relations. A firmer approach was adopted as war approached and the Palestine revolt subsided. The High Commission dissolved the Damascus parliament in July, unceremoniously rejecting dialogue with the Syrian National Bloc in the process.[48] Cowed by the French show of strength, numerous Syrian, Lebanese and Druze politicians as well as the leaders of the Islamic Ulémas in Damascus publicly endorsed the French war effort during September.[49] This allowed Anglo-French military co-operation to proceed from the autumn of 1939 with less thought for its local political consequences.

Towards co-operation with Turkey, 1936–39

Prior to the Abyssinian crisis, the Foreign Office considered the Turkish general staff the main obstacle to Turkish co-operation with Britain.

The French, too, worried that the Turkish military might exploit a crisis in Europe to press irredentist claims against Syria. In September 1935 the French military attaché at Istanbul, Colonel de Courson de la Villeneuve, initiated a war ministry study of measures to combat a Turkish ground offensive north of the Euphrates river.[50] For both countries, this perception of potential Turkish ill-will changed in 1936. Alarmed by Italian expansionism but gratified by the progress of the Montreux conference restoring Turkish sovereignty over the Bosphorus and Dardanelles, the Turkish government edged closer to a formal commitment to Britain and France. The prospect of arms supplies from the western powers catalysed this *détente*.[51] The Turkish general staff lodged the first in a series of armament requests with the British government in February 1936. Subsequent orders for up to 250 French and US military aircraft, including 60 French single-seater fighters, were made later in the year. French military intelligence was impressed by the scale of Turkey's intended rearmament. De Courson de la Villeneuve reported that 56 per cent of the 1936 budget was allocated to military modernization.[52]

As part of the Popular Front's broader attempt to restore French power in eastern Europe, in December 1937 General Huntziger, then French military commander in the Levant, conducted preliminary talks with representatives of the Turkish general staff. Huntziger's message to his Turkish hosts was simple: France's garrison in Syria and Lebanon could be a major strategic asset to the Turks if a European war engulfed the Mediterranean. For the first time, it was directly suggested that French and Turkish forces could act together to end Italy's control of the Dodecanese islands lying immediately off Turkey's Bodrum peninsula. Franco-Turkish collaboration would help ensure the free passage of shipping throughout the eastern Mediterranean, the Straits and the Black Sea whilst facilitating the blockade of Italian supplies to the Dodecanese, Libya and East Africa. Britain's active support was taken for granted.[53] The Turkish foreign minister, Dr Tevfik Rüstü Aras, was non-committal. Though he welcomed Huntziger's initiative, three weeks later Aras applauded the Anglo-Italian Gentlemen's Agreement, confiding to British ambassador Sir Percy Loraine that Turkey could just as easily collaborate with Italy as with France.[54]

For the French the outstanding barrier to bilateral co-operation was Turkey's claim to sovereignty over the Sanjak of Alexandretta, a pocket of coastal territory then in north-west Syria. France could not cede this autonomous region, with its large Arab, Alawite and Armenian minorities, without undermining its status as protector of Syria's national interest, a position reaffirmed in the recently-negotiated Franco-Syrian treaty.[55] However, Turkish goodwill was too important to ignore. In response to Quai d'Orsay enquiries regarding the benefits of Franco-Turkish staff conversations, on 7 May 1937 the war ministry's military intelligence staff confirmed that an 'entente' with Turkey would breathe new life into France's flagging eastern alliance system. With free access through the Straits to Soviet bases in the Crimea and to Romania's Black Sea ports, France could assist Romania, Poland and the USSR more easily. More important in the short term, a Franco-Turkish alignment would probably ensure Bulgaria's neutrality, possibly even its goodwill. This would permit Greece, Turkey and Romania – allied under the 1934 Balkan Pact in opposition to Bulgarian revisionism – to devote greater attention to defence against the Axis powers. Nevertheless, the intelligence staff warned that Franco-Turkish co-operation should not be pursued at the expense of concessions over the Sanjak. Yet it was already apparent that the French were prepared to cede the territory in the teeth of opposition from Jamil Mardam's Damascus government and the Sanjak's minority populations. But this had to be done slowly, ostensibly following the recommendations of a League of Nations inquiry which set the terms for greater local autonomy, elections in the Sanjak and a possible transfer of the region to Turkish rule.[56] In the short term, however, the requirements of French imperial prestige within the Syrian mandate precluded an immediate territorial bargain with the Turks. This frustrated plans for strategic collaboration until 1939, although, as an adjunct to a Franco-Turkish friendship treaty, a preliminary accord between the two general staffs was signed in Antioch on 3–4 July 1938. Conserving only a tenuous autonomy, a day after this agreement, the Sanjak (soon renamed the Hatay Republic) came under Turkish military control.[57]

In the spring of 1938 Léon Blum's short-lived administration was unnerved to discover that the Syrian mandate was discussed during Anglo-Italian talks in Rome. As disquieting as Italian foreign minister Galeazzo Ciano's refusal to offer anything more than verbal assurances of Italy's disinterest in the status of the Middle Eastern mandates was the fact that British ambassador Lord Perth had raised Syria at all. As the Quai d'Orsay's Levant directorate complained, evidently Anglo-French imperial collaboration weighed poorly in the scales of British appeasement policy.[58] Foreign minister Joseph Paul-Boncour's frustration over this in the spring of 1938 was amplified by Daladier once he took over the premiership from Blum in April. The tension between hardening French determination to challenge any Italian aggression in

1938–39 and the lingering British effort to enlist the Italian government as a brake upon German expansionism was never resolved. Only the failure of British appeasement in Rome made possible the final alignment between French and British strategic interests in the eastern Mediterranean.

As prime minister, Daladier grew increasingly pessimistic about the chances of avoiding war with Italy. Though anxious not to denude France's Rhine defences, the premier nonetheless gave fresh impetus to eastern Mediterranean strategic planning. He received strong support from, among others, the minister of marine, César Campinchi, and the minister of colonies, Georges Mandel.[59] Moreover, Daladier's counter-foil, foreign minister Georges Bonnet, though personally sympathetic to Britain's final efforts to appease Rome, inadvertently lent weight to Daladier's more robust diplomacy by removing the Quai d'Orsay's political director, René Massigli, to the Ankara embassy in the winter of 1938. Daladier in Paris and ambassador Massigli on the spot in Turkey formed an effective partnership in support of a Turkish alliance, a policy long advocated by de Courson de la Villeneuve. They were, in turn, strongly backed from 1939 by the chief of the general staff Maurice Gamelin.[60] This helps account for Bonnet's relatively supine abandonment of the appeasement of Italy. Eager to share in British plans for negotiations with the Turks in London, a week before the Munich conference convened Bonnet successfully proposed that France join the London discussions. Although the Franco-Turkish treaty of friendship initialled in July 1938 promised a minimum of benevolent neutrality, thereafter the French government fell in with British efforts to consolidate relations with the Turkish general staff. In late March 1938 de la Villenueve had also urged that France should follow in Britain's slipstream, at least until a Sanjak settlement permitted a more assertive policy.[61]

The Turkish government's response to the crisis over Czechoslovakia was not altogether encouraging. Whilst Atatürk read Hitler shrewdly and the general staff clearly foresaw a long-term German threat to Romania's oil supplies, the Turkish foreign ministry exploited the Sudeten problem to press additional claims against France over the treatment of the Turkish ethnic population in the Sanjak.[62] In October, Aras made plain that Turkey would only undertake detailed strategic co-operation with France as part of a tripartite arrangement with Britain. And, as London ambassador Charles Corbin advised, the Foreign Office expected any such tripartite talks to be extended to include Greece. Any resultant four-power pact would give Mussolini ample pretext to break off dialogue with London, destroying Chamberlain and Halifax's efforts to consolidate the Anglo-Italian agreement of April 1938.[63] To Daladier's annoyance, after Italian irredentist claims against French territory were noisily proclaimed in the Italian Chamber of Deputies on 30 November 1938, wider collaboration with the Turks against Italy still remained on hold throughout the winter of 1938–39 as the British once again pursued the chimera of Italian friendship. The failure of the Chamberlain-Halifax visit to Rome in January 1939, the Anglo-French guarantees to Romania and Greece in the aftermath of Germany's occupation of Prague and, above all, Italy's occupation of Albania in April set discussions with Turkey in train once more.[64]

By this point, comprehensive Anglo-French staff talks were well under way, having opened on 29 March 1939. The principal military and governmental discussions of Near East planning occurred in April and June–July 1939 before the mechanism of the inter-allied Supreme War Council facilitated more regular exchanges once war was declared in September. Differences of emphasis aside, the fundamental tension between the Mediterranean and Middle East proposals of the British COS and Joint Planning Staff on the one hand, and of the French high command on the other, lay in Britain's emphasis upon a strategy of defence in depth and the French tendency to regard the Middle East as the platform for an advance into the Balkans. Where the former was predicated upon Britain's continued naval dominance in the eastern Mediterranean, the latter hinged upon the construction of a multilateral Balkan coalition spearheaded by a French-led expeditionary force.[65] Ironically, just as British appeasement of Italy had stifled Anglo-French strategic planning before 1939, so Italy's neutrality set clear limits to the formulation of detailed operational schemes in the eastern Mediterranean theatre from September 1939 to June 1940.[66] Joint operations in the Near East were therefore unlikely in the short term. This, and the extension of inter-allied staff liaison arrangements, enabled the COS and Gamelin's headquarters staff to iron out their differences. There was little rancour in Anglo-French staff conversations over the eastern Mediterranean. After all was said and done, the first priority remained to get things right in the west.[67] It was also generally agreed that Turkey held the key to any offensive scheme in the Near East. To that end, outward solidarity was essential.

Offensive planning, 1939–40

Though actively supported by Daladier and Gamelin in Paris, the French effort to forge a workable military alliance with Turkey is most readily identifiable with General Maxime Weygand. Immediately after the Turkish government made plain its scepticism about the worth of the Anglo-French guarantees issued to Greece and Romania on 13 April, Massigli suggested that a high-ranking general be sent to Ankara to prove the seriousness of French intent. Massigli read the political situation in Ankara correctly. Marshal Fevzi Çakmak's general staff was 'the hidden hand' in Turkish foreign policy; the generals were suspicious of possible British backsliding, and France, as the major land power in the western alliance, was expected to inject real muscle into military talks. France's new military attaché, General Voirin, agreed. The Turkish military would stand by its Balkan Pact obligations to Romania but naturally expected stronger support from France and Britain. The ever-pragmatic Turks would judge France and Britain on results, measured primarily by the prompt delivery of arms and the elaboration of precise strategic plans for war against Italy.[68] Weygand was the personification of the effort Massigli proposed. In May 1939 he began almost a year of unbroken dialogue with Çakmak's general staff, shuttling back and forth between Paris, Ankara, Beirut and a number of other venues for Franco-British-Turkish discussions. In these exchanges Weygand took the leading role, only briefly stepping aside in July 1939 to allow General Huntziger to reinforce his arguments for a comprehensive military alliance. Indeed, Britain's Middle Eastern commander, General Archibald Wavell, and the BEF's commander, Lord Gort, both suspected that the French general moulded the strategic outlook of his Turkish colleagues.[69] The Quai d'Orsay also played its part. A final agreement over the Sanjak signed by Massigli and foreign minister Sükrü Saraçoglu on 23 June recognized Turkey's *de facto* local control, at last removing this obstacle to a Franco-Turkish alignment.[70]

In addition to the threat of involvement in a European war, by siding with the western powers Turkey stood to lose its pre-eminent role within the quadripartite Saadabad Pact concluded in July 1937 with Iran, Iraq and Afghanistan. Conceived as the basis for an independent, neutralist bloc in the Middle East, the Saadabad Pact could not withstand Turkey's alignment with Britain, whose influence within the Middle East the other three signatories were anxious to limit. After the Anglo-Turkish commitment to alliance was publicized in May 1939 the Saadabad Pact quickly withered despite Turkey's abiding interest in a possible reversion to neutral status alongside Iran. With the Soviet Union a continuing threat, Turkey's final assent to an alliance with Britain and France in October 1939 was a bold step.[71] Between May and October, Turkish staff officers duly bombarded Weygand, Voirin and

Britain's military attaché, Colonel Ross, with urgent pleas for additional arms supplies. The Turkish air force was chronically short of modern fighters and the German annexation of Bohemia prevented the delivery of major equipment orders previously lodged with the Skoda arms works. Anti-aircraft guns, field artillery and anti-tank weapons were priority requirements. On 2 June Voirin was advised by Colonel Baheddine Kuban, head of Turkish military intelligence, that the general staff feared a German thrust towards the Straits before local fortifications were completed. War *matériel* sufficient to increase Turkey's front-line divisional strength from 30 to 42 divisions was immediately requested. The conclusion of the Nazi-Soviet pact on 23 August 1939 compounded these earlier fears regarding the safety of the Bosphorus channel and compromised Turkey's willingness to march in defence of their wavering Balkan Pact allies.[72] Not surprisingly, the Turkish negotiators, capably led by Saraçoglu, resisted British pressure for full reciprocity. The final treaty made Turkish engagement conditional upon prior Anglo-French material support and excluded Turkey from any joint action against the USSR.[73] In an adjunct to the treaty, Britain and France granted Turkey a £25 million credit for war materials. This was consistent with Turkey's existing bilateral commitment to avoid hostile actions against the Soviet Union. Whilst Turkey's urgent need for armaments and its sound respect for the intensified Soviet threat limited the scope of allied strategic planning, between October 1939 and May 1940 it was Italian and Bulgarian neutrality and the swift unravelling of the Balkan Pact, rather than any Turkish equivocation, that undermined the tripartite alliance.[74]

Since the Italians shied away from the fight over the Dodecanese for which the French and Turkish regional commanders had planned in detail, the immediate problem of the October 1939 alliance was its limited offensive potential. Its terms envisaged the creation of an allied bridgehead at Salonika to parry a German thrust into the Balkans but this, too, failed to materialize in the first months of war. Throughout the 'Phoney War' period, British negotiators and French *generalissimo* Gamelin remained unconvinced about the merits of an allied expeditionary force based at Salonika. Unhappy British memories of the Salonika campaign in 1915–18, in particular the domestic political pressure on French commander General Maurice Sarrail, the ill-disguised French effort to consolidate their imperial claim to Syria and the acrimony over command arrangements in the Near East, did not augur well for a similar venture 25 years later.[75] Joint operations at Salonika were initially proposed by Darlan and chief of staff of colonial forces, General

Antoine Bührer, at the Anglo-French Supreme War Council in the dying days of the Polish campaign. A Salonika bridgehead was championed by Weygand who, in the words of the CIGS, General Sir Edmund Ironside, recommended Franco-British intervention in the Balkans not as if 'going to a death bed, but as a good doctor with a syringe of reinvigorating medicine'. However action at Salonika, with up to ten Greek and six French divisions and, possibly, British forces, was losing its strategic rationale by January 1940.[76] The short-term threat of a German thrust towards Romania's oil-fields and the Turkish Straits had receded. Gamelin concurred with the British service chiefs that Greek and Turkish bases lacked adequate fixed defences and local fighter cover to protect major troop landings. And it appeared counter-productive to jeopardize Italian and Bulgarian neutrality by extending the allied military presence in northern Greece in anticipation of potential Italian or Bulgarian attacks. Weygand found himself increasingly isolated in his view that war against the Italians was 'a foregone conclusion'.[77] The Turks were also ambivalent towards a Salonika front. Çakmak was unwilling to commit forces to it, having concentrated over half of his army on manning defensive positions in European Turkey. Unlike Greece, Romania and Yugoslavia, the Turks did not fear Bulgarian irredentism so much as German penetration of Bulgaria for operations elsewhere.[78] Most serious, the requisite Franco-British reinforcements for a Salonika force would have to be drawn off from the western front. Their supply needs would necessitate a dispersal of Mediterranean fleet units to the Aegean at the expense of Suez defence. Neither option was attractive to the allied service chiefs.[79]

On 11 December 1939 the British and French chiefs of staff authorized Weygand and Wavell to formulate more detailed arrangements for the defence of Salonika and Turkish Thrace but without any significant diversion of land and air forces from the western front. Gamelin further stressed that all hinged upon Italy's attitude. Eight days later at the Supreme War Council Daladier's suggestion of a detailed examination of possible allied operations in the Balkans was decisively rejected by Chamberlain, Halifax, Ironside and Chatfield on the grounds that it would jeopardize Italian neutrality.[80] Although Ironside was an advocate of stronger Middle East defences, as Martin Kolinsky has shown, sensitivity towards Italy (typified by Chamberlain and Gamelin), British reluctance to broaden Near East military co-operation to cover possible joint action in the Balkans, and the confusing, poorly defined hierarchy of Anglo-French command impeded the development of a coherent allied strategy throughout the Eastern Mediterranean region.[81]

Anxious to keep the Italians out of the war, on 9 January 1940 the British COS advised Pound's successor at Alexandria, Admiral Andrew Cunningham, that the Mediterranean fleet might still be called upon to protect sea communications to Turkey against German or Soviet attack. Cunningham, in turn, wanted clarification of his precise obligations to provide shipping and support for still uncertain Balkan operations. Denied the opportunity to strike against Italian targets, Weygand and Cunningham were anxious to put their forces to immediate use lest they be transferred elsewhere. Cunningham was prepared to extend blockading operations to the Black Sea whilst Weygand, frustrated over Salonika, spearheaded French military interest in opening a diversionary front against the Soviet Union. This acquired greater momentum once Paul Reynaud took office from Daladier on 21 March.[82] As it became clearer that France and Britain could only complete a tiny proportion of Turkey's armaments orders, greater use of locally available French and British imperial forces to work alongside the Turks assumed a new political importance. But this only produced discord between Turkey's defensive priorities and the rash allied plans to widen the war in the Near East. Weygand's eagerness to direct joint operations in the Balkans also conflicted with the British service chiefs' insistence that the region fell within the Middle Eastern theatre, and was thus subject to British strategic control.[83] On 28 January 1940 Gamelin suggested to his British liaison officer, Major-General R. G. Howard-Vyse, that the British take supreme command in the Scandinavian theatre whilst France assume principal responsibility for Balkan and Near Eastern operations. This held the obvious advantages of enabling the French high command to side-step calls at home for a decisive intervention in Scandinavia whilst also tying Balkan and Middle Eastern planning together once and for all. Not surprisingly, this met with an unenthusiastic British military response. In the event, rather than tackle this question of command head-on, the issue was fudged until the battle for France and Weygand's recall made it academic.[84]

Britain's chronic underestimation of Soviet military potential found no echo in Ankara. Conscious that its forces were too poorly equipped to stave off a Soviet attack, the Turkish government sought to conciliate Moscow over the winter of 1939–40, distancing itself from Anglo-French plans for air strikes at the Soviet oil installations at Baku in the Caucasus. Without the requisite long-range bombers to attack Caucasus refineries from bases outside Turkey, more limited medium bomber sorties were effectively blocked by Turkey's refusal to make airfields available to British and French squadrons from Iraq and Syria.[85] Nor were the Turks willing to permit British warships access to the Black Sea to extend the allied naval blockade against Germany and strike against Soviet targets. During acrimonious staff conversations at Aleppo in mid-March the Turkish delegation concentrated upon consolidating Turkey's air and land defences in eastern Anatolia, and remained determinedly vague when offensive bombardments against the Caucasus were raised at further tripartite staff conversations in Beirut and Haifa between 20 May and 4 June.[86]

Only within the confines of the eastern Mediterranean theatre were the Turks willing to pursue joint offensive planning by the spring of 1940. Available targets were few. General Wavell advised Ironside in late March that British and French reinforcement of Turkish and Greek defences in Thrace took precedence over planning operations against the Dodecanese and the Caucasus.[87] On 1 May Admiral Cunningham discussed Anglo-French Mediterranean war plans with his opposite number, Admiral Jean Esteva. The British admiral reported that the French naval command was not taking the Italian threat seriously. Admiral René Godfroy's eastern Mediterranean cruiser squadron (Force X) sailed to Alexandria without a sufficient destroyer escort to protect it against Italian submarines; Esteva no longer planned to keep a 'light attack force' of three *Galissionnière*-class cruisers and eight large destroyers at Bizerta to offer immediate aid if Malta were attacked; and Esteva's claim that French units would invade Libya immediately Italy entered the war conflicted with information sent to Weygand and Wavell only three weeks earlier. Finally, Esteva brandished an unrealistic French plan to occupy Crete with 6,000 troops from Weygand's command to pre-empt further Italian encroachment into the Aegean.[88]

From early April 1940 French and British military intelligence confirmed Italian preparations for war. But comprehensive Anglo-Franco-Turkish measures to seize the Dodecanese, finalized at the Beirut staff conference on 20–21 May, were still nullified by British and French anxiety to keep Italy neutral.[89] Abortive Anglo-Italian war trade negotiations re-opened on the very day that the Beirut conference closed. A week later Reynaud's Cabinet offered to cede colonial territory in Tunisia, French Somaliland and Chad in a desperate bid to keep Mussolini sweet.[90] Always built on sand, ambitious French strategic planning in the eastern Mediterranean quickly fell apart. In early April Massigli had warned that, without major arms deliveries, President Ismet Inönü and foreign minister Saraçoğlu would soon lose faith in French capacity. Weygand's departure from Beirut to replace Gamelin as supreme commander in late May sealed matters. On 28 May the Turkish authorities blocked the shipment of any further strategic raw materials to Marseilles. Marshal Çakmak only reversed this decision on the understanding that ships making the return journey to Turkey should come laden with French war *matériel*, a promise quickly over-taken by events in France.[91] At a final planning conference in Haifa a week later the three delegations agreed to disagree over a Turkish scheme to invade Rhodes, aware that this was merely a paper plan unlikely to come to fruition.[92] Although Anglo-Turkish collaboration limped on beyond the fall of France, Britain's preoccupation with North and East Africa and the German descent into the Balkans in 1941 ensured Turkey's neutrality.

Anglo-French defence co-operation in the eastern Mediterranean ended much as it had begun – the military crisis of May–June 1940 destroyed the links born out of the Abyssinian crisis five years earlier. The increas-ing importance attached to offensive planning against Italy, common imperial problems in Palestine and Syria and the shared frustrations of the Turkish alliance made for far-reaching dialogue. But this only became fully-fledged strategic planning after April 1939 owing to Britain's reluctance to commit to France. Thereafter, the gulf between Anglo-French ends and means became painfully clear as the require-ments of continental and imperial defence consumed the bulk of western resources. This was repeatedly exposed by their Turkish ally. British nervousness about the defence of Egypt and the unresolved dilemma of a Mediterranean fleet potentially over-stretched by its addi-tional obligation to Far Eastern defence was matched by the French high command's unwillingness to commit the land and air forces nec-essary to make Weygand's Near Eastern planning a viable proposition. After September 1939 Italian neutrality blocked the one joint operation in the eastern Mediterranean – a seizure of the Dodecanese – that might have been swiftly accomplished in order to cement the alliance with the Turks. In its stead, the round of tripartite planning conferences between October 1939 and June 1940 gradually lost credibility. Frus-tration with the requirement to keep Italy neutral, the failure to deliver major arms supplies to the Turks, disagreement over the Salonika bridgehead and the fantasy of an easy knock-out blow against Soviet oil installations all suggest that allied strategic planning in the Near East was at variance with the most salient fact of the 'phoney war' period; namely, that the conflict with Germany in the west would decide everything.

Notes

The author wishes to thank Peter Jackson and Glynn Stone for their comments on earlier drafts of this chapter.

1. S. Morewood, 'The Chiefs of Staff, the "Men on the Spot" and the Italo-Abyssinian Emergency, 1935–36', in D. Richardson and G. Stone (eds), *Decisions and Diplomacy: Essays in Twentieth Century International History* (London: Routledge, 1995), pp. 85–99 *passim*.
2. Eden to Lampson, 20 February 1936, Public Record Office, Kew [PRO], ADM 116/3588; Lampson Diary, 27 and 28 May 1936, Papers of First Baron Killearn, St Antony's College, Middle East Centre archive, Oxford; M. Kolinsky, *Britain's War in the Middle East. Strategy and Diplomacy, 1936–42* (Basingstoke: Macmillan Press [now Palgrave Macmillan] 1999), pp. 29–30.
3. Succinct analyses of Britain's Middle Eastern security concerns are: L. Pratt, *East of Malta, West of Suez: Britain's Mediterranean Crisis, 1936–1939* (Cambridge: Cambridge University Press, 1975); D. Omissi, 'The Mediterranean and the Middle East in British Global Strategy, 1935–39', and M. J. Cohen, 'British Strategy in the Middle East in the Wake of the Abyssinian Crisis, 1936–39', in M. J. Cohen and M. Kolinsky (eds), *Britain and the Middle East in the 1930s: Security Problems, 1935–1939* (Basingstoke: Macmillan Press [now Palgrave Macmillan] 1992), pp. 3–40; M. Kolinsky, *Law, Order and Riots in Mandatory Palestine, 1928–1935* (Basingstoke: Macmillan Press [now Palgrave Macmillan] 1993), pp. 209–16; Morewood, 'The Chiefs of Staff', pp. 83–107.
4. S. Morewood, 'Protecting the Jugular Vein of Empire: the Suez Canal in British Defence Strategy, 1919–1941', *War and Society*, 10 (1992), pp. 86–8.
5. 'Recent emergency in eastern Mediterranean', report by C.-in-C. Mediterranean, 19 March 1936, PRO, ADM 116/3468; 'History of the Italian-Abyssinian emergency', Office of C.-in-C. Mediterranean fleet, 20 December 1937, PRO, ADM 116/3476; CID minutes of the 275th meeting and 'Mediterranean – Counter-bombardment defences', JDC 301, [January 1937], FO 371/21136. For a clear analysis of Italy's actual offensive capability in 1935–6, see R. Mallett, *The Italian Navy and Fascist Expansionism 1935–1940* (London: Frank Cass, 1998), pp. 11–37.
6. 'Situation des bâtiments français en Mediterrannée', Etat-major Général de la Marine [EMM] memorandum, 22 November 1935, PRO, ADM 116/3398.
7. Report on Anglo-French staff conversations, Etat-major Général de la Guerre [EMG], Section d'Etudes, 29 October 1935, Service Historique de la Marine [SHM], Vincennes, 1BB2/182/1; Admiralty to C.-in-C. Mediterranean, 9 December 1935, and Chatfield memorandum for Director of Plans, 3 January 1936, PRO, ADM 116/3398; R. M. Salerno, 'Multilateral Strategy and Diplomacy: the Anglo-German Naval Agreement and the Mediterranean Crisis, 1935–1936', *Journal of Strategic Studies*, 17 (1994), pp. 58–9.
8. 'Note au sujet de mesures à prendre pour ajuster les ressources besoins en 1935 et 1936', EMM premier bureau, no date, SHM, 1BB2/32.
9. 'History of the Italian-Abyssinian emergency', Office of C.-in-C. Mediterranean fleet, 20 December 1937, PRO, ADM 116/3476; Morewood, 'The Chiefs of Staff', pp. 87–8.

10. Captain Hammill report to Director of Naval Intelligence, 8 November 1935, and Report on visit of HMS *Wishart*, Louis Mountbatten, Vice-Admiral Malta, 24 December 1935, PRO, ADM 116/3398.
11. Record of Anglo-French naval conversations, 15 January 1936, EMG Section d'Etudes, SHM, 1BB2/182/1; EMG Section d'Etude des armements navals memorandum, 9 June 1936, SHM, 1BB2/208/14.
12. W. L. French to Chatfield, 3 September 1935, Chatfield papers, National Maritime Museum, Greenwich, CHT/3/1.
13. Pratt, *East of Malta*, pp. 49–52.
14. CID minutes of the 288th meeting, 11 February 1937, PRO, CAB 24/CP (37)65.
15. Lampson Diary, 27 April 1937, Killearn papers.
16. 'Mediterranean Ports: Gibraltar and Malta. Counter-Bombardment Defences', Joint Overseas and Home Defence sub-committee memorandum, 27 April 1937, PRO, FO 371/21136; L. Pratt, 'The Strategic Context: British Policy in the Mediterranean and the Middle East, 1936–1939', in U. Dann (ed.), *The Great Powers in the Middle East, 1919–1939* (New York: Holmes and Meier, 1988), pp. 15–16.
17. 'Négociations franco-italiennes sur les affaires d'Afrique et du Levant', Sous-direction Afrique-Levant, 26 April 1938, Centre des Archives Diplomatiques, Nantes [CADN], Ambassade de Londres, vol. 263.
18. W. Shorrock, *From Ally to Enemy: the Enigma of Fascist Italy in French Diplomacy, 1920–1940* (Kent, Ohio: Kent State University Press, 1988); R. J. Young: 'French Military Intelligence and the Franco-Italian Alliance, 1933–1939', *Historical Journal*, 28 (1985), pp. 157–63.
19. 'Situation générale', report by Parisot, 30 May 1936; De Larosière to EMM deuxième bureau, 30 May 1936, Service Historique de l'Armée de Terre, Vincennes [SHAT], 7N2907/1.
20. See J. Blatt, 'The Parity that Meant Superiority: French Naval Policy towards Italy at the Washington Conference and Interwar French Foreign Policy', French Historical Studies, 12 (1981), pp. 223–48, and 'France and the Washington Conference', *Diplomacy and Statecraft*, 4 (1993), pp. 192–219.
21. R. M. Salerno, 'The French Navy and the Appeasement of Italy, 1937–9', *English Historical Review*, CXII (1997), pp. 66–104; H. Coutau-Bégarie and C. Huan (eds), *Lettres et notes de l'Amiral Darlan* (Paris: Economica, 1992), nos. 41, 42, 52, 53.
22. 'Franco-British action in Libya', French delegation report, 26 April 1939, Anglo-French staff conversations 1939, PRO, WO 193/197/AFC(J)50; 'Note on inter-allied overseas theatres of operations on land', French delegation, 31 May 1939, WO 106/2019/AFC(J)82.
23. Chatfield to Pound, 5 August 1937, Chatfield papers, CHT/4/10.
24. COS sub-committee memoranda, 'Situation in the Mediterranean and Middle East', 1346B and 1364B, 28 July and 26 October 1937, PRO, CAB 4/26; COS sub-committee memorandum, 'Defence of Egypt', 1371B, 24 November 1937; Foreign Office memorandum, 'Concentration of Italian troops in Libya', 1379B, 15 December 1937, CAB 4/27.
25. Admiralty telegram to C.-in-C. Mediterranean, 5 August 1937; Admiral Roger Backhouse to Admiralty Secretary, 6 September 1937, PRO, ADM 1/9533;

M. H. Murfett, 'Living in the Past: a Critical Re-Examination of the Singapore Naval Strategy, 1918–1941', *War and Society*, 11 (1993), pp. 86–94.

26. Lampson Diary, 21 January 1938, Killearn papers; Morewood, 'Protecting the Jugular Vein of Empire', pp. 88–9.

27. Report of Committee on Shipping in the Far East, 12 November 1937, PRO, CAB 24/272/CP270(37); Chatfield to Duff Cooper, 25 January 1938, Chatfield papers, CHT/3/1.

28. 'Mediterranean, Middle East and North East Africa strategic appreciation', 21 February 1938, PRO, WO 33/1507/COS 691; 'The Situation in the Mediterranean and Middle East', Sir Thomas Inskip memorandum, 19 November 1937, PRO, CAB 24/273/CP281(37); Brian Bond, *British Military Policy between the Two World Wars* (Oxford: Oxford University Press, 1980), pp. 263–7.

29. Section Levant to CSDN, 14 May 1936, Ministère des Affaires Etrangères, Paris [MAE], série E, Syrie-Liban 1930–1940, vol. 492; Huntziger report on Franco-Turkish accords, 19 February 1938, SHAT, 7N4190/1.

30. 'Note sur la situation militaire actuelle dans la monde', CSG, 29 March 1938, MAE, Fonds Daladier, D1/1925; Kolinsky, *Britain's War in the Middle East*, pp. 23–5.

31. 'Attitude of the "Arab World" to Great Britain with particular reference to the Palestine conference', 20 February 1939, PRO, WO 106/2018B/COS 847(JIC).

32. MacKereth, to Halifax, 4 November 1938, and 'Memorandum on Lebanese opinion on the Palestine situation', by Havard, 17 May 1938, PRO, CO 733/368/1/E2380/2919/2; P. S. Khoury, *Syria and the French Mandate. The Politics of Arab Nationalism, 1920–1945* (London: I. B. Tauris, 1987), pp. 536–46.

33. Division navale du Levant note, 2 October 1936, SHAT, 7N4190/1; MacKereth to Halifax, 30 November 1938, PRO, CO 733/398/5/E7112/6389/65; Khoury, *Syria and the French Mandate*, p. 493.

34. Hoare to Dill, 10 September 1936, General Sir John Dill papers, PRO, WO 282/4; 'Palestine', memorandum by Eden, 19 November 1937, and 'Policy in Palestine', memorandum by Ormsby-Gore, 1 December 1937, PRO, CAB 24/273/CP 281(37) and CP 289(37).

35. C. M. Andrew and A. S. Kanya Forstner, *France Overseas. The Great War and the Climax of French Imperial Expansion* (London: Thames and Hudson, 1981), pp. 164–208.

36. E. Rabbath, 'L'insurrection syrienne de 1925–1927', *Revue Historique*, 542 (1982), pp. 405–47; I. Rabinovitch, 'The Compact Minorities and the Syrian State, 1918–1945', *Journal of Contemporary History*, 14 (1979), pp. 693–712.

37. Bulletin de renseignements des questions musulmanes, Etat-Major de l'Armée [EMA] Section d'Outre-Mer, 11 September 1937, SHAT, 7N4093.

38. Mediterranean station intelligence report, no. 7, 31 July 1938, PRO, ADM 1/9564.

39. Dill to Jackson, 26 February 1937, PRO, WO 282/1.

40. G. Sheffer, 'Principles of Pragmatism: a Reevaluation of British Policies toward Palestine in the 1930s', in Dann, *The Great Powers in the Middle East*, pp. 110–12.

41. Vansittart memorandum, 29 September 1936, PRO, CAB 16/140/DPR 122; Morewood, 'Protecting the Jugular Vein of Empire', p. 88; 'Note au sujet de l'établissement militaire français au Levant', EMA Section d'Outre-Mer, 10 December 1938, SHAT, 7N4190/1.

42. Admiralty telegram to C.-in-C. Mediterranean fleet, 5 August 1937, PRO, ADM 1/9533; T. Bowden, 'The Politics of the Arab Rebellion in Palestine 1936–39', *Middle Eastern Studies*, 11 (1975), pp. 153–69; M. Kolinsky, 'The Collapse and Restoration of Public Security', in Cohen and Kolinsky, *Britain and the Middle East in the 1930s*, pp. 153–62.

43. Lampson views of Suez Canal Defence Plan, 17 December 1938, PRO, ADM 1/9864.

44. K. W. Stein, *The Land Question in Palestine, 1917–1939* (Chapel Hill, NC: University of North Carolina Press, 1984), pp. 199–202.

45. WO letter to under-secretary of state, Colonial Office, 28 January 1937, PRO, CO 732/79/5; MacKereth to Foreign Office, 27 November 1939, CO 732/86/19/E3195/2413/10. Desertion by Foreign Legion troops and by Palestinian auxiliaries hostile to British policy were persistent problems in 1936–40.

46. Kolinsky, 'The Collapse and Restoration of Public Security', p. 155.

47. Commission d'Etudes de la défense des états du Levant, 1938, 28 December1938, SHAT, 7N4190/1, no. 365.

48. 'Summary of Intelligence', 24 February 1939, HQ British Forces, Palestine and Transjordan, PRO, CO 732/84/15/GSI/4/23; M. J. Cohen, 'Appeasement in the Middle East: the British White Paper on Palestine, May 1939', *Historical Journal*, 16 (1973), pp. 571–96; Khoury, *Syria and the French Mandate*, pp. 485–93, 531–4 and 584–6.

49. Bulletin de renseignements des questions musulmanes, EMA Section d'Outre-Mer, 20 September 1939, SHAT, 7N4093.

50. Vansittart memorandum, 29 September 1936, PRO, CAB 16/140/DPR 122; 'Etude en cas d'une offensive turque contre la frontière syrienne', report by Colonel de Courson de la Villeneuve, 26 September 1935, SHAT, 7N3226/3.

51. B. Millman, 'Turkish Foreign and Strategic Policy, 1934–42', *Middle Eastern Studies*, 31 (1995), pp. 485–8; S. Deringil, *Turkish Foreign Policy during the Second World War: an 'Active' Neutrality* (Cambridge: Cambridge University Press, 1989), pp. 32–6.

52. Vansittart memorandum, 29 September 1936, PRO, CAB 16/140/DPR 122; de la Villeneuve to EMA deuxième bureau, 25 August 1936; de la Villeneuve to EMAA deuxième bureau, 8 December 1936, SHAT, 7N3226/5. Turkey first sought British fighters. This was later altered to a request for Blenheim bombers of which the air ministry only released 12. Their delivery was repeatedly delayed. Twenty-one French PZL fighters were supplied by November 1936.

53. 'Note relative aux accords militaires à établir avec la Turquie', by Huntziger, 19 February 1938, MAE, Papiers d'agents 217, Papiers René Massigli, vol. 24.

54. Loraine, Ankara, to Foreign Office, 12 January 1937, PRO, FO 371/21136/R264/5/67.

55. For analysis of the Sanjak problem, see J. Thobie, 'Le nouveau cours des relations franco-turques et l'affaire du sandjak d'Alexandrette, 1929–1939', *Relations Internationales*, 19 (1979), pp. 355–74; Khoury, *Syria and the French*

Mandate, pp. 494–514; René Massigli, *La Turquie devant la guerre. Mission à Ankara 1939–40* (Paris: Plon, 1964), pp. 42–57.
56. Khoury, *Syria and the French Mandate*, pp. 502–13.
57. 'Conversations d'état-major avec les Turcs concernant le Sandjak d'Alexandrette', EMA deuxième bureau, 7 May 1937, MAE, Papiers 1940, Fonds Daladier, D1; 'Note au sujet de l'établissement militaire français au Levant', EMA Section d'Outre-Mer, 10 December 1938, SHAT, 7N4190/1; D. C. Watt, *How War Came. The Immediate Origins of the Second World War, 1938–1939* (New York: Pantheon, 1989), pp. 285–6.
58. Jules Blondel to Paul-Boncour, 17 April 1938, MAE, Série Z, Italie vol. 278; 'Négociations franco-italiennes sur les affaires d'Afrique et du Levant', Sous-direction Afrique-Levant, 26 April 1938, CADN, Londres, vol. 263.
59. Salerno, 'The French Navy', pp. 79–82; B. Favreau, *Georges Mandel ou la passion de la République 1885–1944* (Paris: Fayard, 1996), p. 356.
60. Massigli, *La Turquie devant la guerre*, chs. I, VI and VIII.
61. Text of Franco-Turkish Treaty of Friendship, 4 July 1938; Ankara Embassy dispatch, 24 September 1938; Bonnet to Henri Ponsot, 8 October 1938, MAE, Massigli papers, vol. 24; de la Villeneuve to EMA deuxième bureau, 28 March 1938, SHAT, 7N3227/1.
62. Captain Leleu to EMA deuxième bureau, 9 September 1938; General Voirin to EMA deuxième bureau, 3 November 1938, SHAT, 7N3227/1; Millman, 'Turkish Foreign and Strategic Policy', pp. 487–8.
63. Charles Corbin to Bonnet, 21 November 1938, MAE, Massigli papers, vol. 24.
64. R. A. C. Parker, *Chamberlain and Appeasement. British Policy and the Coming of War* (Basingstoke: Macmillan Press [now Palgrave Macmillan] 1993), pp. 192–6 and 219–22; Watt, *How War Came*, pp. 274–8.
65. As examples: 'European Appreciation', 20 February 1939, PRO, CAB 16/183A; 'Operations in the Eastern Mediterranean', by General Gamelin, 13 July 1939, PRO, WO 106/2019.
66. Kolinsky, *Britain's War in the Middle East*, pp. 95–9.
67. Lord Gort to Ironside, 26 December 1939, PRO, WO 193/955.
68. Massigli to Bonnet, 'Sur la mission du Général Weygand', 8 May 1939, MAE, Massigli papers, vol. 24; Voirin to EMA deuxième bureau, 21 March 1939, SHAT, 7N3227/3.
69. *DDF*, Ser. II, vol. XVII, nos. 399, 526; Wavell's report on land forces Middle East, August 1939-November 1940, PRO, CAB 106/472; GHQ BEF to Ironside, 26 December 1939, PRO, WO 193/955; B. Millman, *The Ill-Made Alliance. Anglo-Turkish Relations, 1934–1940* (Montreal: McGill University Press, 1998), pp. 294–300.
70. Knatchbull-Hugessen to Foreign Office, 29 June 1939, PRO, CO 733/86/1/E4837/1142/44.
71. D. Cameron Watt, 'The Saadabad Pact of 8 July 1937', in Dann (ed.), *The Great Powers in the Middle East*, pp. 333–52.
72. Voirin to EMA deuxième bureau, 2 June 1939 and 7 October 1939, SHAT, 7N3227/3. Some two-thirds of Turkish munitions orders were placed with Skoda before 1939.
73. Deringil, *Turkish Foreign Policy*, pp. 88–9; for the USSR see A. L. Macfie, 'The Turkish Straits in the Second World War', *Middle Eastern Studies*, 25 (1989), pp. 239–41.

74. Millman, 'Turkish Foreign and Strategic policy', pp. 496–501; B. Millman, 'Toward War with Russia: British Naval and Air Planning for Conflict in the Near East, 1939–40', *Journal of Contemporary History*, 29 (1994), pp. 261–83; Elisabeth du Réau, 'Les Balkans dans la stratégie méditerranéenne de la France, avril 1939-mai 1940', *Balkan Studies*, 29 (1988), pp. 77–8.
75. D. Dutton, *The Politics of Diplomacy. Britain and France in the Balkans in the First World War* (London: I. B. Tauris, 1998), chs. 4 and 6.
76. M. S. Alexander, *The Republic in Danger. General Maurice Gamelin and the Politics of French Defence, 1933–1940* (Cambridge: Cambridge University Press, 1992), pp. 350–1; R. Macleod and D. Kelly (eds), *The Ironside Diaries 1937–1940* (London: Constable, 1962), p. 171.
77. 'Note concerning allied operations in the Balkans', Allied Military Committee, 11 January 1940, PRO, AIR 9/126; Rendel, to Halifax, 2 March 1940, FO 371/24876; Knatchbull-Hugessen to Foreign Office, 12 September1939, CAB 104/137/435.
78. Millman, 'Turkish Foreign and Strategic Policy', pp. 498–9. In collaboration with Germany, Bulgaria later annexed the southern Dobruja in September 1940 and Yugoslav and Greek Macedonia and Greek Thrace in April 1941.
79. 'Note on eventual military co-operation with Turkey', PRO, WO 193/197/AFC(J)80; M.O. 1 Notes on Middle East planning, 8 September 1939; Note on Middle East discussion for C.-in-C. BEF, n.d., December 1939, PRO, WO 193/955.
80. Record of meeting held at Gamelin's HQ, 11 December 1939, PRO, CAB 104/138; du Réau, 'Les Balkans', pp. 80–1; Kolinsky, *Britain's War in the Middle East*, pp. 110–11.
81. Kolinsky, *Britain's War in the Middle East*, pp. 99–121.
82. 'War Policy in the Mediterranean', Cunningham memorandum, 26 November 1939; Admiralty to Cunningham, 9 January 1940, PRO, ADM 1/10358; Millman, *The Ill-Made Alliance*, pp. 326–7.
83. 'Allied command in the Near East', 8 January1940, PRO, AIR 9/126/COS (40)186; Kolinsky, *Britain's War in the Middle East*, pp. 107 and 115–17.
84. 'Note on conversation with General Gamelin', British Military Mission No. 1, 28 January 1940, and 'Control of Theatres of Operations', Howard-Vyse memorandum to DMO, 29 January 1940, PRO, WO 208/618.
85. Millman, 'Toward War with Russia', pp. 268–75; P. Buffotot, 'Le projet de bombardement des pétroles soviétiques de Caucase en 1940, un exemple des projets alliés dans la drôle de guerre', *Revue Historique des Armées*, 4 (1979), pp. 79–101.
86. Aleppo conference reports, April 1940, PRO, WO 106/2049; C.-in-C. RAF Middle East to Air Ministry, 16 June 1940, AIR 9/145.
87. Wavell to CIGS, 30 March 1940, PRO, WO 106/2049.
88. Report on Bizerta conversations by Cunningham, 2 May 1940, PRO, ADM 1/10599.
89. General d'Arbonneau to EMA deuxième bureau, 31 March 1940; d'Arbonneau record of conversation with deputy chief of general staff, General Assim Gündüz, 30 April 1940, SHAT, 7N3227/4; Minutes of Beirut conference, 20 May 1940, PRO, AIR 9/145; du Réau, 'Les Balkans', p. 83.
90. R. Mallett, 'The Anglo-Italian War Trade Negotiations, Contraband Control and the Failure to Appease Mussolini, 1939–40', *Diplomacy and Statecraft*, 8

(1997), pp. 137–67; French government message to Churchill, 28 May 1940, PRO, AIR 8/351.

91. Massigli meeting with Inönü and Saraçoglü, 5 April 1940; Massigli telegrams to Section Afrique-Levant, 24 May 1940 and 1 June 1940, MAE, Massigli papers, vol. 24.

92. DMO to CIGS, 9 June 1940, PRO, WO 106/2066.

8
Preparing to Feed Mars: Anglo-French Economic Co-ordination and the Coming of War, 1937–40

Martin S. Alexander

The experience of 1914–18 demonstrated incontrovertibly that the success or failure of a nation – or alliance – in modern war depended as much on economic organization as it did on courage at the front or talented generalship. Above all, episodes in the first world war such as the 'shells scandal' in Britain in the spring of 1915, as well as the need to enhance the efficiency of French war industries discovered and subsequently undertaken by Etienne Clémentel and Louis Loucheur in 1917, exposed the vital importance of a professional preparation and management of defence industries.[1] Victory in the 'age of industrialized war' demanded a ruthless and integrated regime to ensure timely and almost unlimited supply to the armed forces of weapons, equipment and munitions. Such a regime had to do this without bankrupting the nation. Yet, whilst meeting military needs, it had to avoid neglecting civilian requirements for food and fuel to the point of provoking serious pressure to end the war before victory was achieved. Britain and France both sought to learn and embed these 'lessons' of 1914–18. Both powers established bodies responsible, in peacetime, for planning and administering a rapid expansion and balanced distribution of productive resources in the event of another war. This chapter will, first, briefly review the British and French administrative arrangements. It then examines in more detail the far-sighted, but in crucial respects incomplete, measures taken by 1939–40 towards forging an integrated allied, or 'joint', war economy.

In France, rather than economic preparations for war being clearly and simply under one specialist ministry or planning organ, such preparations were a playground for competing ambitions, aggrandisement and empire building. The lack of clarity and simplicity of the French

186

army and air-force chain of command has been identified by many writers as a key structural shortcoming that contributed to French defeat in 1940. In parallel with this, complex, confused and overlapping responsibilities also marred French preparations on the economic side of contingency planning for war. The bodies chiefly involved down to 1939 were, first, the Conseil Supérieur de la Défense Nationale (CSDN) and, second, a series of government ministries.

The CSDN had been established in 1906. Its capabilities were steadily enhanced, first through the addition of a Studies Section (later the Studies Commission) in 1911, then by the formation of a Secretariat in 1913 (expanded to a Secretariat-General in 1921). Finally the CSDN's Studies Commission was reorganized in March 1922 into four sections, one of which was charged with economic planning for war. For the first decade after the first world war the CSDN was a highly professional and active body. In the 1920s it generated valuable reports on the technical aspects of fortifications policy that led to construction of the Maginot Line. From 1930 onwards it supported the work of the French members of the preparatory commission for the World Disarmament Conference which opened in Geneva in February 1932.[2] Another of its key roles was to examine and draft advisory papers on the steps France would need to take to mobilize, financially and industrially, for another war. Several of its studies on this topic were undertaken by Charles de Gaulle who, as a lieutenant colonel, served on the secretariat from 1932 to 1937.[3]

In the second half of the 1930s, however, the CSDN's influence declined. Alternative bodies were set up, charged with the higher direction of French defence and military policy. These were, most notably, the Haut Comité Militaire (HCM) created in May 1932 and its successor, the Comité Permanent de la Défense Nationale (CPDN) established in June 1936 at the same moment as the ministry of national defence and war. Though its Studies Commission continued at work, there was no plenary meeting of the council after spring 1935. As Eugenia Kiesling aptly observes, 'the CSDN and its study committee slumbered during the mid-1930s'.[4] Its diminished activity and effectiveness reflected the preoccupation of successive prime ministers with domestic political unrest (the February 1934 Paris riots and their aftermath) and with budget crises triggered in 1933 when the world depression hit the French economy.

The CSDN was unduly dependent on prime ministerial impetus. This was because its successive secretaries-general, Generals Bernard Serrigny, Pierre Chabert and Louis Jamet, reported directly to the head of government. This placed the CSDN outside the normal chain of command alongside the senior military advisers – the chiefs of the army, navy and air staffs, who reported to their respective cabinet ministers. Greatest responsibility for failing to reactivate the CSDN, its secretariat and its research and investigative resources, lies with Edouard Daladier, the senior Radical Party politician. This is because in April 1938 he became prime minister again (having already led governments in 1933 and 1934), whilst retaining his defence and strategic planning responsibilities as minister for national defence and war, the department over which he had an unbroken tenure from June 1936 to March 1940.[5] In theory Jamet had direct access to the prime minister. In practice, however, most heads of government were swept up by the political, social and economic turbulence of the later Third Republic and remained partly or wholly deaf to strategic and military issues.

Lacking a firm lead from the prime minister's office, numerous departments staked out claims to run parts of the defence economy. Among the departments within the government bureaucracy most involved in economic preparations for war were: the ministry of national defence and war (constituted in June 1936); the ministry of labour; the ministry of commerce and industry; and the ministry of public works. A damaging consequence of this was an approach to economic preparation for future war that remained fragmented, rather than clear and centralized. In certain cases, such as the action of the Direction des Charbonnages at the Ministry of Public Works discussed in greater detail below, excellent work was done to prepare wartime substitute sources of coal that was, in peacetime, purchased by French steel foundries from German suppliers. Elsewhere, however, the proliferation of multiple departmental interests in all aspects of the planning of France's conversion to a war economy proved a recipe for bureaucratic rivalries, inefficiency and a job still unfinished when war came in September 1939. France's ill-preparedness made its ministers and high command desperately grateful for every month that Hitler delayed his expected offensive in the West. Belatedly trying to tackle the deficiencies, Daladier reshuffled his government on 13 September 1939, creating a new and independent ministry of armaments. To run this he brought in a businessman, Raoul Dautry, a successful, highly respected and dynamic former head of French state railways.[6] Yet even in the autumn and winter of 1939–40, as will be seen, serious handicaps continued to cripple sectors of France's war industries. Worse, on-going bureaucratic bickering between the many ministries that kept fingers in the pie continued to undermine the aim of turning France into a lean, well-honed combatant at one with itself over the aims and methods best suited to defeating the Third Reich.[7]

Perhaps one aim and method with which nobody in Paris took issue was the vital need for France to have a full-scale British economic and military commitment to help first to defend her and then, later in a war, to go on and defeat Germany. But how well had Britain, for her part, been preparing to convert to a war economy? In 1927 Stanley Baldwin's Conservative government gave the Principal Supply Officers' Committee the task of investigating supply matters in the eventuality of a future war. In December 1933 an advisory group of leading industrialists was formed to provide expert advice to the government and to the supply committees of the War Office, Admiralty and air ministry. These developments were supplemented by the establishment of specialist departments within the service ministries themselves during 1936. At the War Office, Sir Harold Brown was appointed that year to a new post, Director-General of Munitions Production, assuming responsibility for the progress of the army's part of British rearmament. The Directorate of Industrial Planning provided blueprints for the production of army equipment during wartime. By the spring of 1939 – the point at which Britain finally entered comprehensive staff talks with France – it had compiled a set of 'process manuals'. The work of these departments and of the respective supply committees in the British service ministries ensured that, before September 1939, detailed plans had been formulated for wartime military-industrial requirements, and on how to reorganize industry from a peacetime to a war footing.

Formulating workable plans for wartime production, with which the relevant officials and industrialists were closely acquainted, was vital if Britain's war economy was to cope with the expected 'long haul' characteristics of another war with Germany (the *guerre de longue durée* as the French termed it).[8] The war economy, however, had something of the characteristics of a pipeline: the service ministries placed orders, creating a flow of war manufactures beginning at one end, and a tap was opened at the other from which the flow would emerge to the armed forces in the field. But the pipeline in between was a long one and it contained twists and bottlenecks, both of industrial plant and skilled labour. Turning on even a well-greased tap could not, therefore, produce an instant surge of output. Before hostilities began the British government remained anxious about the nation's financial and economic health and the fragility of the recovery from the slump of 1931–33. These had been the primary concerns of Neville Chamberlain during his years as Chancellor of the Exchequer (1931–37). To this eye for national economic prosperity was added Chamberlain's determined – and, till the winter of 1938–39, confident – search for a general settlement or 'appeasement' with Germany and Italy. The result was that Britain's economy was rendered capable of transition to a war footing, but was held back from going onto such a footing until all possibilities for peaceful accommodation had been exhausted.

Financial prudence was a wise policy. British gold and foreign-exchange reserves had been severely depleted by the nation's war effort in 1914–18. This legacy left the Treasury concerned to balance the need for munitions in the short run with the need to husband the financial strength to survive in the long run. Sir Robert Vansittart, from 1930 to January 1938 permanent under-secretary at the Foreign Office and an inveterate sceptic about appeasing Germany, complained in a minute in mid-summer 1939 that 'the Treasury worry too much about how we shall live five years hence, not whether we shall be alive one year hence'.[9] But it was essential to balance the short term and the long term in preparing Britain for a war that the chiefs of staff expected to last at least four or five years.

Nevertheless, what George Peden has termed 'Treasury rationing', and the maintenance of British industrial output for civilian export markets right down into 1939, meant that aircraft production to re-equip the RAF remained limited even after 1938.[10] It also saw plans in 1939 for a 55-division British army being scaled back in favour of a planned 32-division army by the end of the second year of war. Government planning for a war of three years' duration or longer was reasonable. But as the official historian of British wartime production, M. M. Postan, has remarked:

> the decisive strategic events of the period came before the culminating dates in the calendar of preparations. Neither the declaration of war in September 1939 nor the beginning of active operations in the spring of 1940 took account of the timetable of His Majesty's Government.[11]

Even at the time there were complaints from the service chiefs about the inadequacy of the measures taken to mobilize industry and generate large-scale deliveries of the most up-to-date weapons and munitions in the first eight months of the conflict – the so-called 'phoney war' from September 1939 to April 1940. General Sir Edmund Ironside, the Chief of the Imperial General Staff (CIGS) during this time, sent agents from the War Office around Britain to report on the output of factories. 'They said that few were working all-out, many only for eight hours out of twenty-four, practically none worked at night, and there appeared to be no sense of urgency.'[12] Government measures to ensure the provision of the necessary supplies of materials and skilled labour could have alleviated these problems. Leslie Hore-Belisha, the Secretary of State for War, declared in September 1939: 'The Empire is faced with a situation of great peril . . . the country should be roused to make far greater efforts and far greater sacrifices than are at present contemplated.'[13]

More comprehensive economic preparations for war might have been developed had the British authorities taken an earlier decision to institute a wider system of controls and directed priorities for industry. But before the summer crisis of 1940 stirred up a new sense of urgency, there was, as Postan notes, no 'economic regimentation'. Indeed during the phoney war the discipline and single-minded focus on output of military stores of a war economy were still 'being merely coaxed into existence'.[14] It remained possible for civilian manufacturers of non-essential goods to compete with war production for increasingly scarce resources such as fuel, labour and raw materials. Business-as-usual may have ceased. Postan has argued, however, that this was replaced by a philosophy of 'life as usual'.[15] Some controls were introduced at the outbreak of war for priority materials such as iron and steel. A ministerial Priority Committee was established in the first weeks of war to regulate the allocation of national economic resources. Also the Ministerial Committee on Economic Policy was assigned the role of co-ordinating the economy of Britain in wartime. Yet the overall system of regulation and prioritization remained 'embryonic' down to mid-1940.[16]

The application of controls and the determination of priorities in the labour market were equally inadequate in the early months of war. As 1939 turned into 1940 it became plain that more draconian steps were needed to counteract the scarcity of skilled workers for essential industries (and especially for ones such as airframe and aero-engine construction, in which massive expansion was required). At first a redistribution of existing labour would have reduced many of the difficulties faced by the armaments industries. Yet it was found that measures of 'dilution' and de-skilling were also essential. In the early months of the war measures to address the problems of skilled-labour bottlenecks and shortages were not taken as swiftly as they might have been, through concern over the attitude of the British trade unions. This delayed full-scale mobilization of labour. In the war's first year British industry had to bear the mounting manufacturing costs that resulted from competitive pay rises obtained by men with sought-after skills.

One crucial measure that was taken towards establishment of a British wartime economy was the formation of a ministry of supply. In October

1938, after Munich, the Cabinet had postponed indefinitely the idea of creating such a body. It was not till July 1939 that this decision was reversed and the ministry of supply, under Leslie Burgin, was at last established – very much a response to the worsening European crisis. One official deeply involved in Britain's wartime organization of logistics, Sir Arthur Salter (later Lord Salter), later criticized the way Chamberlain's government inched its way 'from resistance, then reluctant and dilatory acceptance' towards this decision.[17] Even when the ministry was set up, Salter censured the government's policy of permitting the contract departments of the War Office, Admiralty and air ministry to decide whether or not to transfer to the new body. General Ironside was another who aimed barbed comments at the ministry of supply. He, along with Hore-Belisha and Winston Churchill, once again First Lord of the Admiralty from September 1939, had argued for establishing an organization analogous to the 1915–18 ministry of munitions. There was a feeling that the ministry of supply was apart from, rather than fully integrated with, the existing defence bureaucracies. In one example, Ironside criticized the procedures that prevented consultation between the army and the ministry of supply. This led to poor co-ordination over crucial matters of weapon design and weapons manufacturing priorities. Even in June 1940 Ironside complained of the ministry of supply's failure to understand army requirements: 'The Army cannot get its demands fulfilled by the Ministry of Supply. The user has had little say in what he requires.'[18] In sum, measures towards a comprehensively organized, efficient and balanced British war economy were slow and incomplete before the summer crisis of 1940 provided a sharp spur to resolve many long-shelved but lingering issues previously regarded as too difficult to deal with.

But what of Anglo-French co-operation to ensure the best distribution and application of the combined economic resources of each country and its overseas empire? Paradoxically, greater progress had been made before the war in joint planning in this area than in the resolution of purely domestic aspects of British wartime economic management. Measures taken to regulate the supply and apportioning of foodstuffs is an interesting and rarely considered case study. Preparations for providing sufficient food in wartime to the populations of the British Isles and metropolitan France were well advanced and successful before the coming of hostilities. In July 1938 a memorandum from Sir Thomas Inskip, Britain's minister for the co-ordination of defence, expressed concern that the food talks were proceeding too far, too fast, and threatened to lead 'to little short of a civilian War Plan concerted between the two countries'.[19] Inskip was worried that the French would plan their own resources for war from a base-line that assumed a guaranteed quality to what were supposed to be provisional British undertakings to furnish certain commodities to France. This was, in the economic sphere, evidence of what Peter Jackson and Joe Maiolo note in respect of steps towards Anglo-French intelligence co-operation: anxiety among British ministers and officials still trusting in appeasement, that excessively firm, detailed strategic arrangements with France might embolden a government in Paris to a hard-line stance capable of provoking Germany to start a war.[20]

Undoubtedly, however, the discussions between officials from Britain's Food (Defence Plans) Department in the Board of Trade and their French counterparts led to important results well before September 1939. It was agreed to make co-ordinated purchases of foodstuffs from third-party supplier nations on the outbreak of war. This was done to avoid wasteful competition created by allocating merchant shipping by both nations to convoying identical foodstuffs from the same exporting countries, and to prevent over-charging by neutrals.

This success in preparing co-ordinated food-supply arrangements was not, however, extended to other areas where essential commodities and resources needed to be managed as a whole. During early 1938 the French requested an extension of joint planning into requirements for oil, coal and industrial raw materials such as ores and precious metals. In coal there was progress. Officials from Britain's Department of Mines had long-running negotiations with their opposite numbers in Anatole de Monzie's ministry of commerce and industry.[21] By September 1939 the French had been assured that their requirement for 20 million tons of coal per year would be met from Britain (much of it high-grade coking coal from South Wales, to replace supplies that the French steel industry obtained in peacetime from the Ruhr mines of its potential enemy, Germany). Margaret Gowing, however, has judged that this planning to supply coal to France was 'optimistic' in the light of foreseeable strains on British merchant shipping as a war exacted its inevitable attrition.[22] The French departure from the war in June 1940 faced Britain with a mortal threat to its existence but may, ironically, have spared her from having to confront an unsustainable pre-war economic commitment.

Plans for the supply, sharing and distribution of oil did not advance as far as those for adequate provision of foodstuffs or, arguably, those for coal. No agreements for co-ordinated oil purchase existed when war broke out. Moreover, in so far as the issue had been considered, plentiful tanker capacity to ship oil imports to British and French ports was simply and unwisely assumed. Equally troubling was the position in regard to Anglo-French co-operation in the supply of raw materials to the two countries' manufacturing industries. Talks between French and British civil servants did take place, but few purchasing arrangements eventuated. All in all there was little progress before 1939 in harmonizing and integrating the manufacturing sectors of the allies' war economies.

Furthermore, a widespread complacency that merchant shipping would be available in the quantities likely to be required led to only rudimentary planning in the area of merchant navy 'pooling'. Only with the establishment of a ministry of shipping in Britain in the first weeks of the war was a start made to improve this sorry state of affairs. The need for a general requisition of vessels from the merchant navy was belatedly recognized and instituted early in the war. Salter, appointed parliamentary under-secretary to the ministry of shipping in November 1939, recorded that the organization of shipping remained one of Britain's weaker sinews as she honed her body politic for the marathon that the war of 1939 was expected to become. Shipowners were at first disappointed at the overturn of pre-war understandings that their vessels would remain under their control, subject to a government licensing system. Gradually civil servants and employees of the shipping lines worked together, so that 'the machine as a whole, with a larger task, acquired after about two years the same degree of efficiency which had only been reached before in the fourth year of war'. [23] Taking two years rather than four to organize the pooling of shipping was of no consolation to France, however, which by late 1941 had lain defeated and occupied for over 12 months.

Another criticism of British preparations for sustaining the war effort economically was that, till the summer of 1940, little was done to accumulate reserve stocks of essential raw materials and foodstuffs. In principle, stockpiling was accepted by the Defence Policy and Requirements sub-committee of the Committee of Imperial Defence in June 1936. Indeed some reserves of raw materials were amassed thereafter. But this stockpiling was very limited, and reserves were modest. A major obstacle was the susceptibilities of the neutrals. The Food (Plans) Department and the War Office heavy-handedly informed Belgium's military attaché in London, Lieutenant General Baron Vinçotte, in June 1937, that 'the neutrals must, for better or worse, fall into line with Britain's policy of buying up all kinds of merchandise in order to prevent a global rise in prices'. Neutral hostility in the face of such brusque treatment obliged

Whitehall to soften its tone. In September 1937 Vinçotte reported to the Belgian general staff and defence ministry in Brussels that he suspected the Foreign Office had contacted the Food Department to 'advise moderation as far as Belgium was concerned'.[24]

If Belgium's perception was at all typical, nations not yet sucked into the war harboured few illusions about British (and almost certainly French) policy: that it aimed to 'draw the neutrals into their commercial orbit'. This, the neutrals suspected, was part of an Anglo-French grand strategy for economic warfare. They were close to the mark. The design had two pillars. The first was defensive and intended to stifle price inflation at source. The other was offensive. It aimed to use the Allies' maritime supremacy to sweep German shipping from the seas and, simultaneously, impose a trade blockade on the Reich, exactly as in 1914–18. On 23 September 1939 Vinçotte reported to Brussels that, since the war's outbreak, he had 'frequently had occasion to gauge the vital importanc of the economic side of the war for the British'. A civil servant in the London Foreign Office had confided that British plans to wage economic warfare upon Germany had been laid as long ago as 1933. Such commercial and strategic considerations revealed the preponderant importance of the blockade in British eyes, according to the Belgian attaché; 'it appears by some distance to be the chief means on which they are relying to win the war'.[25] There was a great deal of accuracy in the Belgian estimate. France also immediately initiated economic warfare against Germany. Indeed, the emphasis on economics was signalled by Daladier, the prime minister, when he used the government reshuffle of 13 September 1939 to add a new ministry for blockade headed by Georges Pernod to his government, along with another new ministry, for armaments, under Dautry.

In the planning for both offensively and defensively configured economic warfare, Salter repeatedly argued for the stockpiling of reserves of raw materials and food. Stockpiling promised to render the shipping of food, fuel and industrial raw materials a less urgent call on the allied merchant fleets and navies than it had been in 1914–18. Food, fuel and ores would, moreover, cost less if pre-purchased during peacetime. The British government was, however, slow to respond to these calls to build up precautionary stockpiles. Salter alleged that the Food (Defence Plans) Department was an authority without teeth. It could bark but not bite because it did not have one single government ministry behind it. Instead the responsibility for the department was divided between the ministry for the co-ordination of defence and the Board of Trade. 'This late-born, unwillingly conceived, miserable child was handed over to the niggardly alimony of one Minister and the step-fatherly neglect of another. Unhappily endowed, unhappily baptised, its prospects in life were poor'.[26] Better things were promised by the publication of the Essential Commodities Reserves Bill in June 1938. Subsequently, however, Salter discovered that its sweeping new powers were not being exploited. Useful stocks were assembled before the outbreak of war in 1939, yet Salter concluded that it was a 'shameful . . . tale of lost opportunities'.[27]

Therefore, although economic warfare was at the heart of the Anglo-French vision of how to defeat Germany, much work remained in September 1939 if there were to be a genuinely integrated set of structures for the efficient management of the Allied war economies. Hence the civil servants in the supply and industrial ministries, in Paris and London, were delighted to see the tempo of military operations slacken during the phoney war, after Germany had conquered Poland. Few doubted that time would work to the advantage of the Allies. The passage of the months was expected to enable the French and British to increase their mobilized strength, economic as well as military, at a proportionately faster rate than could the Germans.

Anglo-French economic war co-ordination encompassed an enormous range of initiatives, worthy of book-length study by themselves.[28] One area was the joint procurement and production of weapons. When the Chamberlain government decided in February 1939 to treat Belgian and Dutch territorial inviolability as vital British security interests Charles Corbin, the French ambassador to London, seized the moment. He immediately recommended a more integrated and accelerated approach to arms design and manufacture.[29]

One of the first areas to give rise to discussions between officials and industrialists was the aviation sector. Yet satisfactory results proved elusive. A meeting took place in the rooms of the British prime minister at the House of Commons on 22 March 1939. The British participants were led by Chamberlain himself. On the French side, the foreign minister, Georges Bonnet, attended, as did the ambassador to London, Charles Corbin, and Robert Bressy from the Quai d'Orsay. Bonnet informed Chamberlain that Daladier intended to use the special powers to govern by decree which had been given him by the French parliament in 1938, and recently renewed in March 1939, to 'considerably step up the activity of French armaments factories in general and aviation factories in particular'. He drew Chamberlain's attention to the fact that the French government had recently placed orders in the USA for 1,000 Curtiss fighter aircraft. This was an outcome of a CPDN decision on 5 December 1938 to make up the deficient output from French aero-engine and airframe factories by making emergency 'off the shelf' purchases overseas. The British prime minister, however, was sceptical. He retorted that American aircraft production was, according to British sources, geared primarily to civilian aircraft types and was ill-equipped to respond swiftly to French orders for warplanes. Chamberlain added a claim that British aircraft production had risen from 280 machines per month in September 1938 (the month of the Munich crisis) to 580 per month. With an air of superiority, he pronounced Britain 'wholly disposed to help France if the latter would like assistance, notably by means of meetings between technical experts'. Bonnet inquired whether France 'might in due course buy aircraft in Britain?' At this Chamberlain turned defensive. He replied that 'he did not know, but he did not think that Britain had a sufficient excess of aircraft to enable her to sell any'. Then, perhaps remembering that attack can be the best form of defence, Chamberlain adroitly shifted his ground, remarking that British experience suggested Bonnet should investigate whether France's problem resulted from the inadequate size of orders placed by the French air force with the French aviation industries.[30]

If there were difficulties in co-ordinating aircraft purchases to circumvent the ill-effects of the dislocation of the French aviation industry's nationalization and decentralization in 1937–38, the small size and slow deployment to the continent of a British field army was another worry for the French. Nor was French concern simply a matter of the scale of the British effort on land. It also stemmed from the dominance of infantry in the make-up of the first echelon of two divisions that the British agreed to send to France. Ambassador Corbin broached the possibility, in January 1939, that France might provide a small number of armoured vehicles to British companies, for the latter to copy them and thereby expand tank production. There seems to have been a twin hope behind the offer: first, that British industry would make up for inadequate French tank production and, second, that a more standardized and inter-operable inventory of Allied armoured equipment would eventually result. On 29 January 1939 Daladier met Sir Eric Phipps, the British ambassador in Paris, when he again offered French technical assistance to hasten the conversion of the British army from an infantry-based force to a predominantly mechanized one.[31]

Progress was not achieved until the Anglo-French staff talks commenced after Germany had annexed Bohemia, Moravia and Memel. Following the first stage of the staff conversations (29 March–4 April 1939), Daladier's personal staff noted with some anxiety that the British 'had explained their difficulties in regard to the despatch of an expeditionary corps; they have less trouble recruiting the force's manpower than in providing its essential equipment'.[32] French officials reckoned that Britain possessed the industrial resources to strengthen the Allied land forces, but lacked the prototypes to put into immediate mass-production. The French had, in contrast, developed various high-performance, modern armoured vehicles such as the fast, well-armed and well-defended Somua S35 cavalry tank and the Panhard Auto-mitrailleuse de Découverte (AMD) armoured car. But France faced a shortfall of modern tooling in her factories. She also had insufficient skilled engineering workers to manufacture the quantities of armoured fighting vehicles likely to be required. Co-operation, greater integration of manufacturing facilities, and some role-specialization between the French and British armies was indicated, in order to maximize the potential complementarity of French and British capabilities.

On 17 April 1939, on the eve of the second stage of the staff talks (24 April–5 May 1939), four British army officers were sent from the War Office to look at tank designs and prototypes in France. They listened to what the Direction des Fabrications d'Armement at the French ministry for national defence and war suggested be done in Britain to accelerate and expand armoured vehicle production. French ideas were sufficiently well received that, two days later, on 19 April, General Julien Martin, the French army's Inspector of Armoured Forces, travelled to Britain to see prototypes under development at the Royal Ordnance Establishment, Farnborough, and at the Nuffield motor company's factory at Birmingham. The French team was disappointed. 'The overall impression formed by our technicians', reported General Albert Lelong, the French military attaché in London, 'was that the British equipment is noticeably less advanced than our own in respect of design and manufacture'.[33] At the end of the second stage of the staff conversations, on 4 May 1939, one of the four 'Measures agreed for Immediate Execution' was the establishment of a French technical delegation that was to proceed to London to assume responsibility for questions of joint manufacture of war material.

From 6 to 9 June 1939 General Maurice Gamelin, chief of the French defence staff, visited Britain. Under the cover of attending ceremonial events (the army Tattoo at Tidworth and the Trooping the Colour for the King's official birthday), he held talks with Admiral Lord Chatfield, who had in January succeeded Inskip as minister for the co-ordination of defence, and with Major-General Hastings Ismay, secretary to the Committee of Imperial Defence. It was agreed to study production requirements and priorities in the next stages of the staff talks. It was also agreed that the Foreign Office and Quai d'Orsay should discuss the creation of an inter-Allied body to handle joint war finance, rearmament and associated issues.

Tank production remained an area that officials on both sides of Channel regarded as crucial. It was, more than anything else, the cause of delays in establishing further British and French mechanized divisions. In April 1939, just after the first stage of the staff talks, Lelong warned Daladier that Britain's deployment of two armoured divisions to the continent would be delayed until 15 months into a war. Consequently, the French returned to the possibility of meshing their industrial successes in the field of tank design and manufacture with those of British firms. During the summer and autumn of 1939 consideration was given to adapting the bodies of Hotchkiss H39 medium cavalry tanks to take British-manufactured turrets and guns. Though embryonic, the initiative marked the first step towards design and production of a standardized, inter-operable Anglo-French tank. This would be a hybrid for which the French were to be responsible for hulls, engines and drive-trains, the British for turrets, turret armour and armament (components that demanded high-grade steel which French steel mills could not manufacture in sufficient quantity).

In discussions and correspondence in early 1940, the ministry of supply and Dautry's ministry of armaments went further. They concluded an agreement in principle for Hotchkiss to furnish completely assembled tanks direct to the British Expeditionary Force (BEF). Ironside wrote to Gamelin in February 1940, requesting that 12 H39 tanks be sent to Lord Gort's troops to enable them to conduct trials and familiarization, prior to taking delivery of a full consignment from the Hotchkiss factory. Two weeks later, though cautioning that the 'French army's own requirements in Hotchkiss tanks are very important because of my establishment of additional armoured and mechanised divisions', Gamelin agreed to supply the 12 tanks to the BEF.

Within a month, however, the French high command applied the brakes to this promising area of Anglo-French co-operation. Gamelin took fright, it seems, from a letter on 1 March from Dautry. This covered a detailed 17-page report about the latest trends in French weapons production. Dautry underlined the appalling difficulties he had encountered since his appointment, in setting up his nascent ministry in September 1939. His report especially emphasized the inability of the antiquated, inefficient artillery ammunition arsenal at Roanne to produce the required quantities of 75mm shells. He also stressed the handicap facing his officials in raising weapons output to meet wartime targets because of France's structural shortages of welders, fitters, machine-tool operatives, engineers and managers throughout the arms and munitions industries. Dautry closed by noting that the position was not unremittingly pessimistic: 'The situation is serious, and the difficulties to be overcome are great, but by resolutely confronting the problem I am certain we shall resolve it.'[34] Whatever note he sought to sound, however, the tone had been set by the preceding 16 pages of complaints and warnings.

On 11 March 1940 Gamelin, in his turn, wrote to General Louis Colson, formerly the French army chief of staff and now in charge of the 'military zone of the interior'. Gamelin at this point cast a dark shadow over the prospects of France aiding Britain's military build-up on the Continent. An itemized list of weapons required for the BEF was presented; some 275 anti-tank guns and 165 medium and heavy tanks were required every month. The key to Gamelin's paper was his insistence on the *prior* need to fill all existing gaps in the order of battle of the French army's divisions before diverting any French munitions output to BEF units. Gamelin described the number of formations on the northern and north-eastern frontiers as yet equipped with modern armour as 'manifestly inadequate, having regard to the potential of our adversary'. He instructed Colson that equipping the BEF 'will therefore only be possible once our own deficits have been made good *and so long as there are no active military operations during the course of this summer'.*[35]

Meanwhile, French and British overseas-purchasing missions were established, representing another and less problematic dimension to a co-ordinated management of the allies' war economies. A French office under the businessman René Mayer was opened in London in November 1939. It represented Dautry's ministry and had the task of co-ordinating raw-materials purchases and joint manufacturing with the British ministry of supply. Meanwhile an Anglo-French Purchasing Commission was formed, under a British civil servant, Arthur Purvis, and dispatched to New York. These bodies operated under the overall direction of an Anglo-French Economic Co-ordinating Committee (Comité des programmes et des achats alliés), authorized in France by a decree of 2 November 1939 and chaired by another French business-man, Jean Monnet, who had extensive experience of overseas muni-tions purchasing in the United States both in 1917–18 and in 1938–39.[36]

Monnet and his committee were responsible for ensuring a co-ordinated, harmonious and prioritized Anglo-French approach to the acquisition of raw materials, machine tools and war material from all sources outside the French and British empires. These joint procurement missions signified, above all, the determination in London and Paris to avoid competitive bidding in neutral market places, especially in the United States. The priority in 1939–40 remained, as it had been since December 1938, the purchase of American combat aircraft, particularly defensive fighter-interceptors. Writing to Daladier on 10 February 1940, Chamberlain referred to the Anglo-French governmental agreement, reached at the 5 February Supreme War Council meeting, to 'utilise the productive facilities of the US aircraft industry and to invite their respective experts to examine the question with a view to action accordingly'.[37]

On 24 February a French treasury already reeling under the unexpectedly heavy depletion of its gold and foreign-exchange reserves nevertheless decided to exempt direct purchases of combat-ready American aircraft from tight new restrictions on expenditures in US dollars. Daladier issued a prime-ministerial directive supporting the 'creation of a manufacturing potential [for aircraft and munitions] in the United States'. This was, the directive noted:

> a heavy financial charge that we are sharing with our British ally – but an essential one. It is an indispensable insurance. The possible destruction by the enemy of certain French or British manufacturing centres . . . could have fatal consequences. If, on the other hand, we have the good luck to escape serious damage being done us by Germany, the aircraft . . . from America may then represent an essential element in achieving a quicker [allied] victory.[38]

This passage is indicative of the on-going significance of financial calculations behind every aspect of Anglo-French rearmament and conversion to a war economy. From as early as 1937, France and Britain explored how, rationally and equitably, to apportion the monetary costs of waging another war. Beginning in 1937, negotiations took place between the Direction des Charbonnages of France's ministry of public works and the Department of Mines at the Board of Trade in London. It was eventually agreed that the charges accruing for billets, dedicated railway lines and provisions in France for the British army would be offset against the cost of coal from South Wales that would be supplied to France to make up lost sources from the Ruhr.

The broadest possible co-ordination was essential in the management of Anglo-French war finances. An internal French note of 30 September 1939 cautioned that a fully integrated scheme for purchases outside the sterling and franc zones would see France rapidly run up a 'consider-able' indebtedness in sterling. The chief causes would be: French purchases direct from Britain (chiefly coal); purchases in the British Dominions and colonies comprising the sterling area; purchases in neutral markets settled in sterling. Monnet and Emmanuel Monick, the French financial attaché and treasury delegate in London in 1938–40, were therefore instructed to negotiate a compensation mechanism to regulate the consequences of allied joint purchasing settled in the British currency. From the war's earliest days, therefore, the French ministry of finance recognized that the size of their pre-war sterling debt and the expected increase in this during the first year of hostilities would create a franc credit account for Britain. The French decided to permit the British to use this credit balance 'either for purchasing prod-ucts from us, or for the maintenance of her armies [in France]'.[39]

On 30 September 1939 officials from the French ministry of com-merce and industry conferred at the ministry of economic warfare in London with a team of British officials led by Sir Frederick Leith-Ross from the Treasury and also containing representatives of the Board of Trade and the Foreign Office. Hervé Alphand, head of the Directorate of Commercial Agreements at the Quai d'Orsay, handed Leith-Ross a list of France's purchasing requirements from Britain in the first year of war. The British agreed to reciprocate with a list of their needs. The French government, explained Alphand, 'hoped to maintain as normal a flow as possible of France's traditional exports to Britain'. It was agreed that British goods exported to the French market be sold at the same price as on the British domestic market. Leith-Ross requested France to 'reduce its purchases of coal from Britain as far as possible' in order to maximize what would remain available for purchase in hard currency by the European neutrals. Britain wished to use coal as a weapon of economic warfare, to exclude German coal from neutral markets and limit the ability of a Third Reich starved of hard currency to barter for imports of foodstuffs, raw materials and commodities. Finally, the British emphasized to the French the importance of strictly limiting non-sterling payments, so as to eke out the Allies' war chest of gold and foreign-exchange reserves that British ministers from Chamberlain downwards had long regarded as Britain's 'fourth arm of defence'. Were similar measures to be implemented by France, asked the British offi-cials? Everything possible would be done, replied Alphand, to restrict paying foreign currency for imports. Some expenditure in US dollars would, he opined, be unavoidable. France had concluded a commercial protocol with the Italian government on 25 September that provided for part-payment in dollars of imports from Italy. This was part of a broader grand strategy of seeking to detach Mussolini from his May 1939 'Pact of Steel' with Hitler and preserve Italian neutrality in the war. Furthermore, in pursuit of the disruption of German trade with the neutrals, added Alphand, the Allies should be ready to pay in foreign exchange to deny strategic commodities to the enemy.[40]

In general, however, French leaders were keen to husband gold and hard currency reserves as they steeled themselves for another long, costly war. Ministers and civil servants in Paris were haunted by the memory of how the first world war had drained national finances and caused the financial vulnerability reflected in the franc's 80 per cent devaluation in the 1920s. Many French politicians and journalists remained convinced that after the 1914–18 war France had been swindled out of her rightful rewards – or appropriate compensation – for the disproportionately heavy sacrifices she had borne in the Allied cause.

At the onset of the second world war, therefore, French ministers resisted an unrestricted militarization of the national economy. They remained anxious to ensure that France did not 'forfeit the peace' a second time. Some, such as Paul Reynaud, finance minister from November 1938 to March 1940, thought the military stalemate of the autumn of 1939 a godsend. He judged the profit-and-loss account of the phoney war in material, measurable terms. At the forefront of his calculations were the numbers of men in uniform and the numbers of divisions that Britain and France were amassing. 'Why risk Hitler parading under the Arc de Triomphe', he asked Gamelin during a visit to the general's headquarters at the Château de Vincennes in mid-October 1939, 'especially if a few weeks' or few months' respite can lessen the imbalance between France's [war] potential and that of Germany?' Gamelin agreed that it would 'be good to gain time to continue the material preparation of the nation and the units [of the army]'; but he warned Reynaud to remember there was 'the home front to hold, too, and that demands we maintain high and undivided morale'.[41]

However other French civilian leaders shared Reynaud's boundless confidence that the Anglo-French defences were strong enough to withstand the German offensive when it came. Some were already thinking ahead to the post-war challenges for France. Fernand Gentin, the minister for trade and industry in Daladier's government of 13 September 1939–21 March 1940, energetically resisted any further encroachment by Dautry's new ministry or by French armaments firms on the productive capacity and workforce remaining in non-military consumer manufacturing for export. 'We need to continue to produce for the export market to ensure we still have our customers . . . when the war is over'.[42] Rather than insuring against French military defeat in the short term, French leaders of this view took Allied victory for granted. They set their sights on planning France's commercial prosperity, *vis-à-vis* her wartime alliance partners, in the postwar era when state-directed economic co-operation would give way to cut-throat competition and a liberal free-for-all in overseas markets.

Daladier was shocked to look out of the windows of his aeroplane and see the fields of the *départements* of the Aisne and Somme full of spoiled, unharvested crops, as he flew from Le Bourget to Abbeville on 12 September 1939 to see Chamberlain at the first meeting of the Anglo-French Supreme War Council (SWC). In the days after the SWC, Daladier provoked an acrimonious exchange with Gamelin by urging the general to demobilize thousands of agricultural labourers for harvesting duties, just two weeks after they had been called up and deployed to the eastern and north-eastern frontiers.[43]

In striking this stance, Daladier was only reflecting a wider view among French politicians in late 1939. This view held that it was crucial for France to conserve her economic strength – not simply in order to win the war, but to hold her own after Allied victory in the postwar order where burgeoning American economic power was much feared. Only economic strength carefully conserved could enable France to withstand the long haul of a three-year war, or more, without paying the price of loss of her position as a major international trading nation. With hindsight, this objective of French leaders may appear naive. After all, the 1939–45 war imposed unprecedented costs on all the belligerents and wrought unimagined changes in the global balance – and locus – of power. Yet French ministers and their officials sought in 1939 and 1940 to make the most rational, prudent preparations possible in relation to the challenge of Nazi Germany as they perceived it.[44] As defined by Daladier in a directive of 24 February 1940, the French aim was:

> on the one hand to establish a balance between our military effort and our means to meet it . . . on the other, to apportion the effort of France and England judiciously . . . our entire policy must be directed at permitting us to hold on in the long term as much from the viewpoint of our financial resources as from that of our military effort [and] must be framed as though England and France have to win this war by themselves without the aid – even financial – of the United States. A balance . . . will be the best guarantee that we shall be able to sustain our effort until we achieve total victory.[45]

Three weeks after this directive was issued, on 11 March 1940, Gamelin found Daladier opining that he 'no longer thought there would be a battle [in 1940] and that men could be released from the armies for other duties in the interior'. Gamelin was shocked to realize how few politicians feared any sort of military crisis arising in the initial defensive phase of the war.[46]

Yet in the autumn of 1939 some French officials pointed out exactly this sort of danger. From London ambassador Corbin wrote to Daladier in mid-October, warning about the leisurely pace of mobilization of the British army destined to help defend France. Nobody in London thought that a knock-out blow could be delivered by the Wehrmacht against France and Belgium, complained Corbin. 'In a general manner', warned the French ambassador, 'the British have such confidence in the French army that they are inclined to consider their provision of military support as a token of allied solidarity rather than a vital military necessity.' Even Winston Churchill, the most 'broad minded and imaginative' of British ministers, had expressed the view to Corbin in late September 1939 that a German attack in the west that autumn was unlikely. Even Churchill was said to have 'difficulty' grasping the continental dimension to the war and understanding 'that however effective the blockade [of Germany] the final decision always depends on troops on the ground'.[47]

The Anglo-French coalition hardened its economic muscles for war during the winter of 1939–40. But by May 1940 it resembled two athletes preparing for a team event who had done all their weight training and road work separately. They had prepared their economic sinews of war – but they had prepared as two individuals rather than as partners in a genuine team effort. It was also as though they had discussed team-tactics, but not practised them. Many far-sighted and essential preparations had been made by May 1940. Captains of industry and the civil servants in the economic ministries, as well as the French and British populations and their political leaders, were more realistic than their forebears in 1914–15 as to the sacrifices and economic dislocations that a long, industrialized war would necessitate. The mismanagement, mutual antagonisms and oversights that took three years to rectify in 1914–18 were largely avoided in 1939–40. In the view of Jean-Louis Crémieux-Brilhac, author of the most detailed study of the topic of French industry's phoney-war performance: 'When all is said and done, the factory front was the one that best fulfilled its mission. It worked better than the military front: it was better directed, better staffed and

... better meshed together.'[48] It is a judgement that can equally be applied to British war production in 1939–40. But what two comparatively efficient sets of war industries left unresolved was the question of integration and collaborative manufacture. Britain and France had parallel, albeit partially co-ordinated, war economies by 10 May 1940 – not an integrated Allied war economy. Frictions and the 'not invented here' syndrome in the realms of money and manufacturing, as much as divergences over strategy, marked the limits to the economic and industrial pillars of Anglo-French defence relations as the Second World War commenced.

Notes

1. See J. F. Godfrey, *Capitalism at War: Industrial Policy and Bureaucracy in France, 1914–1918* (Leamington Spa: Berg, 1987).
2. See M. S. Alexander, *The Republic in Danger: General Maurice Gamelin and the Politics of French Defence, 1933–1940* (Cambridge: Cambridge University Press, 1992), pp. 34–49, 88–95 and 120–31.
3. J. Lacouture, *Charles de Gaulle, Vol. I: the Rebel, 1890–1944* (London: Collins-Harvill, 1990), pp. 118–26.
4. E. C. Kiesling, *Arming against Hitler: France and the Limits of Military Planning* (Lawrence, KS: University Press of Kansas, 1996), pp. 14–35.
5. E. du Réau, *Edouard Daladier, 1884–1970* (Paris: Fayard, 1993), esp. pp. 175–88.
6. *Ibid.*, pp. 372–4 and 378–83.
7. Cf. R. Baudouï, *Raoul Dautry (1880–1951): le technocrate de la République* (Paris: Balland, 1992), pp. 182–217; M. Avril, *Raoul Dautry (1880–1951), ou la passion de servir* (Paris: France-Empire, 1993), pp. 104–37; V. Halpérin, *Raoul Dautry: du rail à l'atome* (Paris: Fayard, 1997), pp. 123–48; J.-L. Crémieux-Brilhac, *Les Français de l'an 40, vol. II: Ouvriers et soldats* (Paris: Gallimard, 1990), pp. 105–14; M. S. Alexander, 'Les hommes, les munitions et la mobilisation de 1939', in A. Crémieux (ed.), *Histoire de l'armement en France de 1914 à 1962* (Paris: Editions Addim, 1994), pp. 55–79.
8. See R. J. Young, 'La Guerre de Longue Durée: Some Reflections on French Strategy and Diplomacy in the 1930s', in A. Preston (ed.), *General Staffs and Diplomacy before the Second World War* (London: Croom Helm, 1978), pp. 41–64.
9. Vansittart minute, 11 February 1939, on 'The Strategic Position of France in a European War', report by the Chiefs of Staff sub-committee, 1 February 1939, Public Record Office, Kew [PRO], FO 371/22915/C1503/130/17.
10. G. C. Peden, *British Rearmament and the Treasury, 1932–1939* (Edinburgh: Scottish Academic Press, 1979), *passim*.
11. M. M. Postan, *British War Production, 1939–1945* (London: HMSO, 1975), p. 114.
12. R. Macleod and D. Kelly (eds), *The Ironside Diaries, 1937–1940* (London: Constable, 1962), p. 128.

13. R. J. Minney, *The Private Papers of Hore-Belisha* (London: Collins, 1960), pp. 240–1.
14. Postan, *British War Production*, p. 76.
15. *Ibid.*, p. 88.
16. *Ibid.*, p. 93.
17. Lord Salter, *Memoirs of a Public Servant* (London: Faber and Faber, 1961), p. 261.
18. Macleod and Kelly, *Ironside Diaries*, p. 361.
19. Cabinet paper, 1 July 1938, PRO, CAB 53/153 (38).
20. See Jackson and Maiolo's chapter (Chapter 6) in the present volume.
21. A. de Monzie, *Ci-devant* (Paris: Flammarion, 1941), pp. 67–8, 93, 124–5, 138, 178–9, 196–8, 200 and 208.
22. M. Gowing, 'Anglo-French Economic Collaboration: Oil and Coal', in *Les relations franco-britanniques de 1935 à 1939* (Paris: Editions du CNRS, 1975), pp. 263–75.
23. Salter, *Memoirs*, pp. 259 and 264–6.
24. Le Lieutenant-Général Baron Vinçotte (attaché militaire en Grande-Bretagne) au Lieutenant-Général, Chef de la Maison militaire du Roi; au Lieutenant-Général, Chef d'Etat-major général de l'armée, à M. le Ministre de la Défense, 23 September 1939, Archives du Ministère des Affaires Etrangères et du Commerce Extérieur, Brussels, no. 6210.
25. *Ibid.*
26. Salter, *Memoirs*, pp. 257–8.
27. *Ibid.*, p. 258.
28. See Alexander, *Republic in Danger*, pp. 349–72. The author is engaged in writing a further volume, provisionally entitled *The Republic at War: Franco-British Strategy, Politics and Defeat, 1939–40*, which will explore these questions in greater detail.
29. Halifax to Phipps, 28 January 1939, in Sir E. L. Woodward and R. Butler (eds), *Documents on British Foreign Policy, 1919–1939* (London: HMSO, 1968 et seq.) [*DBFP*], ser. III, vol. IV, no. 44; also Corbin to Bonnet, 28 January 1939, in J.-B. Duroselle, J. Laloy and Y. Lacaze (eds), *Documents Diplomatiques Français, 1932–1939* (Paris: Imprimerie Nationale, 1963 et seq), 2nd ser., vol. XIII, no. 445.
30. Corbin to Quai d'Orsay, 23 March 1939, *DDF*, 2nd ser., vol. XIV, no. 27.
31. Phipps to Halifax, 29 January 1939, *DBFP*, ser. III, vol. IV, no. 52.
32. 'Note du 12 avril 1939', by CSDN, *Service Historique de l'Armée de Terre*, Vincennes [SHAT], 5N579.
33. Lelong to Gamelin, 14 and 21 April 1939, SHAT, 7N2816.
34. 'Le problème des effectifs, 1939–40', Dautry report to Gamelin, 1 March 1940, fonds Gamelin, SHAT, 1K224/7.
35. Gamelin to Colson, 11 March 1940, fonds Gamelin, SHAT, 1K224/7, emphasis added. Cf. Halpérin, *Raoul Dautry*, p. 138; du Réau, *Edouard Daladier*, pp. 378–83.
36. Monnet had been part of André Tardieu's munitions purchasing missions in Washington in 1917–18. He was sent back to the USA by Daladier after Munich, to explore prospects for purchasing American military aircraft. In May 1939 he was in the USA once more for talks with the US Treasury Department about a one-off French partial settlement of unpaid 1914–18

war debts that, it was hoped in Paris, might unfreeze American credit to France. See du Réau, *Edouard Daladier*, pp. 383–7; J. Monnet, *Memoirs* (trans. R. Mayne, London: Collins, 1977); J. McV. Haight Jr, *American Aid to France, 1938–1940* (New York: Atheneum, 1970); *idem*, 'Jean Monnet and the American Arsenal after the Beginning of the War', in E. M. Acomb and M. C. Brown (eds), *French Society and Culture since the Old Régime* (New York: Holt Rinehart and Winston, 1966), pp. 269–96.

37. Chamberlain to Daladier, 10 February 1940, papiers Daladier, Archives Nationales, Paris [AN], AP 496, 3DA5/2/a.

38. Présidence du Conseil: 'Directives de la politique économique française: programmes de production et d'achat pour 1940', 24 February 1940, *ibid.*, 3DA5/2/c, pp. 4–5.

39. Dautry to Gamelin, 1 March 1940, fonds Gamelin, SHAT, 1K224/7.

40. 'Procès-verbal. Réunion tenue le samedi 30 septembre 1939, au "Ministry of Economic Warfare", à Londres, sous la présidence de Sir Frédérick Leith-Ross', papiers Daladier, AN, 3DA2/3/c.

41. 'Journal de marche', 9 October 1939, fonds Gamelin, SHAT, 1K224/9.

42. Chambre des Députés. Commission du Commerce et de l'Industrie: 'Audition de M. Fernand Gentin, ministre du commerce et de l'industrie, le 18 octobre 1939', procès-verbal, pp. 13–14, Archives de l'Assemblée Nationale, Paris.

43. 'Journal de marche' (18 September 1939), fonds Gamelin, SHAT, 1K224/9 Cf. M.-G. Gamelin, *Servir, vol. III: la Guerre* (Paris: Plon, 3 vols, 1946–7), pp. 236–43; Avril, *Raoul Dautry*, pp. 131–2.

44. See more detail in R. Frankenstein, 'Le financement français de la guerre et les accords avec les britanniques, 1939–40', and L. S. Pressnell, 'Les finances de guerre britanniques et la coopération économique franco-britannique en 1939 et 1940', in *Français et Britanniques dans la drôle de guerre: Actes du colloque franco-britannique tenu à Paris du 8 au 12 décembre 1975* (Paris: Editions du Centre Nationale de la Recherche Scientifique, 1979), pp. 461–87, and 489–510.

45. 'Directives de la politique économique française', papiers Daladier, AN, 3DA5/2/c, pp. 2–3.

46. 'Journal de marche', 11 March 1940, fonds Gamelin, SHAT, 1K224/9.

47. Corbin to Daladier: Compte-rendu d'un entretien avec M. Churchill, le 25 septembre 1939', *ibid.*, 1K224/7.

48. Crémieux-Brilhac, *Les Français de l'an 40, vol. II*, p. 351.

9
The Benefit of Experience? The Supreme War Council and the Higher Management of Coalition War, 1939–40

William J. Philpott

On 13 December 1939, three months after the outbreak of war with Germany, the British Minister for Co-ordination of Defence, Admiral of the Fleet Lord Chatfield, addressed the National Defence Public Interest Committee. He was able to reassure his listeners:

> Further, we have the closest cooperation with *our great Ally*. Here again in the months before the war was organised the closest and most complete understanding. Not only had we at the outbreak of war a Supreme War Council, but Anglo-French staffs in all sections are completely organised and sit together daily to study the problems of war. It is true to say that never have allies started fighting with such a complete mechanism, such complete plans and such identity of spirit.[1]

While strictly accurate, Chatfield's statement, as might be expected in a ministerial address intended for public consumption, is disingenuous. The establishment of the allied Supreme War Council was a hasty response to the rapid deterioration of the international situation in the summer of 1939. The organization existed on paper by August 1939, but the actual machinery had to be rather hurriedly improvised on the outbreak of war. While it cannot be denied that this was a considerable improvement on the situation in the first world war, in which the allies spent three years, against a background of strategic rivalry and personal mistrust, evolving an effective co-ordination machinery,[2] in 1939 there was no opportunity for the inter-allied machinery, in practice a resurrection of that from the earlier conflict, to function in peacetime, as had been intended, to iron out any teething troubles in the machinery and to accustom the higher personalities of the alliance to working together.

The circumstances of the resurrection of the Supreme War Council are indicative of the allies' half-hearted approach to the coming war. Hitler's dismemberment of Czechoslovakia in March 1939 forced Britain and France to address their joint preparations for another general European conflict directly. Hitherto their policy had been restrained by an 'appeasing' mind-set, anxious not to provoke Hitler by making obvious preparations for war, and especially Britain's reluctance to enter into any formal commitment to France that might constitute such provocation. In March and April 1939 joint staff talks were finally formalized and political and military contacts increased, with a sense of resignation rather than enthusiasm. It was still hoped that a more forceful diplomatic policy, based on the resurrection of an anti-German bloc in central and eastern Europe and Anglo-French security guarantees, could deter or at least delay German aggression in that region. Meanwhile preparations to contain any German threat in the west could be taken over a period of years.

It was one thing to plan together for war, quite another to set up the inter-allied institutions for fighting it before it started. For the French a British commitment to creating joint political and military organizations would confirm Britain's commitment to a joint military effort, in lieu of a formal alliance. In Britain, where the prevailing inter-war attitude to continental war was 'no more Sommes', such a commitment was resisted for that very reason.[3] Staff talks implied a willingness to prepare for a war but, unlike the creation of joint directing machinery, did not involve any obligation to participate in it. Here the pre-1914 situation, when Britain had developed detailed logistical plans for sending a British Expeditionary Force to France while remaining determined to retain a completely free hand in military policy until war broke out, set an unfortunate precedent. Fortunately for the allies there were also some valuable precedents from the Great War which could be drawn upon when the decision was belatedly taken to establish joint directing machinery. The allied Supreme War Council established at Versailles in November 1917 and developed over the following year could provide both a model for the institution and valuable experience of its operation which could be drawn on in 1939. It is certainly true that the 1917–18 model was closely studied and replicated in many of its features, although it is evident that not all the mistakes made in the first war were avoided in the second.

General Maurice Gamelin, chief of the French defence staff, was the first to identify the need for an inter-allied body to co-ordinate strategic plans and military activity, during the first Czechoslovakian crisis. His dealings with the British during the crisis convinced him that the best way to ensure co-ordination between the British and French service staffs was by means of:

> un *haut comité militaire franco-anglais* (tout au moins, pour débuter, une réunion des personalités interessées – civils et militiaires) leur donne les directives nécessaires et assume la charge de coordonner la préparation des actions à prévoir pour l'ensemble des forces terrestres, maritimes et aériennes des deux pays.[4]

The Conseil Supérieur de la Défense Nationale (CSDN), France's central defence committee, had already considered the problem of Anglo-French co-operation in April 1938. They concluded that effective direction in a coalition war required an inter-allied body of responsible statesmen and military commanders (something that had been lacking between 1914 and 1917). Moreover, they judged that it was appropriate to establish such an organization in peacetime to make the necessary joint diplomatic, economic and strategic preparations for war.[5] This remained academic, however, while the British were reluctant to commit themselves formally to military and economic co-operation. The French premier, Edouard Daladier, raised the issue of close political and military co-operation with his opposite number Neville Chamberlain when in London in November 1938, but his suggestion fell on deaf ears.[6]

Formal military staff talks in the spring of 1939 presented the first realistic opportunity to consider the higher directing machinery of the alliance, an opportunity which the French were determined to seize. It seemed that British political and public opinion was finally coming to accept the prospect of a war with Hitler, and to recognize the need to be prepared; in February 1939 Brigadier-General Sir Edward Spears, a member of the House of Commons and expert on Anglo-French relations,[7] called for the creation of an allied war council in the press.[8] Nevertheless, the French chiefs of staff recognized the need to proceed with caution, in order not to stir British susceptibilities on the question of military subordination to France. Although it seemed to Gamelin that a supreme military command like that exercised by General Foch in 1918 was impossible, he intended at least to broach the subject of establishing a higher military committee of allied commanders-in-chief, to which the British seemed disposed, if not a full Supreme War Council (SWC).[9] Although not raised during the first stage of the talks in March, the French delegation considered that the talks had been conducted in a mood of such openness and cordiality that the question of co-ordination could be placed on the agenda for the second phase of the talks in late April.[10]

Gamelin was particularly anxious to sort out the arrangements for joint military command in time of war, which were inseparable from the question of higher co-ordination. Gamelin hoped to go beyond the 1918 arrangements and establish what in practice would be an executive inter-allied politico-military organization. At the top of the executive pyramid would sit an allied 'Comité de Guerre' or 'Conseil Supérieur' of political and military representatives (composed of prime ministers, defence ministers and chiefs of staff) to co-ordinate alliance policy. There would also be a 'Haut Comité Militaire' of the chiefs of staff and commanders-in-chief, for determining allied strategy and directing military operations, with authority over four subordinate military committees, one for each of the three services, and one for the colonies. The latter arrangement would address the problem of co-ordinating the military operations of the allies in the field which had proved so difficult in the earlier conflict; a difficulty of which Gamelin had had first-hand experience while serving on General Joffre's staff between 1914 and 1916. Although this experience suggested to him that it would be impossible to appoint a single allied supreme commander who had the confidence of all the allied armies on the outbreak of hostilities, Gamelin envisaged that the president of the allied military committee would gain the trust of his allied collaborators and in time be able to give orders to the other forces of the coalition, as the *generalissimo* Foch had been able to do in 1918.[11] Of course Gamelin also had every expectation that as the senior military official of the leading military power of the coalition he would be president of the allied military committee. Leaving aside this personal ambition, Gamelin's organization did go some way towards addressing some of the weaknesses of the executive organization of the previous war, in which relations between the SWC and the allied commanders-in-chief had been ill-defined and fractious before Foch's appointment.[12] It might be speculated that his proposed military committee might have had a dynamic input into the strategic direction of the war; the analogous Anglo-American Joint Chiefs of Staff Committee created later in the war certainly fulfilled this role. The command structure proposed by Gamelin would certainly have defined more clearly the relationship between the allies' political and military leaders, although in practice it would have increased military influence considerably. Without such a committee tensions in civil-military relations, particularly rivalry between Gamelin and

Daladier for control of French military policy in the early months of the war, were to compromise the cohesion and dynamism of allied policy-making as they had done in the previous war.[13]

Although raised during the later stages of the staff talks in the spring of 1939, it was recognized from the start that the issue of higher allied direction, and with it the linked question of the higher command of the British Field Force deployed in France, could not be settled by the junior officers delegated to conduct the talks.[14] In Britain the matter was passed to the Committee of Imperial Defence (CID) for consideration. Chatfield took it upon himself to prepare a paper for the CID,[15] which was ultimately delivered and approved in mid-July.[16] Although submitted under the Minister for Co-ordination of Defence's signature, much of the work behind this paper was carried out by the CID's secretary, Major-General Hastings Ismay. Ismay concluded that 'we could do no better than repeat the arrangements which were made towards the end of the 1914–18 war'.[17] Consequently the letter sent by Chamberlain to Daladier at the end of July proposed a non-executive council exactly like that which had existed at the end of the last war. Only the premier and one other minister from each country were to be permanent members of the council, other ministers, officials and service chiefs being summoned when required. The council was to be advised by a staff of permanent military representatives drawn from the three services of each country. Ismay was to follow Chamberlain's letter to Paris, where he was to meet Gamelin and other French officials to discuss the implementation of the scheme.[18]

It is evident, but perhaps not too surprising, that the CID made no real attempt to evaluate the effectiveness of the earlier SWC. Chamberlain, notorious as a peacemaker, showed no real interest in organization for war, and left this important task to his deputy on the CID and his permanent officials. As is often the way with civil servants, the latter looked to precedents from the past. Over the whole process hung the spectral presence of Lord Hankey, the architect of the CID system and the British official who had overseen the smooth running of the Versailles SWC in the absence of a permanent secretariat. As Ismay's mentor,[19] Hankey's methods had a powerful influence over his successor as CID secretary, and his written recollections of the earlier SWC were drawn on heavily in Ismay's work.[20] Yet there is no evidence that Hankey was approached in person for his thoughts on the strengths and weaknesses of the earlier organization. Nor was the former prime minister, David Lloyd George, who had been a permanent member of the first SWC for its whole existence, approached.[21] In extenuation of this rather perfunctory approach, we should note it was still thought while this examination was going on that war was some way off and there would be time to test the new inter-allied institutions in the less demanding circumstances of peacetime.[22]

The French were naturally receptive to the British approach. Gamelin himself had been apprised of the trend of British thought on the matter when he visited London in early June. He had talks with both Chatfield and Ismay, the latter briefing him on his proposals for a war council along the lines of that of the Great War and suggesting the possibility of setting up a peacetime inter-allied body.[23] Immediately on his return to Paris Gamelin had taken up the matter, recirculating his earlier memorandum.[24] No action was taken until Chamberlain's letter arrived in late July, although then Gamelin and his staff set about preparing a reply to the British proposals. While raising no objection to the principle of an inter-allied council – indeed going further and suggesting that the council as well as the permanent military staff should start to function in peacetime[25] – Gamelin sought to create an organization in which the allied commanders-in-chief had greater influence. He felt that Chamberlain's proposed organization confused the higher direction of war and the conduct of military operations – in particular the establishment of a separate SWC staff would interfere with the functions of the responsible allied chiefs of staff. He still argued for a 'Haut Comité Militiare Interallié' in addition to the 'Conseil Suprême', which should be constituted once war broke out. As far as the relations between the military and political councils were concerned, it was expected that the allied commanders-in-chief and chiefs of staff would, as in the last war, be seconded to the SWC in a consultative role, while not being permanent members of it. Gamelin also hoped to restrict the role of the permanent military representatives, who he feared might come to rival the commanders and military staffs in their role of advising ministers and executing policy. Gamelin was well aware of the mistakes made in the earlier conflict: firstly when the British had appointed Sir Henry Wilson to the Versailles SWC as an alternative source of strategic advice to the Chief of the Imperial General Staff, Sir William Robertson; and secondly, when the Versailles SWC had attempted to create an executive War Board under Foch to restrict the operational independence of the allied field commanders, General Philippe Pétain and Field Marshal Sir Douglas Haig. Consequently Gamelin pressed for an advisory 'Comité d'Etudes Militaire Interallié' of officers subordinate to the allied military staffs, rather than an independent permanent staff organization. These officers would examine common problems in peacetime, laying the groundwork for the expansion of the allied organization in wartime, when they would function as the secretariat of the 'Haut Comité Militiare Interallié'. It was in these terms that Daladier replied to Chamberlain's letter on 3 August.[26]

Another contentious issue was the location of the inter-allied organization,[27] indicative of deep-rooted *amour-propre* on both sides of the Channel. Chamberlain had suggested that it should be based in London;[28] but Ismay's rationale for this – that the British capital was more secure from air attack, and that questions of mercantile shipping would be of vital importance in the next war and Britain was the principal mercantile power of the alliance – seems rather lame.[29] The French naturally wished it to sit in Paris, although they were prepared to accept that it should meet alternately in the two capitals.[30]

On 17 August Chamberlain replied to Daladier's letter, indicating his complete agreement with the French proposals.[31] This was not quite the case. Chamberlain accepted the proposed arrangements for the attendance of military chiefs at the council, but made no mention of the idea of setting up a separate 'Haut Comité Militiare' parallel to the 'Conseil Suprême'. It is not clear why the British rejected, or ignored, this proposal, but such a committee was not established after war broke out.[32] The French political authorities certainly voiced no objection to this omission.[33] The most likely explanation is that since by this time the British government had accepted the Chiefs of Staff Committee's (COS) recommendation that the British Field Force sent to France should be placed under French military control, this perhaps obviated one of the main functions of the higher military committee, the co-ordination of allied field operations.[34] Similarly, Chamberlain made no mention of the venue for the inter-allied organization, although it seems that the principle that the SWC should meet alternately in Britain and France, as became the case after war broke out, was accepted by default. Administrative details, Chamberlain suggested, should be left to the appointed allied military representatives to work out.[35] The French concurred with this arrangement.[36]

Chamberlain had already referred the matter of the 'Comité d'Etudes' to the COS. After interviewing the French military attaché, Brigadier-General Albert Lelong, they recommended that a staff on the lines proposed by Gamelin be set up at once, so that the nominated British and French officers could get used to working together; and, equally importantly, so that if it came to war they would be united enough to force the Anglo-French point of view over the opinions of other members of the alliance.[37] Indeed, the question of how Anglo-French authority was to be imposed over lesser allies was one of the preoccupations of these negotiations. It was agreed, on Chatfield's recommendation, that in wartime other allies should be invited to send representatives to the SWC, and appoint officers to the 'Comité d'Etudes'. However, communications problems indicated that eastern European allies would only be able to nominate their ambassadors as members of the SWC, and that they would therefore have less influence over alliance business than the principal partners. This rather authoritarian arrangement satisfied both allies, who anticipated that on the outbreak of war Anglo-French military missions would be sent to lesser allies to 'assist in the co-ordination of allied effort by explaining and elaborating the recommendations of the Supreme War Council to the authorities of these countries, and by sending the Supreme War Council accurate information, which might not be otherwise available, of the situation in their respective theatres of war'.[38]

The other outstanding issue referred to the COS was whether the organization should have a permanent secretariat, drawn from the secretariats of the CID and the CSDN, to manage SWC business. This had not been the case with the Versailles organization, and ultimately it was decided, again following the precedent of the earlier war, that rather than establishing a separate administrative body Ismay and the head of the CSDN secretariat, General Louis-Marie Jamet, should liaise over war council business through an Anglo-French liaison section drawn from their staffs.[39] The Inter-allied Military Committee, as it became known, was to have its own secretariat drawn from the allied defence staffs, to ensure liaison between London and Paris.[40] The personnel of the new committee were quickly chosen. The French appointed the officers who had represented the French service staffs during the recent round of staff talks, while the British appointed three new officers, chosen because they were not burdened with other responsibilities. This, the French military representative, Lelong, complained, would impede the rapid operation of the new body, since the new British officers were unacquainted with both allied business and their French counterparts.[41] Nevertheless, the new organization was to meet on 28 August to discuss the most pressing strategic matters, aid to Poland and the impact of the Nazi-Soviet Pact. As this agenda makes clear, these negotiations had been overtaken by events – the allies were at war six days later.[42] The committee's other task, to consider the nature and functions of inter-allied organizations,[43] would not now be possible in peacetime.

While Chatfield had been truthful in his declaration that the allies had established co-ordination machinery before war broke out, his statement covered up the fact that the new organization was both untried, and potentially obsolescent. The intention had been to get this organization functioning effectively in peacetime at least, and to allow it to consider at leisure the expansion and functioning of inter-allied machinery. However, in 1939 the new machinery, or more accurately the revived old machinery, was going to have to be constituted and to evolve against a background of conflict, rather than in the relative tranquillity of peacetime. As the British secretary of the Anglo-French liaison section remarked: 'Experience only can show what final organisation will best serve requirements.'[44]

On the outbreak of war Gamelin warned against repeating the mistakes of the last war, stressing the need for co-ordination of the allied high command. The principal strategic problems facing the allies echoed those of the last war – offence or defence in response to the German attack on Poland, and economic organization for a long war of blockade[45] – and would require the sort of management which the Versailles SWC had belatedly brought to the Allies in these fields. Although the eight months of 'phoney war' allowed the allies some time to develop the new SWC and to iron out any teething troubles, it is clear that similar problems to those which had undermined the cohesion of the coalition in the first world war persisted. Personal and institutional factors, as well as tensions in civil-military relations which had been apparent in the pre-war discussions over co-ordinating machinery, determined the way that the SWC would operate in practice.

At the most basic level the allies had to fashion an effective means of communicating their ideas and settling their differences. While the armies mobilized, the soldiers and diplomats communicated and organized and the allied liaison structure blossomed. Military and civilian missions were exchanged, and offices established, so that by the end of September there was a functioning, if somewhat complex and as yet untested, mechanism for communication between the allied governments and armies.[46] The SWC itself sat at the pinnacle of this elaborate network of liaison missions and sub-committees.

At the pinnacle of the SWC itself sat the allied premiers; it was their attitudes and methods which were to determine how the SWC functioned in practice. Chamberlain the peacemonger brought his negotiating style to the management of war. He had always found conferences with the French 'difficult and delicate . . . [and] very fatiguing'.[47] To manage the French 'I have supplied most of the ideas and taken the lead throughout',[48] and this attitude underpinned his careful stage-managing of SWC meetings. Having had experience of Chamberlain's obstinacy in diplomatic negotiations, Daladier's hope was that the SWC organization could be used to impose a French strategic agenda on the alliance. The first instruction issued by Daladier to Gamelin was that he should study the French war plan 'd'établir, en fonction des résultes de cette étude, un avant-projet des décisions à proposer au Conseil Suprême pour la conduite de la Guerre sur le Plan interallié'.[49] The stage was set for the friction which had characterized high-level Anglo-French talks in peacetime to continue.[50]

While the allies were preoccupied with mobilization the new organization was given little thought. During the first weeks of September the Inter-allied Military Committee met daily so that its members could get to know one another and exchange information, but since it had no authority to undertake work which had not been referred to it by higher allied authorities it found itself with nothing practical to do.[51] The SWC itself took time to develop effective procedures. The first meeting, called rather hurriedly in Abbeville on 12 September to address mobilization and planning issues, had no formal agenda. Chamberlain's private account of the meeting is revealing;

> I had thought out beforehand the subjects I wanted to discuss and I took and kept the lead in the conversations all through as the French did not seem to have any points of their own. It was the most satisfactory conference I have ever attended. There was no point on which there was any disagreement between us and when we parted we felt both of us fresh hope and confidence. Moreover I think it did a lot of good throughout to know that the Supreme Council had met. ... I shall I suppose have to go again some day, but it is Daladier's turn to come here next.[52]

Clearly the British prime minster intended to use the SWC as a means to demonstrate alliance solidarity when necessary, rather than a organ for regular alliance management and decision-making. In this, at least, the first meeting 'was a great success', and brought the British and French premiers closer together after their peacetime differences.[53] However, superficial accord masked their fundamental disagreement on strategy.[54]

The first meeting exposed the administrative lacunae in the new organization. As well as the lack of a formal agenda, rectified for future sessions, the SWC had no formal procedures for taking minutes and drawing up resolutions. The problem of drawing up an effective record of the SWC's meetings preoccupied Ismay and Jamet over the ensuing months. It was not until January 1940 that administrative procedures were settled. Eventually a procedure similar to that during the previous war, whereby joint resolutions would be drawn up and agreed at the meeting, while separate English and French minutes would be prepared afterwards, was adopted.[55] As well as perfecting administrative procedures, the organization itself expanded in the early months. Economic co-ordination, which the allies had learned by trial and error in the earlier war, was one area in which the Versailles SWC produced great results. Here the allies learned from experience, and acted quickly to extend the purview of the SWC from strategic and diplomatic affairs to economic practicalities. At Abbeville agreement was reached to follow the precedents of the earlier war, and by October 1939 an Anglo-French Co-ordinating Committee and six executive sub-committees analogous to those which had operated in Versailles were set up to deal with the management of common economic questions.[56] It was contemplated that in time the organization would expand to cover other raw materials and commercial undertakings, the whole being overseen by a separate allied Supreme Economic Council.[57] By the end of 1939 a complex multi-level committee organization was up and running, and administrative procedures, if not perfect, were effective.

Despite this rapid evolution, the SWC never became the dynamic flywheel of a well-co-ordinated war effort, remaining a consultative rather than an executive or policy-making body.[58] It met only irregularly when one or other of the allied governments had something for discussion. As in the first world war, as time went on the membership increased to such an extent that the organization became unwieldy and difficult to manage.[59] An indication of how the SWC worked can be gathered from the diary record of the meeting of 28 March 1940 made by the British Chief of the Imperial General Staff, General Sir Edmund Ironside;

> The Supreme War Council was far better than I expected. These old *rusés* politicians like Chamberlain have a strategy their own and he certainly had a good one this time. He started off with a ninety minutes' monologue upon the general situation, apologizing every now and then for taking so long. He took all the thunder out of Reynaud's mouth and left him gasping with no electric power left. All the 'projects' that Reynaud had to bring forward, Chamberlain took away. It was most masterly and very well done. Little Reynaud

sat there with his head nodding in a sort of 'tik', understanding it all for he speaks English very well, and having to have it translated all over again for the benefit of others. He was for all the world like a little marmoset.

The new Air Minster, Laurent d'Eynac . . . and Vuillemin, his Service Chief, were asleep. . . . Darlan, the French Admiral, smoked his pipe all the time and drew pictures on his bit of paper.

. . . The whole War Council took in all five and a half hours and it was conducted completely from beginning to end by Chamberlain and Reynaud. Nobody else said a single word. A battle of wits, and I am quite sure that Chamberlain won.[60]

The SWC's sessions were carefully managed by the allied prime ministers to produce a show of consensus and alliance solidarity to the nation and the world.[61] Military leaders recognized that this system hindered strategic decision-making; prior agreement between the allied general staffs was necessary to gain a rapid decision by the SWC, and disagreement was unlikely to be resolved in that forum.[62] Potentially contentious issues, such as the general examination of the manpower and material resources of the two Allied nations proposed by the chairman of the Anglo-French Co-ordinating Committee, Jean Monnet, would in general not be put on the agenda 'until the two Prime Ministers had had the opportunity for informal discussion on the matter'.[63] Most important business was discussed and settled between the relevant authorities before the SWC assembled. For example the decision to evacuate the allied landings around Trondheim in Norway, formally taken at the SWC on 27 April 1940, was the consequence of three days of shuttle diplomacy and tense negotiations between the allies' military and political authorities, following a unilateral British decision to evacuate which the French opposed.[64] The real purpose of the institution might be surmised from the bland press releases put out after each session. After the third meeting on 17 November it was announced: 'Complete agreement was reached on the best method of combined employment of French and British forces for the most effective conduct of operations'.[65] But as one who was present later caustically commented, 'Quelle que soit la bonne volonté de ses membres, on ne conduit pas la guerre avec un conclave'.[66]

In time the pressure of business became too much for the existing structure.[67] When faced in the spring of 1940 with the likelihood that the war would soon become a real one, some thought was given to strengthening the SWC. Chamberlain detected a more 'foxy' adversary in the new French premier, Paul Reynaud, who at the SWC on 28 March proposed more frequent and regular meetings and the creation of a permanent secretariat to drive the institution.[68] While the British government agreed to the former, the vested interests of the British Cabinet secretariat prevented the latter, forgoing the last chance to strengthen the inter-allied organization before the war started in earnest.[69] The German attack on Norway in April presented the alliance with its first major military challenge, and exposed the inadequacies of the higher directive machinery.[70] As the allied response to the Russian attack on Finland had already demonstrated, it could not take rapid decisions,[71] and therefore surrendered military initiative to the enemy. The institution all but collapsed after the German invasion of France in May, the last meetings of the SWC being hurriedly improvised and tense.[72] While this might be expected in the circumstances, it is nevertheless a reflection on the lack of solidarity in the alliance, something which could not be compensated for by an institution which was primarily intended to present a united front to the world, while avoiding wherever possible differences of opinion and masking fundamental disagreements over policy and strategy.

Generals are often accused of fighting the last war, and this is said particularly of the French generals in 1939–40. Study of the SWC suggests that the same might be said of the politicians. It is to the allies' credit that, unlike in 1914, they did not ignore the question of co-ordinating machinery during peacetime, leaving it to be improvised by a lengthy process of trial and error against a background of military reverse and political disagreement. However, the allies had clearly benefited little from their earlier experience of coalition war. Spears, who had served at the heart of the Anglo-French liaison system in the Great War, commented prophetically on the eve of the second war:

> It is all too evident that centuries of peaceful intercourse will be needed to achieve what even the common suffering of the war failed to accomplish, a capacity to view a given situation from the point of view of the man of another nationality. To do so calls for a degree of education, knowledge and imagination that the men of the war generation did not possess.[73]

The men of the inter-war generation were to prove that they also lacked these qualities.

The Versailles SWC had evolved as a means to mitigate years of personality clashes, strategic disagreements and civil-military disputes, and to give the Entente unity of purpose, an important factor in the eventual allied victory. The 1939 SWC was never likely to achieve this unity of purpose, being created for the war that the allies planned to fight – one of static defence, attrition and economic blockade. Although this machinery functioned well enough in 'une guerre d'attente et inaction', it proved ill-suited to the needs of modern 'lightning' warfare. The historian of the SWC, François Bédarida, has suggested that this was not a fault of the institution itself, but of the mental attitudes of its members, pursuing a strategy 'paralysée par la passívitée, l'attentisme et les illusions'.[74] Nevertheless, stronger institutions with real executive power, which had been contemplated and rejected before the war, might have injected greater realism, dynamism and consensus into the allied war effort. But in 1939 the focus was too much on structure rather than process – the end product of 1918, not its origins. The allies looked to tried institutions to alleviate the inevitable tensions of coalition war, but these proved no substitute for open minds and positive attitudes. The 1939 SWC was dominated by two prime ministers with different points of view, whose show of agreement in council rarely survived in practice. Its debates over Scandinavia, for example, parallel those over Salonika which had so troubled the Entente before the establishment of the Versailles SWC.[75] Innovations which might have tempered the influence of the prime minsters and allowed a more united and dynamic prosecution of the allied war effort, such as a higher military committee and a permanent secretariat, were never tried, as they were not present in the 1917–18 organization, and they threatened vested interests. Therefore, while the SWC ensured close allied liaison at the highest level,[76] it gave no real direction, and did not serve to reconcile fundamental Anglo-French and civil-military differences. A new British prime minster, Winston Churchill, who from the start had argued for making the SWC the pivot of the Anglo-French alliance,[77] was to draw more appropriate conclusions from the events in France in May 1940, and create an Anglo-American apparatus more suited to the conduct of coalition war.

Notes

1. 'Speech to National Defence Public Interest Committee Lunch', 13 December 1939, Admiral of the Fleet Lord Chatfield papers, National Maritime Museum, Greenwich, CHT/6/4.
2. For the first world war see W. J. Philpott, *Anglo-French Relations and Strategy on the Western Front, 1914–1918* (Basingstoke: Macmillan Press [now Palgrave Macmillan]: 1996); *Idem*, 'Squaring the Circle: the Higher Coordination of the Entente in the Winter of 1915–16', *English Historical Review*, cxiv (1999), pp. 875–98.

3. For the struggles over a continental military commitment between the wars see B. J. Bond, *British Military Policy Between the Two World Wars* (Oxford: Clarendon Press, 1980).

4. 'Note sur la collaboration militaire franco-britannique', by Gamelin, 23 November 1938 (original emphasis), Service Historique de l'Armée de Terre, Vincennes (SHAT), 2N227/3.

5. 'Note sur la collaboration militaire franco-britannique', unattributed CSDN memorandum, 24 April 1938, SHAT, 2N227/2.

6. F. Bédarida, *La stratégie secrète de la drôle de guerre: la Conseil Suprême Inter-allié, septembre 1939–avril 1940* (Paris: Presses de la Fondation Nationale des Sciences Politiques, 1979), p. 21.

7. Spears had been active in Anglo-French liaison in the first world war and was to play a similar role in the second. See M. Egremont, *Under Two Flags: the Life of Major-General Sir Edward Spears* (London: Weidenfeld, 1997).

8. 'Article du général Spears sur la solidarité franco-britannique', report by Lelong, 23 February 1939, SHAT, 7N2816.

9. Minutes of the 'reunion des chefs de l'Etat-Major Général', 17 February 1939, SHAT, 2N225; 'Note sur la collaboration franco-britannique', 2 March 1939; 'Note sur les accords d'états-majors franco-anglais (directive pour la délégation envoyée à Londres)', c. 8 March 1939, SHAT, 5N579/2.

10. 'Note sur diverses questions traitées au cours de la première phase des conversations franco-britanniques ou pouvant être traitées dans la 2ème phase', unsigned, 11 April 1939, SHAT, 2N229/1; 'Information du President: conversations d'état-major franco-britanniques', unsigned, 12 April 1939, SHAT, 5N579/2.

11. 'Note sur diverses questions traitées...' *ibid.*; 'Analyse', by Gamelin for Daladier, 8 March 1939, SHAT, 5N579/2; 'Note sur la préparation du haut commandement de la coalition', by Gamelin, 10 June 1939; 'Note sur la direction d'une guerre de coalition', by Gamelin, 10 June 1939, SHAT, 2N229/1.

12. In fact Gamelin overlooked or deliberately ignored the fact that Foch's appointment as *generalissimo* of the allied armies resulted from the failure of just such a military committee under Foch's chairmanship, the Executive War Board of the Versailles Supreme War Council. Philpott, *Anglo-French Relations and Strategy*, pp. 150–3.

13. M. S. Alexander, *The Republic in Danger: General Maurice Gamelin and the Politics of French Defence, 1933–40* (Cambridge: Cambridge University Press, 1992), pp. 88–93.

14. Minutes of the 'reunion des chefs de l'Etat-Major Général', 27 March 1939, SHAT, 2N225.

15. CID, minutes of the 355th meeting, 2 May 1939, Cabinet Office: Committee of Imperial Defence minutes, Public Record Office (PRO), Kew (CAB 2): CAB 2/8.

16. CID, minutes of the 364th and 365th meetings, 6 and 13 July 1939, CAB 2/9; 'Supreme Control in War', memorandum by the Minister for Co-ordination of Defence, 3 July 1939, Cabinet Office: Committee of Imperial Defence ad-hoc sub-committees of enquiry: proceedings and memoranda, PRO (CAB 16): CAB 16/183A/DP(p)64.

17. Lord Ismay, *The Memoirs of Lord Ismay* (London: Heinemann, 1960), p. 87. See also 'Supreme Control in War', unattributed memorandum, 3 July 1939,

which was clearly the precursor of the memorandum of the same title submitted to the CID (see note 16), SHAT, 2N229/3.

18. Chamberlain to Daladier, 26 July 1939, SHAT, 2N229/3; Ismay, *Memoirs*, p. 87. See also CID, minutes of the 365th meeting, 13 July 1939, PRO, CAB 2/9; 'Supreme Control in War', by the Minister for Co-ordination of Defence, 3 July 1939.

19. Ismay, *Memoirs*, p. 44.

20. See 'Supreme Control in War', unattributed memo, 3 July 1939.

21. Ismay did draw on Lloyd George's war memoirs for his analysis of the Versailles SWC, *ibid*. The French too seem not to have consulted former members of the Versailles SWC for their recollections of its organization and efficiency. General Maxime Weygand, the French military representative in 1917, was still on the active list although inaccessible in the Middle East.

22. CID, minutes of the 365th meeting, 13 July 1939, PRO, CAB 2/9.

23. Lelong to Daladier, 13 June 1939, SHAT, 7N2816.

24. 'Note sur la préparation du haut commandement de la coalition', by Gamelin, 10 June 1939; 'Note sur la direction d'une guerre de coalition', by Gamelin, 10 June 1939, SHAT, 2N229/1.

25. 'Note of Major-General H. L. Ismay's Conversations in Paris on the 29th July, 1939'; Ismay to Rucker, 31 July 1939, prime minister's papers, PRO (PREM 1): PREM 1/311.

26. Minutes of the 'reunion des chefs de l'Etat-Major Général', 1 August 1939, SHAT, 2N225; 'Direction de la Guerre et Commandement', by Gamelin (n.d), SHAT, 2N233; Gamelin to Daladier, 2 August 1939, SHAT, 5N579/2; 'Signature du President: projet du réponse à Monsieur Chamberlain au sujet de l'organisation du commandement interallié', 2 August 1939, SHAT, 5N579/2; Daladier to Chamberlain, 3 August 1939, SHAT, 2N229/3. See also untitled note on the functioning of the Versailles Supreme War Council, [July 1939?], SHAT, 2N229/3.

27. 'Note of Major-General H. L. Ismay's Conversations in Paris on the 29th July, 1939'.

28. Chamberlain to Daladier, 26 July 1939, SHAT, 2N229/3.

29. 'Supreme Control in War', memorandum by the Minister for Co-ordination of Defence, 3 July 1939.

30. Gamelin to Daladier, 2 August 1939, SHAT, 5N579/2; Daladier to Chamberlain, 3 August 1939, SHAT, 2N229/3.

31. Chamberlain to Daladier, 17 August 1939, SHAT, 2N229/3.

32. In the wartime organization the service chiefs were called to the council 'whenever important decisions on military matters require [sic] to be taken, with a consultative voice and with not only the right but the duty to state their opinions on military matters'. 'Inter-Allied Military Organisation', 22 November 1939, Cabinet Office: Registered Files, PRO (CAB 21): CAB 21/1377.

33. 'Je suis en particulier heureux de constater que notre point de vue est le même pour tout ce qui a trait à la responsabilité à laisser, au sein même du Conseil Suprême, aux hautes authorités militaires de nos deux Pays.' Daladier to Chamberlain, 28 August 1939, SHAT, 2N229/3.

34. CID, minutes of the 368th meeting, 24 July 1939, PRO, CAB 2/9. Significantly, in his draft reply to Chamberlain's letter of 17 August Gamelin made

no mention of the 'Haut Comité Militaire'. Gamelin to Daladier, 24 August 1939, SHAT, 5N579/2.

35. Chamberlain to Daladier, 17 August 1939, SHAT, 2N229/3.
36. Daladier to Chamberlain, 28 August 1939, SHAT, 2N229/3.
37. Lelong to Gamelin, 10 August 1939, SHAT, 7N2817.
38. 'Supreme Control in War', memorandum by the Minister for Co-ordination of Defence, 3 July 1939; Chamberlain to Daladier, 26 July 1939, SHAT, 2N229/3; Daladier to Chamberlain, 3 August 1939, SHAT, 2N229/3.
39. Lelong to Gamelin, 10 August 1939, SHAT, 7N2817. This solution had been suggested by Ismay when he visited Paris. 'Note of Major General H. L. Ismay's Conversations in Paris on the 29th July 1939'.
40. Gamelin to Lelong, 19 August 1939, SHAT, 2N229/3.
41. In practice Lelong found that his other responsibilities left him little time for this new task. Lelong to Gamelin, 25 August 1939, SHAT, 7N2817.
42. CID, minutes of the 368th meeting, 24 July 1939, PRO, CAB 2/9; Lelong to Gamelin, 24 August 1939, SHAT, 7N2817. In fact the Inter-allied Military Committee was not yet up and running, and this meeting was designated a further session of the inter-allied staff talks. *Procès-verbal* of the 14th meeting, 28 August 1939, SHAT, 2N229/2.
43. Note for Gamelin, 25 August 1939, SHAT, 2N229/3.
44. Secretary of the Anglo-French liaison section to Ismay, 1 September 1939, SHAT, 27N189.
45. 'Note concernant la conduite générale de la guerre', by Gamelin, [c. 8] August 1939, Daladier papers, Archives Nationales, Paris, 3DA1/1a.
46. For the structure and personnel of these many missions see the organization tables, 'Liaisons franco-britanniques en France', SHAT, 27N189; 'Diagramme de la liaison franco-britannique sur les questions militaires et civils', SHAT, 2N229/3. For an example of the negotiations behind the creation and functions of this liaison structure see untitled memorandum of a meeting to organize Anglo-French liaison, [c. 5] September 1939, SHAT, 2N231.
47. Chamberlain to Ida Chamberlain, 14 March 1936, Neville Chamberlain papers, Birmingham University Library, NC18/1/951.
48. Chamberlain to Hilda Chamberlain, 21 March 1936, Chamberlain papers, NC18/1/952.
49. Daladier to Gamelin, 6 September 1939, SHAT, 5N580/3.
50. For contrasting pre-war accounts from both allies see Chamberlain to Ida Chamberlain, 1 May 1938, Chamberlain papers, NC18/1/1049, and Daladier's typescript account of events surrounding the dismemberment of Czechoslovakia, pp. 42–8, Daladier papers, 2DA1/3.
51. Admiral Odend'hal to 'Mon Général' [Jamet?], 13 September 1939, SHAT, 2N231.
52. Chamberlain to Hilda Chamberlain, 17 September 1939, Chamberlain papers, NC18/1/1121.
53. Ismay to Hankey, 12 September 1939, PRO, CAB 21/746; Halifax to Phipps, 8th September 1939, PRO, PREM 1/410; 'Note for the prime minster', no date, PRO, PREM 1/437; Bédarida, *La stratégie secrète*, pp. 33 and 87.
54. E. du Réau, *Edouard Daladier, 1884–1970* (Paris: Fayard, 1993), pp. 392–3.
55. An account of the process can be found in Bédarida, *La stratégie secrète*, pp. 35–40. Details of the negotiations are in PRO, CAB 21/764 and CAB 21/1377.

56. 'Première Séance du Conseil Suprême Interallié', 12 September 1939, Bédarida, *La stratégie secrète*, p. 9; Chamberlain to Daladier, 27 September 1939, Daladier papers, 3DA2/3/b. The committees covered air production and supply, armaments and raw materials, shipping, economic warfare, oil and food.

57. Monnet to Bridges, 1 October 1939, PRO, CAB 21/747; Daladier to Chamberlain, 18 October 1939; Chamberlain to Daladier, 22 October 1939, PRO, PREM 1/437.

58. Bédarida, *La stratégie secrète*, p. 29.

59. *Ibid.*, pp. 30–1. There is evidence that various British ministers and officials attended on the off-chance that the French would raise matters not on the formal agenda of the meeting. Bridges to Wilson, 15 November 1939, PRO, CAB 21/764.

60. R. Macleod and D. Kelly (eds), *The Ironside Diaries, 1937–40* (London: Constable, 1962), pp. 237–8.

61. Bédarida, *La stratégie secrète*, pp. 32–3. See also Chamberlain's speech to the House of Commons, 8 February 1940, PRO, CAB 21/1377, and Chamberlain to Hilda Chamberlain, 9 February 1940, Chamberlain papers, NC18/1/1142.

62. Weygand to Gamelin, 13 December 1939, Daladier papers, 4DA5/2.

63. 'Explanatory note' by Bridges to Rucker, 27 March 1940, PRO, PREM 1/437.

64. 'Historique sommaire des journées des 26, 27 et 28 Avril 1940', SHAT 27N4/1. Chamberlain to Ida Chamberlain, 27 April 1940, Chamberlain papers, NC18/1/1152.

65. Press communiqué on the 17 November 1939 meeting, PRO, CAB 21/1377.

66. Admiral Auphan, quoted in Bédarida, *La stratégie secrète*, p. 33.

67. Ismay to Howard-Vyse, 26 March 1940, PRO, CAB 21/1377.

68. Chamberlain to Ida Chamberlain, 30 March 1940, Chamberlain papers, NC18/1/1148.

69. Bédarida, *La stratégie secrète*, pp. 44–9.

70. *Ibid.*, p. 34.

71. *Ibid.*, pp. 235–3.

72. F. Bédarida, 'La rupture Franco-Britannique de 1940: le Conseil Suprême Interallié de l'invasion à la défaite de la France', *Vingtième siècle*, 25 (1990), pp. 37–48.

73. E. L. Spears, *Prelude to Victory* (London: Jonathan Cape, 1939), p. 81.

74. *Ibid.*, p. 34.

75. For details see D. Dutton, *The Politics of Diplomacy: Britain and France in the Balkans in the First World War* (London: I. B. Tauris, 1998).

76. Certainly much closer than in the first world war, when the Allied prime ministers did not meet until the war had been in progress for 11 months. See R. A. Prete, 'Le conflit stratégique franco-brittanique sur le front occidental et la conférence de Calais du 6 Juillet 1915', *Guerres mondiales et conflits contemporains*, 187 (1997), pp. 17–49.

77. Bédarida, *La stratégie secrète*, pp. 85–6.

Index